An Introduction to Multilevel Modeling Techniques

QUANTITATIVE METHODOLOGY SERIES
Methodology for Business and Management

George A. Marcoulides, Series Editor

An Introduction to Multilevel Modeling Techniques

Ronald H. Heck

and

Scott L. Thomas

University of Hawai'i at Manoa

2000

LAWRENCE ERLBAUM ASSOCIATES, PUBLISHERS

Mahwah, New Jersey   London

Lawrence Erlbaum Associates, Inc., Publishers
10 Industrial Avenue
Mahwah, NJ 07430

Cover design by Kathryn Houghtaling Lacey

Library of Congress Cataloging-in-Publication Data

Heck, Ronald H.
An introduction to multilevel modeling techniques /
Ronald H. Heck and Scott L. Thomas
    p. cm.—(Quantitative methodology series)
  Includes bibliographical references and index.
  ISBN 0-8058-2963-6 (alk. paper)
    1. Social sciences—Mathematical models.   2. Social
sciences—Research—Mathematical models.   I. Heck,
Ronald H.; Thomas, Scott Loring. II. Title. III. Series.
  H61.25.H43 1999
  300'.1'5118—dc21   99-19115
                                                                        CIP

Books published by Lawrence Erlbaum Associates are printed
on acid-free paper, and their bindings are chosen for strength
and durability.

Printed in the United States of America
10 9 8 7 6 5 4 3 2 1

Series Editor's Introduction

The book by Heck and Thomas presents an introduction to the statistical method of multilevel data modeling. Many data sets can be termed *multilevel* because they are organized and described through various levels of aggregation. The term *hierarchical* has also been used as an appropriate way to describe such data. For example, data collected about the attitudes and beliefs of employees toward sexual harassment in the workplace can be hierarchically organized by specific department or by organization. Because it is not possible for an individual employee to be in more than one department or for the department to be in more than one organization, the employees are said to be *nested* within departments and the departments are nested within organizations.

Until recently, the most common approach for the statistical analysis of multilevel data would be to first either aggregate data to the group level or disaggregate data to the individual level. Unfortunately, neither approach is adequate for a proper analysis of multilevel data. The statistical method of multilevel modeling (sometimes also referred to as hierarchical, random-coefficient, or variance-component modeling) allows for the appropriate analysis of multilevel data. Two major obstacles have hindered the more widespread use of multilevel modeling: the complexity of the original treatments of the theory provided by its developers, and the lack of tailored computer programs for performing a multilevel analysis. Although tailored computer programs for calculating a multilevel analysis are becoming more widely available and some commercial statistical packages now provide procedures for computing the estimates needed in a multilevel analysis, few nontechnical introductions to the method have appeared in the literature.

In this volume, Heck and Thomas make the theory and methods of multilevel analysis available to anyone who has mastered the most basic rudiments of regression analysis. Although the book is written at an introductory level, the examples do an excellent job covering necessary computational procedures and available software in detail. The steps from the simple models to the more complicated ones are clearly described and illustrated, and thus the reader can begin at a relatively low level and proceed slowly to the more general class of models described in later chapters. I believe readers will find this book to be an excellent research companion for conducting multilevel analyses. This book provides an important addition to the *Quantitative Methodology Series*.

—George A. Marcoulides
California State University, Fullerton

Contents

Preface

In this book we present an introductory approach to the use of multilevel modeling techniques for conducting research within organizational and educational settings. These techniques are relatively new and they have not yet been fully integrated into most textbooks on univariate and multivariate data analytic methods. Similarly, they are not yet an integral part of the analytic techniques available in most commonly used statistical software programs. We believe that the multilevel approach to modeling univariate and multivariate relationships, however, will become increasingly relevant in social science research. For this reason, multilevel modeling should become an important alternative in mainstream quantitative analysis.

Organizational and educational research present an opportunity to study phenomena that are multilevel, or hierarchical, in nature. For example, individuals work within particular departments, organizations, and geographic regions. The individuals are seen as interacting with their social contexts. Individuals within particular organizations may share certain properties, for example, socialization patterns, traditions, attitudes, and work goals. Similarly, properties of groups may also be influenced by the individuals in them (e.g., leadership abilities, attitudes, and motivations). In the past, researchers have had considerable difficulty analyzing such models where individuals are "nested" within a series of multilevel socioorganizational groups. Ignoring such nested structures can lead to false inferences about the relations among variables, as well as missed insights about the social processes one is studying.

Increasingly, both the concepts and analytical tools are becoming available that allow a more rigorous and thorough approach to investigating organizational and educational processes. While a number of methodologists have led the way in developing multilevel models in the social sciences, we believe there is a need to introduce a wider audience of applied researchers in these disciplines to an overview of the general principles and possibilities of these techniques. We hope that readers of this book will be encouraged to seek opportunities to use these various techniques within their own research agendas. Multilevel modeling has the potential to answer many questions of interest to researchers. It should always be remembered, however, that the *map* is not the *terrain*; that is, statistical models are representations of reality and not the reality itself. As we will develop subsequently, any statistical application, or model, is never a substitute for strong theory and a thorough understanding of one's data.

We would like to help you clarify and recognize when multilevel features are present in data, as well as how to plan for and ask questions of a multilevel nature within organizational and educational research settings. Multilevel analysis can enable researchers to make informed interpretations about relationships in more complex data structures. Of course, in applying any statistical model, one must still give attention and care to selecting the sample, including the theoretically important variables in the model, measuring them adequately, and accounting for variation from unexpected sources related to the processes of interest. Our inferences through statistical modeling can only be as good as the data on which they are based and the adequacy of the assumptions that we make.

These issues aside, multilevel modeling is an attractive approach for social scientists because it allows the incorporation of substantive theory about organizational effects at different levels into the clustered nature of the data often collected in surveys. Despite this attractiveness, however, there are a variety of issues that still need to be resolved in applying multilevel models to organizational research. While the field of multilevel analysis is rapidly unfolding, it has also brought confusion in basic terminology, analytic approaches, and available software to test the models. One issue is the slightly different notation that is used in describing the models (e.g., using the letters c, g, or j to represent level-two units), stemming from tradition in how writers in various disciplines approach the representation of the relevant mathematical models.

A second issue is choice of analytic approach. We develop the notion that these decisions should be related to the study's design (research questions, theoretical model, sampling). One concern is sample size and its relevance to topics such as the determination of statistical power, especially because the number of groups (e.g., organizations) available for study is usually considerably less than the total number of individuals. Smaller sample sizes present a variety of problems in statistical inference. Associated with choice of analytic approach is the range of statistical software available to conduct the analysis. Although this has been a limitation in the past, fortunately, there is currently much software development that is taking place including the ability to handle more complex theoretical models, a variety of nonnormal distributions, and greater attention to parameter estimation and model fit under varied conditions.

This book attempts to provide a broad overview of basic multilevel modeling issues and an illustration of different multilevel techniques through building analyses around several organizational data sets. Although our focus is primarily on educational and organizational settings because these are the ones we encounter in our own research, we hope that the examples help you discover the possibilities of applying these techniques to your own research interests.

We develop two basic classes of multilevel models: multilevel regression models and multilevel models for analyzing covariance structures. Our intent is to develop the rationale behind the specification of these models and to provide an introduction to the design and analysis of research studies using the two respective analytic techniques of hierarchical linear modeling and structural equation modeling. In actuality, there are a great many similarities in these techniques, and a few differences. As background, we provide introductions to single-level analyses using both techniques and then extend each into several multilevel examples.

Our examples are intended to show you, in simple terms, how to set up and conduct the analyses, step by step. For this reason, we keep substantive issues at a minimum and focus on the methodological and practical issues. Of course, we had to make other choices about what content to cover and what areas to refer readers to others who have provided extended treatments of the issues. We have also provided a number of preliminary exercises that can be completed using data employed in the various examples presented in the book.

There are a variety of statistical programs currently available that can be directly used (or adapted) for multilevel analysis. As we suggested, currently these fall into two general groups: multilevel regression programs (i.e., focusing primarily on single outcomes and the investigation of random intercepts and slopes) and multilevel covariance structure analysis (i.e., focusing on relations among latent variables). As a practical matter, however, there is considerable overlap between these two basic approaches. Although a comparison of software programs' ease of use, advantages, and disadvantages is outside the scope of this book (e.g., see Kreft, de Leeuw, & Kim, 1990 or Kreft & de Leeuw, 1998) we have chosen to demonstrate multilevel modeling techniques using four software packages with which we are familiar—HLM (Bryk, Raudenbush, & Condon 1996), LISREL (Jöreskog & Sörbom, 1993), STREAMS (Gustaffson & Stahl, 1996), and *Mplus* (Muthén & Muthén, 1998). Users familiar with other programs (e.g., MLWin, SAS, AMOS, EQS), however, can use those programs to conduct some of the analyses we present in the book. Our choice of software packages is in no way meant to imply that these packages are superior or inferior to other alternatives. Indeed, each program we have used, including those we have not mentioned here, has its own set of important strengths and weaknesses.

HLM (Bryk, Raudenbush, & Condon, 1996) is a multilevel modeling routine designed to test hypotheses about effects at each organizational level and across levels. The program can include predictor variables associated with individuals, groups within organizations, and organizations; incorporate variation occurring at more than one level that is distinct from measurement error variance; and estimate models with multivariate outcomes (Bryk & Raudenbush, 1992; Supovitz & Brennan, 1997).

LISREL is a flexible modeling approach to estimate unknown coefficients in a set of linear structural equations—particularly models including latent variables, measurement errors, reciprocal causation, simultaneity, and independence. Unlike HLM, however, LISREL was not specifically designed to handle multilevel data. The newest version of LISREL (8.30) allows the specification of multilevel regression models similar to HLM. Although multilevel models with latent variables can be specified and tested with LISREL, in practice, the procedures are somewhat more difficult to implement (e.g., requiring the computation of special matrices and under some conditions, correcting degrees of freedom in the model, and re-calculating fit indices by hand). To address some of these difficulties, Gustaffson and Stahl (1996) recently developed a software program called STREAMS that allows the relatively easy specification and testing of two-level structural equation models (including latent variables) using LISREL. This program produces the necessary within- and between-group covariance matrices and fit index modifications.

Mplus (Muthén & Muthén, 1998) is a comprehensive modeling program for applied researchers that can be used for a variety of different modeling purposes involving continuous, categorical, and binary outcome variables. Some of the techniques include linear regression with univariate and multivariate outcomes, probit regression for binary and ordered categorical variables, exploratory and confirmatory factor analysis, growth models, and structural equation models. The program can be used to estimate a variety of different multilevel models (e.g., path models, latent variables models, direct and indirect effects, multilevel growth models).

In chapter 1, we develop the rationale for using multilevel data analytic techniques in doing organizational and educational research. Chapter 2 provides an overview of the development of multilevel techniques, detailing a number of general advantages of multilevel modeling approaches and some problems with previous approaches. In Chapter 3, we present an overview of single-level regression models. Chapter 4 extends the regression discussion to multilevel regression models and introduces HLM procedures and setups for running an example. The analysis is built around an educational data set (i.e., looking at reading improvement of sixth grade students as a function of their backgrounds and school-level variables) to demonstrate how such an analysis can be conducted.

Next, we shift to the structural equation modeling (SEM) approach to multilevel data analysis. In chapter 5 we present a basic overview of SEM techniques, focusing specifically on confirmatory factor analysis (CFA). Chapter 6 extends the CFA approach to multilevel confirmatory factor analysis (MCFA). We use MCFA to investigate the construct validity of a simplified two-level model of organizational leadership. In chapter 7, we then expand the factor-analytic approach to include predictors at two different organizational levels—referred to as a multilevel structural model. Finally, in chapter 8 we present a common data set analyzed with both approaches and focus on a discussion of similarities and differences between the multilevel approaches presented. We also address a number of issues for further consideration in conducting multilevel research.

ACKNOWLEDGMENTS

We would like to thank a number of people for their help at various stages of the writing process. We are indebted to those who read and critically reviewed several versions of the manuscript: Marian Crislip, Terry Duncan, Sarah Gronna, Stacey Himeda, Vicki Rosser—your time spent, insights, and helpful comments were gratefully appreciated. Thank you to Linda Muthén of *Mplus* for helpful advice and Stephen du Toit of *Scientific Software International* for discussions regarding LISREL 8.30's new multilevel program. For years of inspiration and training in these areas we are indebted to George Marcoulides and Russell Rumberger. Thanks are again due to George Marcoulides, our series editor, who provided guidance throughout and kept us on track.

We are ever grateful to those who taught us and those whose work in this area over the years has been an inspiration to our own research efforts. A thank you is also extended to our colleagues in our department and our students who supported, encouraged, and put up with our efforts! Finally, we thank our families and friends for their patience and support during the months when this project consumed our energies and attention. Thank you all.

—Ronald H. Heck
—Scott L. Thomas

Chapter 1

An Introduction to Multilevel Models in Organizational Research

Multilevel modeling refers to a variety of statistical methods that may be used to handle the hierarchical, or nested, data structures present in social research on organizations. These types of data structures are typical in the social sciences. A researcher may investigate a sample that includes a number of students within a set of classrooms within a set of schools. For decades, researchers have taken advantage of the multilevel nature of such data in designing investigations (e.g., through surveys employing various sampling schemes including clustered random sampling). Only recently, however, has the multilevel nature of sampling designs directly figured into the techniques used to analyze such data (Draper, 1995). Unfortunately, standard analytic methods are biased by any deviation from simple random sampling (Bryk & Raudenbush, 1992). Standard statistical tests depend heavily on the assumption of independence of the observations (Hox, 1995). In contrast, nested data are likely to produce sizable pockets of similarity among the individuals comprising each group. If the assumption of independent observations is violated, the standard errors of parameters in the model are underestimated—potentially resulting in a greater likelihood of the false attribution of statistical effects where none should exist.

In this introductory chapter, we discuss a number of conceptual and methodological issues associated with the use of multilevel methods. We take care to locate multilevel modeling within a larger framework of quantitative methods of data analysis. Within this larger framework of quantitative methods, we identify four general types of analyses involving single or multiple dependent variables that are often relevant to analyzing organizational data. Broadly speaking, they are all methods of analyzing the variability of outcome measures (e.g., dependent variables, criterion variables). The goal of these analyses may be either prediction or explanation (see Pedhazur & Schmelkin, 1991, for further discussion). In the former instance, the focus may be more on efficiency of prediction and parsimony of variables included in the prediction equation, whereas in the latter case, the focus rests more on the correct specification of a theoretical model under consideration.

Our approach toward multilevel modeling takes us generally in the direction of explanation—more specifically, in explaining variability in a dependent variable or variables through a set of independent variables. The researcher formulates a model from theory and then tests this model against the data. Obviously, there is overlap between the predictive and explanatory approaches to data analysis (Pedhazur & Schmelkin, 1991). We call attention to this distinction, however, because in predictive studies, variables might be retained in an analysis only because they are statistically significant and dropped simply because they are not. In other words, theory may not enter into decisions about model efficiency. Because of the nature of the data structures in multilevel modeling (e.g., individuals nested within groups), however, there would seem to be an inherent need for the application of theory to guide the kinds of relationships investigated within, between, and across levels. This is because for purely predictive purposes, it would often be more efficient to just ignore the underlying structure of the data. In contrast, in the explanatory approach to modeling (i.e., especially in testing structural equation models), model specification should be carefully considered, and subsequent changes should be made sparingly, and also with regard to theory; otherwise, it may be difficult to attach any substantive meaning to the final model.

Decisions about analysis are located with a framework that begins with questions, designs, and data structures (Raudenbush, 1998). As summarized in Table 1.1, quantitative analyses of organizations have often been categorized into univariate or multivariate analysis. Univariate (one dependent variable) analysis might entail correlation, analysis of variance (ANOVA), or regression within the framework of the general linear model. In fact, univariate techniques can be seen as special cases of the multivariate model. Within multivariate analysis, there are various related techniques including canonical correlation (correlations between two sets of variables), multivariate analysis of variance (MANOVA) for multiple, continuous dependent variables (or repeated measures on individuals), discriminant analysis for predicting group membership on a categorical dependent variable, factor analysis, path analysis, and a variety of time-series analyses.

More recently, structural equation modeling (SEM) has been employed in handling a range of complex theoretical relations involving both cross-sectional and longitudinal data within a multivariate setting. As conceptu-

TABLE 1.1
Summary of Quantitative Approaches
to the Analysis of Organizational Data

Analytic Approach	Example Techniques
Single-level data structure	
1. Univariate (one dependent variable)	Correlation, analysis of variance, regression
2. Multivariate (two or more dependent variables)	Canonical correlation, multivariate analysis of variance, discriminant analysis, factor analysis, path analysis, time-series analysis, structural equation modeling
Multilevel data structure	
3. Univariate (one dependent variable)	Multilevel regression or random-coefficients models, variance-components models, mixed linear models, time-series analysis, growth-curve models
4. Multivariate (two or more dependent variables)	Multilevel factor analysis, multilevel structural equation modeling, multivariate variance-components models, multilevel multivariate regression, time-series analysis, latent growth-curve models

alized in most texts and commercial statistics packages, both the univariate and multivariate approaches are typically confined to single-level analyses; that is, either individuals are the unit of analysis, or groups are the unit of analysis. In a way, this represented a "blind spot" in how we approach the analysis of organizational data, although relevant concerns were periodically raised (e.g., Burstein, 1980; Cronbach & Webb, 1975; Goldstein, 1987; Lindley & Smith, 1972; Walsh, 1947).

Appropriate analysis of organizational data, however, acknowledges the individual and group relationships present in the sampling scheme. Multilevel models require us to extend single-level univariate and multivariate analyses to more complex models, often with variables measured at different levels of analysis. For the univariate, multilevel case, we can use multilevel regression models (also referred to as random coefficients, or random effects models). An example would be formulating a theoretical model that decomposes the outcome of interest (e.g., organizational productivity) into the clusters represented in the sample (Muthén, 1994).

A two-level analysis might contain a set of variables explaining how individuals rate their organization's leadership and another set explaining differences in leadership between organizations. The lowest level measurements are called the *micro level*, with all higher level measurements called the *macro level*. A three-level analysis might include variables relating to the individual, departmental, and organizational levels. From this perspective, the relationships among variables observed for the individuals in a study have parameters that can take on values different from those of the departments or organizations. Macrolevel variables are frequently referred to as groups or *contexts* (Kreft & de Leeuw, 1998). With a contextual model, therefore, one could envision successive levels extending beyond the organization. Empirical work, however, for many years has lagged behind the substantive theory of contextual models because of the constraints of analytic techniques. Although analysis of variance methods offered partial answers to some of the questions posed with nested data (Draper, 1995), the general formulation of the multilevel linear model was not developed until the early 1970s (e.g., see Lindley & Smith, 1972).

We can also identify a fourth analytic situation: multilevel, multivariate analyses. In these cases, we might apply multilevel factor analysis or multilevel structural models consisting of separate unobserved (latent) and observed-variable models at different levels of analysis as needed. Similarly, we can also formulate multilevel, multivariate regression models in situations where there are multiple dependent variables, as well as individual and group effects within a three-level model. A variety of longitudinal and latent-growth models involving individuals within groups may also be incorporated into the multilevel, multivariate analytic framework.

As the reader will no doubt realize, the multilevel analytic approach opens up a variety of new possibilities for asking questions of the data. In this book, we concentrate on approaches 3 and 4 summarized in Table 1.1: that is, extensions of univariate and multivariate statistics to multilevel data analysis. We emphasize that the choice of analytic paradigm first requires the investigator to consider the research questions, the theoretical model, and the structure of the data before considering the strengths and limitations of various techniques and software programs.

As multilevel modeling techniques have become better understood and better supported with software programs, their applications have begun to appear in diverse fields including education, medicine, and business. Besides their usefulness in accounting for the nested nature of organizational data, they are also useful in analyzing longitudinal survey data and individual growth studies.

INVESTIGATING ORGANIZATIONAL PROCESSES

Multilevel modeling offers a number of important benefits to researchers examining theories about organizational life. Organizations have special features that can influence the analysis of their processes and outcomes. Individuals bring certain skills and attitudes to the workplace; they are clustered in departments or work units having certain characteristics; and they are also clustered within organizations having particular characteristics. All of these clusters may exert effects on productivity in the workplace. Outcomes may result from various sets of variables related to the backgrounds and attitudes of employees (e.g., experience, education, and work-related skills, attitudes and motivations), the processes of organizational work (e.g., leadership, decision making, staff development, organizational values), and the interactions of these variables with the structure of the organization (e.g., its clustered groupings).

As we have suggested, past research strategies for dealing with the complexity of the multilevel, or contextual, features of organizations have been somewhat limited. Researchers have not always considered the implications of the assumptions they made about measuring variables at their natural level, or moving them from one level to another through aggregation or disaggregation. *Aggregation*, for example, means that the productivity level of individuals within departments or organizations would be combined to a higher level (e.g., the organizational level). This reduces the variability in productivity within each individual and within each unit to a single organizational-level variable. The comparison is then made between organizations' mean productivity outcomes. Of course, failing to acknowledge the within-group variability present in the data can potentially distort relationships examined between such units.

In contrast, *disaggregation* refers to moving a variable conceptualized at a higher level to a lower level. For example, in a different analysis we may have productivity measured at the organizational level, but also have data on individuals' attitudes and motivation. In this case, we intend to analyze the data at the individual level to see whether employee attitudes influence productivity. If we assign to all individuals the same value on the organizational productivity variable (and possibly other organizational variables such as size), we attribute properties of the organization to individuals, which can also confound the analysis.

These examples suggest that analyses conducted at the micro or macro level may produce different results. Treating individuals as if they were independent of these various organizational groupings ignores the complexity inherent in the data and introduces a potentially important source of bias into the analysis. This is because individuals in a group or context tend to be more similar on many important variables (e.g., attitudes, behaviors) than individuals in different contexts. If such clustering effects are ignored, important relationships may be overlooked and erroneous conclusions drawn. As the reader can surmise, it is important to develop a scheme to place the explanatory variables hypothesized to affect individuals and other types of organizational processes in their proper locations (Hox, 1995). This helps to clarify the organizational level to which they rightly belong. Different sets of variables associated with each level, or cluster, in the data quite likely affect productivity in the workplace. There are also likely effects that may result from various interactions across such organizational levels. Mapping these sorts of relations, however, has often been problematic—often focusing on single, discrete elements while ignoring the multidimensional and interrelated aspects of organizational processes.

One important contribution of multilevel modeling, therefore, is to allow the researcher to avoid the aggregation (i.e., assigning the same organizational mean to each member) or disaggregation (i.e., treating subjects without reference to their organizations) problem by considering both levels simultaneously in the analysis. Developing a conceptual framework of organizational relations can also help the researcher avoid another potential source of bias within the analysis—that of ignoring the different levels of the explanatory (independent) variables. Through examining the variation in outcomes that exists at different levels of the organization, we can develop more refined theories about how explanatory variables at each level contribute to outcomes. Analytical procedures that allow outcome intercepts (means) to vary across levels have been referred to as *random-effects, mixed-effects,* and *multilevel linear models* (Bryk & Raudenbush, 1992).

Partitioning the variance in an outcome variable into its within- and between-group components is often the first step in determining whether a multilevel analysis is even necessary. The percent of variance that lies between organizations will be a portion of the total variance to be explained. If there were little or no variation between organizations in the outcome, there would be no need for a multilevel analysis. The extent of homogeneity of groups can be described by an intraclass correlation. If the intraclass correlation is low, the groups are only slightly different from each other. In this case, a simple regression analysis conducted at the micro (individual) level would be adequate. If the intraclass correlation is higher, it suggests that the groups are relatively homogeneous and likely quite different from each other.

If there were significant variation to be explained at the organizational level, however, and if this variation were not incorporated into the analysis, the standard errors will be underestimated for the individual parameters in the model. Because the statistical test of the significance of a variable is defined as the ratio of the size of its parameter coefficient to its standard error, an underestimated standard error could result in a finding of significance when one does not really exist. The effect of this violation can be to increase the probability *Type I* errors (false rejection of the null hypothesis). The effects of clustering can dramatically increase the alpha level associated with a hypothesis test (Barcikowski, 1981).

Acknowledging the existence of an intraclass correlation is important because it changes the error variance in single-level regression analyses (Kreft & de Leeuw, 1998). Error variance represents the effects of variables not included in the model and measurement error, with the assumption that these errors are unrelated. Where clusters are present, this assumption of independent errors is likely violated. Single-level analyses such as multiple regression or analysis of covariance do not correct for the intraclass correlation. Multilevel modeling, then, also contributes to our understanding of organizational processes by allowing researchers to estimate the importance of model parameters more efficiently and accurately.

After the researcher determines that organizational outcomes vary sufficiently across organizational levels to conduct a multilevel analysis, she or he can investigate how various organizational processes are related to outcomes. For example, organizational culture is one construct that has received attention in the literature concerning how employee background, organizational structure, and process may affect outcomes (e.g., Hofstede, Neuijen, Ohayv, & Sanders, 1990). Although organizations are acknowledged to be socially constructed by their members, there is little agreement about what the concept of culture means (Schein, 1990), how it should be observed and measured, and at what organizational level it should be formulated. Several researchers, however, have attempted to conceptualize and measure culture within organizational settings and to assess its effects on organizational outcomes (e.g., Hofstede et al., 1990; Marcoulides & Heck, 1993; Smart & St. John, 1996).

After defining and measuring culture through one or more theoretical lenses suggested from previous research, we would then decide whether to treat organizational culture as exerting a *fixed* or a *random* effect on productivity. In a single-level analysis, we would have no control over how culture is hypothesized to affect productivity. We would have to assume it exerts the *same* (fixed) impact within every organization. The slope coefficient would represent the average effect of culture on productivity across our sample of individuals or organizations. In a multilevel analysis, however, we can treat the slope describing culture's impact on productivity as a random variable, which means we can allow its impact on productivity to vary across the organizations in the sample. This latter formulation would be more consistent with our theory that organizational culture exerts a differential impact on productivity.

We could then develop (or test) a theoretical model that explains this variation in the slopes across the organizations by including of a set of variables at the organizational level. In our analysis, therefore, we would formulate one model to explain differences in organizational productivity (intercepts) as a result of organizational-level variables (size, type of organization), controlling for a set of within-organization variables (e.g., culture, worker backgrounds). A second model would explain the variation in culture's impact (slope) on productivity using organizational-level variables. As suggested, it is important to develop clarity regarding what explanatory variables are assigned to what level in the analysis. Only with such clarity can these variables be appropriately measured and entered into the analysis in a manner that is consistent with the organizational theory being tested.

Of course, there are many other ways in which we could investigate the effects of organizational culture. As the reader can see, the multilevel analysis used in this example—showing how organizational culture affects outcomes—puts the focus squarely on the researcher to use theory beforehand to explain proposed relationships. It is important to caution, however, that the complexity of most organizational theories cannot be reduced to a single model attempting to explain organizational outcomes. One can always be criticized for omitting a potentially important variable in the analysis. Because all possible causes cannot be included, the problem is reduced to using previous theory to construct a model such that all known, relevant causes are included, while recognizing that this will almost assuredly be incomplete (Marcoulides & Heck, 1993).

MEASURING CONSTRUCTS IN ORGANIZATIONAL STUDIES

Because of concerns with how theoretically important organizational processes may account for variations in organizational outcomes, researchers often need to define and investigate various organizational constructs. Constructs are theoretical abstractions that help us explain and organize our environment (National Council on Measurement, 1984). They are frequently mentioned in the literature on people's attitudes toward political issues, consumers' buying habits, and organizational leadership. Because constructs cannot be seen, however, they cannot be directly measured. Instead, they must be defined by measuring several "indicators" or observed variables (e.g., items on a survey) thought to represent each construct. The advantage of this approach is that several observed variables can be used to operationalize a construct, which allows the researcher to incorporate measurement error into the analysis. The researcher can then assess which items measure the construct well and which ones do not.

For example, we might be interested in defining how teachers' career satisfaction affects their turnover. We would not want to define career satisfaction through using only one item from a survey. It would likely be a very ambiguous statement (e.g., How satisfied are you with your career as a teacher?). We would have no real way to determine whether we have reliably and validly measured it. Instead, if we included several items on our survey that define different aspects of satisfaction with teaching as a career, we could look at the various correlations among the items and determine the extent to which the items form a data pattern. We could, for example, create some type of career satisfaction scale and describe the level of consistency in this measure across a set of individuals. One simple description of relative consistency in subjects' responses on a scale is Cronbach's alpha. Alternately, we could examine several other potential sources of error through generalizability theory (e.g., Shavelson & Webb, 1991), where we could describe variance in perceptions due to the persons who respond, the items used to define the scale, and perhaps the occasions of measurement (as well as possible interaction effects).

Another approach we could use to define a construct like career satisfaction through several items is factor analysis. Factor analysis allows us the advantage of incorporating an individual error term for each observed variable defining the underlying construct, as opposed to only an overall measure of error, as when using a unidimensional scale for satisfaction. Whether using some type of scaling or factor analysis, however, we are likely to sample the domain of possible items more adequately. In contrast, it is important to note that in studies using only single items to define variables, we have to assume that each variable is measured without error. As we might expect, when we do not incorporate measurement error into the analysis, there is a likely bias in the estimates of the model's parameters.

In many organizational investigations, researchers are concerned with the relationships between constructs. An example might be the relationship between teacher career satisfaction and teacher productivity. As we have suggested, an important step in conducting such analyses is to measure the constructs well, so that estimates of their interrelationships will be accurate. Structural equation modeling (SEM) is well suited to investigating how constructs in theoretical models are defined by their indicators, as well as the structural relationships among constructs. The first part of an SEM analysis is referred to as *developing the measurement model*, because the focus is on defining the constructs through their hypothesized observed indicators. The analytical procedure is known as *confirmatory factor analysis*, because of the emphasis on defining the theoretical relationships first and then "confirming" the fit of proposed theoretical relations against the data. The usefulness of the measurement model is that it allows researchers to account for measurement errors in the model.

In the past, factor models of organizational constructs have often been developed without regard to the separate organizations in which members work. This is because they were conducted at a single level (i.e., the individual level) of analysis. As the reader will recall, failing to acknowledge the nested nature of the data can affect the conclusions that a researcher draws about the stability and validity of the factor model (i.e., how well it holds across groups), as well as its psychometric properties (i.e., how well each construct is measured). Another related shortcoming is that single-level factor-analytic methods make the assumption that the data have been obtained as a simple random sample from a given population. For studies of organizational constructs, however, violation of the assumption of independent observations can be particularly important, because individuals in the same organization may produce sizable intraclass correlations (i.e., because of their clustering) due to common sources of variation (Muthén, 1991).

Multilevel factor analysis provides us one means of examining the intraclass correlations of the observed variables used to measure a construct. Through the multilevel analysis, the construct becomes adjusted for the different properties (e.g., differing intraclass correlations, individual measurement errors) of the observed variables that comprise it. It is important to note that in a multilevel factor analysis, measurement error contributes to errors in the partitioning of an observed variable's variance into its between- and within-level components. Using this type of multilevel analysis, therefore, we can examine the reliability of responses from the individuals providing the information within each organization. This is useful because subjects' precision in providing information may vary widely in a typical sample of organizations. Multilevel factor analysis therefore produces results that correspond to those that would be obtained from perfectly reliable measurements (Muthén, 1994). This adjustment yields a much more accurate assessment of the relationships between constructs such as job satisfaction and performance.

After the constructs are adequately defined, structural relations among the constructs, including an assessment of direct and indirect effects on outcomes, can be investigated. Applications of the basic multilevel regression model in multivariate situations using multilevel SEM, however, are just emerging (Kaplan, 1998). Computer software that can be used to perform these latter analyses is evolving rapidly. Undoubtedly, researchers will continue to develop and refine these techniques in the near future.

SUMMARY

The use of multilevel analysis can add substantive information about how organizational processes can be affected by the hierarchical nature of the data and by the features of the organizations and their contexts. As we have discussed, these techniques therefore allow the specification of more complex theoretical relationships than is possible using traditional single-level regression analyses. Analytical approaches that can be used to model complex organizational relationships have greatly expanded over the past couple of decades. These analytical means allow us to investigate organizational processes in more theoretically appropriate ways.

Multilevel techniques allow us to investigate several types of univariate models involving clustered sampling schemes and a number of fixed and random effects (e.g., De Leeuw & Kreft, 1986; Hartley & Rao, 1967; Lindley & Smith, 1972; Raudenbush & Bryk, 1986; Shigemasu, 1976; Wong & Mason, 1985). Extensions of the basic multilevel regression model to a variety multivariate situations—multiple dependent variables and direct or indirect effects—are also being developed. For example, multilevel factor analysis allows investigation of constructs within and across organizations, taking into consideration their measurement properties. Multilevel models can also be used to examine organizational change by including multiple measurements and by modeling what factors account for the change (or growth) over time (e.g., see Duncan & Duncan, 1996; Kiecolt-Glaser, 1997; Laird & Ware, 1982; McArdle & Hamagami, 1996; Muthén, 1997; Muthén & Muthén, 1998; Ware, 1985; Willett & Sayer, 1996). Within a three-level model, for example, we could incorporate repeated measures on individuals at the first level, individual background variables at the second level, and organizational variables at the third level.

There is no doubt that multilevel modeling has a number of useful applications to social science research in both cross-sectional and longitudinal data situations. Because of the increasing availability of computer software that can analyze such data structures, there is a need to explicate these methods for use in organizational research, so that they can be effectively utilized. Our attention in this introductory book is divided between the univariate case of multilevel modeling (developed in chaps. 3 and 4), and situations where the multivariate case may be required (chaps. 5–8).

We emphasize the importance of casting multilevel analyses within the context of multilevel theories about organizational processes. We return to this theme several times in our presentation of multilevel modeling. Ideally, substantive progress in a field is achieved when headway occurs simultaneously on conceptual and methodological fronts.

Chapter 2

The Development of Multilevel Modeling Techniques

In this chapter, we outline a few of the conceptual debates and shortcomings with previous approaches to the analysis of multilevel data, some advantages and limitations of multilevel models, and the basic research objectives and issues regarding the multilevel regression and structural equation modeling approaches.

A HISTORICAL PERSPECTIVE ON MULTILEVEL MODELING

Over the past two decades, concerns with conceptual and methodological issues in conducting social science research with nested data have led to the development of multilevel analytic techniques. Various terms have been used to refer to these methods: multilevel linear models, hierarchical linear models, mixed-effects and random-effects models, random-coefficients models, and covariance-components models. The use of these different labels is related to their use within different fields of inquiry (Kaplan & Elliott, 1997). The statistical theory for multilevel models, therefore, has developed out of several streams of methodological work including biometric applications of mixed-model analysis of variance (ANOVA), random-coefficients regression models in econometrics, and developments in the statistical theory of covariance component models and Bayesian estimation of linear models (Bock, 1989; de Leeuw & Kreft, 1986; Efron & Morris, 1975; Fisher, 1918, 1925; Goldstein, 1987; Hartley & Rao, 1967; Laird & Ware, 1982; Lindley & Smith, 1972; Morris, 1995; Raudenbush, 1988; Raudenbush &

Bryk, 1986; Rubin, 1950; Shigemasu, 1976; Wald, 1947; Wong & Mason, 1985).

It is important to emphasize that much of this methodological work is continuing at present, so there is still considerable debate over specific issues in multilevel modeling that have surfaced within initial modeling efforts. The varied terminology, analytic approaches, and software can be confusing. As multilevel methods become more accepted into the "mainstream" of quantitative modeling, we expect that many of these issues will be resolved. We use the term *multilevel model* with respect to two separate statistical objectives described within one theoretical model (Morris, 1995).

The first objective concerns inferences made about the model's structural parameters (e.g., intercepts, regression coefficients), which describe between-unit (or level-2) distributions (variance) of the group intercepts or slopes (Morris, 1995). These are often called *random effects* or *random coefficients* from various statistical perspectives. In experimental research, a *random* effect describes where the levels of a treatment (e.g., groups) are assumed to be a sample from a universe of possible relevant treatments. Because the effect is considered as randomly varying across the groups in the study, the intent is to make inferences beyond the specific treatment levels included. Therefore, the effects are not assumed to be constant. In contrast, a *fixed* effect is where all possible treatments are present in the experiment (Kreft & de Leeuw, 1998). Inferences can only be made about the specific treatments used in the experiment. The effects are considered to be constant and measured without error (because all possible cases are included).

Random coefficients models describe a type of linear (or nonlinear) model where the values of the coefficients are assumed to vary as a probability distribution. In a single-level regression, the coefficients describing the linear model, such as the intercept and slope, are considered as fixed values estimated from the sample data. For example, the regression coefficient (slope) describing the impact of socioeconomic status (SES) on student achievement would be fixed at some weight (beta) for the model. In contrast, in the multilevel model, the coefficients at level 1, the individual level, can be treated as random coefficients. As opposed to being fixed for the entire data set, the slope describing the impact of SES on student achievement would be viewed as randomly varying across the set of schools. In some schools the coefficient might be larger, and in some it might be smaller. The researcher might be interested in the average SES effect across the schools, as well as in how particular schools deviate from the overall average SES slope.

The second objective of the multilevel analysis concerns inferences about how particular individual parameters vary from the overall distribution across the units. This is the probabilistic part that describes the random behavior of the parameters (e.g., student achievement intercepts, SES-achievement slopes). In most cases, the researcher's primary concern is with estimating the structural parameters (i.e., random coefficients) that have been hypothesized to vary across units. In other cases, however, estimating the distribution of unknown individual parameters (e.g., the variance of standard errors of the effect estimates) is the researcher's main interest (Morris, 1995). Especially where the sample size is small, the methods used to estimate the model's parameters may provide biased estimates that understate the between-groups variance of the effect estimates.

For either analytic objective, the model's structural parameters, their variances, and standard errors can be estimated by several means including maximum likelihood, restricted maximum likelihood, or Bayesian methods (Hartley & Rao, 1967; Lindley & Smith, 1972; Efron & Morris, 1975; Raudenbush, 1988). As we develop later in a bit more detail, there is currently considerable debate over which methods of estimation to use under particular sampling conditions. When the number of level-2 units is large, any consistent method of estimation may be used, but with small numbers of units, parameter estimation is more problematic, and therefore greater care must be taken to ensure accurate estimation (Morris, 1995; Raudenbush, 1995). This is because the level-2 regression coefficients and individual effects are conditional on estimates of the level-2 variance, which may be underestimated when there are small numbers of groups in the study (Morris, 1995).

Although statistical concerns about multivariate modeling under different sampling conditions and emerging solutions are more recent concerns of researchers, the substantive concerns about multilevel modeling, including proper model specification (e.g., unit of analysis, aggregation effects, contextual effects) and the precision of parameter estimates with single-level analyses, are older concerns (e.g., Burstein, 1980; Cronbach & Webb, 1975; Lindley & Smith, 1972; Strenio, 1981; Walsh, 1947). Attempts to solve the unit of analysis issue often centered on aggregating or disaggregating variables in a nested structure to yield a data set that could be analyzed on a single level. For example, the researcher might collect data on individuals who belong to particular departments or subunits within a variety of companies—a typical three-level nesting structure. Analysis of variance (ANOVA) would be problematic because of the complexity of the grouping structure (i.e., three organizational levels containing many subunits and organizations).

Instead, the researcher might attempt an ordinary least squares (OLS) regression, using either a disaggregation or aggregation approach (e.g., de Leeuw, 1992). The single-level regression model also produces several analytical difficulties including a forced choice over the proper unit of analysis (i.e., whether to conduct the analysis among individuals or at a higher group level), trade-offs in measurement precision, and limitations in the regression models employed (Raudenbush, 1995). In the disaggregation approach, the researcher would analyze the data at the individual level—that is, considering only the total number of individuals in the sample without regard to the higher level organizational structures. This approach, however, violates the required assumption of independence of errors among individuals in the sample. In other words, single-level analyses require the researcher to assume incorrectly that individuals within similar subunits and organizations share no common characteristics or perceptions, which leads to the possibility of biased regression coefficients and associated standard errors. It is important to recognize, therefore, that if the researcher uses an individual-level analysis, it implies that no systematic influence of macrolevel variables is expected and therefore all macro influence is incorporated into the error term of the model (Kreft & de Leeuw, 1998).

Instead of using the disaggregation approach, the researcher might attempt to avoid potential individual-level biases by aggregating data from individuals and subunits within each organization and then building a linear model that explores between-organizational differences in the aggregates (i.e., usually organizational means are examined). In this manner, the individual and department data may be used to obtain a mean for each organization. Unfortunately, this approach with OLS regression also presents problems because the differences at the aggregate level typically appear stronger than they would be if within-organizational variation were also considered (Draper, 1995; Kaplan & Elliott, 1997). This is because organizational-level analyses reduce the variability present within each organizational unit (or subunit) to a single mean. Because the numer of groups in the study can be small, the statistical problems of small sample sizes all apply including unreliable estimates, low statistical power, and misleading statistical inference. Ignoring individual variability and then making statements about individuals through conducting a group-level analysis is known as the *ecological fallacy* (Robinson, 1950). As the reader will no doubt realize, attempting to use OLS regression estimates in a three-level setting (i.e., individuals nested in departments nested in organizations) complicates the problem even more and would require a different algorithm. The unit of analysis problem suggests that OLS regression estimates are not robust to misspecification of the number of levels in the data structure (Raudenbush, 1995).

In contrast to single-level regression models, the multilevel regression model specification facilitates the consideration of a variety of substantive issues about the relationships of individuals to their organizational contexts. One example of this is whether perceptions about organizational processes (e.g., culture, morale) are basic properties of the organization (and should be measured at the organizational level), or merely properties of the individuals who perceive them (Burstein, 1980). Prior to the development of multilevel analytic techniques, few satisfactory solutions to the measurement and analysis of these types of organizational variables emerged, although concerns were raised repeatedly (e.g., Burstein, 1980; Kish, 1957; Walsh, 1947) and corresponding approaches were laid out (e.g., Aitken & Longford, 1986; Cronbach & Webb, 1975; Dempster, Laird, & Rubin, 1977; Goldstein, 1987; Lindley & Smith, 1972; Muthén, 1989, 1991; Schmidt, 1969; Wong & Mason, 1985).

Although psychologists have argued that perceptions are individual measures and therefore that individual-level analyses should prevail, sociologists have pointed out that individuals and their organizational units influence each other. Because of this interdependence, the statistical assumptions of the analysis are violated and too many independent degrees of freedom are utilized in the model—that is, corresponding to the number of individuals rather than the number of organizations. An early solution to this conceptual and methodological problem was to conduct analyses at both the individual and aggregate levels and look for findings consistent across models. These separate analyses, however, did not really address contextual issues about how individuals may influence their contextual settings, as well as how they may be influenced by those contexts. Ultimately, the question of the "proper" unit of analysis and model specification became one of developing statistical models that could provide an explicit representation of the multiple organizational levels frequently encountered in social science research (Bryk & Raudenbush, 1992). While some of the problems of single-level analyses remain in multilevel analyses (e.g., small numbers of groups), the approach gives expanded options for improving the investigated model's estimates.

Along with the possibilities presented by multilevel approaches, it should be emphasized that often single-level analyses conducted at either the individual or group level suffice quite well, depending on the structure and characteristics of specific data sets (de Leeuw & Kreft, 1995). In many practical applications to organizational studies to date, for example, most of the variance in outcome or other process variables has been found to exist at the individual level (e.g., see Lee & Bryk, 1989). We should always be mindful of the multilevel structure of data present in organizational research, but even if the multilevel nature of the data is taken into account, there are various modeling options that can be considered (de Leeuw & Kreft, 1995).

MULTILEVEL REGRESSION MODELING

If we determine that there is sufficient variance in an outcome to be explained at different organizational levels, multilevel regression models offer a number of advantages, both conceptual and technical, over the previous OLS regression and ANOVA approaches (Draper, 1995) and the single-level multivariate framework. Most importantly, multilevel regression encompasses a mathematical modeling environment within which researchers can investigate theories about functional relationships among variables at each level of the organizational or sampling hierarchy. Multilevel analysis provides a means of partitioning the outcome variable's variance into different levels (e.g., within and between units) and within the analysis, a means of assigning explanatory variables to different organizational levels.

An example may help illustrate the point. In accounting for learning outcomes, educational theorists have often expressed concern with the relationship between individual variables (e.g., gender, previous learning, socioeconomic background, motivation), classroom (teacher variables), and school characteristics (e.g., size, academic environment, goal structures). Multilevel regression analysis provides a more refined environment in which to test these theoretical relationships, because the variables comprising the models can be specified correctly (i.e., according to educational theory) within the analysis. Of course, where within-unit similarities are hypothesized to be present due to context or organizational structure, it is also reasonable to question the extent to which individuals in a particular context all share a similar view of that context, whether there might be multiple, overlapping contexts of relevance, and whether the impact of a particular context is distributed evenly across individuals (Mason, 1995).

Second, with respect to nested data structures where variability is actually present across levels, multilevel analyses yield better calibrated uncertainty estimates of the individual parameters (e.g., variance in standard errors). More specifically, this is often an issue of the extent to which multilevel models offer an improvement in the precision of these measurements over previously used analytic approaches such as OLS regression (Longford, 1993). This is important because ignoring the clustering effects on individuals results in smaller standard errors and hence more findings of significant parameters in the model. On the other hand, in the absence of between-unit variability (i.e., where the intraclass correlation is nearly zero), there is little need to perform a multilevel analysis. The single-level analysis would provide correct estimates of the standard errors.

In typical situations, multilevel regression involves at least two submodels: one for the data at level 1 (the individual level), and another specifying the unknown distributions for each individual parameter at level 2 (the group level). A variety of models can be specified, from those where the outcome (e.g., an intercept) only is treated as a random coefficient (and the individual-level predictors are fixed, or assumed to have constant variance across units), to ones where some or all of the individual variables may be treated as random coefficients that vary across level-2 units. The general 2-level model can be extended to include other organizational levels. Another useful extension of the multilevel regression model is the investigation of multivariate outcomes for each individual (e.g., using several measures of productivity). We develop this latter model in more detail in chapter 8.

Finally, multilevel linear models offer a single framework that combines the information within and across units (called exchangeability) to produce more accurate explanations of outcomes (Draper, 1995). Thus, they bring together regression equations at the individual level and the group level into a single statistical model. In this manner, multilevel models allow the comparison of differences between schools or other types of organizations after adjusting for differences attributable to their individual members.

Estimating Level-1 Intercepts and Slopes

As we noted earlier, one advantage of multilevel modeling is that it allows us to treat a level-1 intercept or regression coefficient (slope) as randomly varying across the number of groups in the sample. We can begin our multilevel analysis by estimating an individual regression equation for each group using OLS regression. If the errors in the model are normally distributed, the OLS estimates are be the unique, minimum-variance, unbiased estimators of the parameters (Bryk & Raudenbush, 1992). Developing a separate regression equation for each unit would require us to estimate a large number of separate models. Because organizational units would likely vary in size, some groups might be too small to give accurate estimates of the relationships. For example, if an organization had a small sample or a restricted range on a particular variable of interest, its slope estimates would tend to be imprecise. The sum of the slope estimates across the organizational units would then appear to be more variable than the true parameters were in actuality. Because group sample size affects measurement precision, we should take into consideration the precision of the estimation of parameters within each organizational unit if we are to achieve an accurate estimation of the model's parameters (Bryk & Raudenbush, 1992).

On the other hand, we could decide to ignore the precision of measurement within each group. Instead, we could just pool all the information for each group together and conduct the analysis at the group level. Each group would have one coefficient, regardless of the number of individuals within the group that contributed to calculating the coefficient. In cases where the number of individuals within a particular unit is small, however, the results are "shrunk" to the overall solution (Kreft & de Leeuw, 1998). What this means is that we would lose important information about the variability of individual units because of differences in their sample sizes and corresponding precision of measurement. This results in biased parameter estimation.

We must therefore improve on the OLS estimates within each group in order to be able to compare intercepts and slopes across groups of different sizes and measurement precision. Random-coefficient, or multilevel regression, models represent a compromise between modeling each organization separately and modeling all contexts simultaneously within the same model (Kreft & de Leeuw, 1998). They avoid the pitfall associated with conducting either a microlevel or macrolevel OLS regression analysis. In this way, multilevel models account for individual variability associated with each unit and also avoid the tendency for individual units to be shrunk into an overall solution. Although this framework has many conceptual benefits in studying organizations, providing estimates of the multilevel parameters has proven to be much more complex than OLS regression and has drawn considerable attention from researchers over the past couple of decades.

As Bryk and Raudenbush (1992) indicated, three conceptually distinct approaches have been used to estimate random coefficients models: Bayes estimation, full information maximum likelihood (FIML), and restricted maximum likelihood (REML) (see Dempster, Rubin, & Tsutakawa, 1981, for a discussion of the differences among these approaches). Each method rests on a slightly different set of assumptions, and we emphasize that the statistical theory underlying multilevel models is relatively complex. As we have suggested, we can start with OLS estimates of each unit's intercept and slope coefficients. In the Bayesian approach, the optimal estimator of a level-1 intercept or slope is a weighted combination of the within-group and between-group components based on the relative reliability of the group's data. Bayes (or shrinkage) estimators take into consideration the precision of each group's regression line (Lindley & Smith, 1972). For example, if the sample mean for the group is highly reliable, more weight will be placed upon the within-group portion of the estimate. If the sample mean is relatively unreliable, the estimated grand mean will be given more weight in composing the estimate (Bryk & Raudenbush, 1992). Because these estimates are weighted according to their precision, they represent an improvement over the OLS regression estimates across a variety of conditions found in the level-2 units (e.g., unbalanced within-unit sample sizes, situations where some groups have sparse data, small sample sizes).

Multilevel modeling also allows the researcher to investigate the variation in regression coefficients (slopes) comprising each unit's regression equation across the set of units. Of course, the precision of the slope coefficients is of concern in accurately estimating the structural parameters of multilevel models. As we have suggested, the interaction of measurement precision in estimating a level-1 intercept or slope and the sampling distribution of level-2 units in the study is known as *shrinkage*. *Unconditional* shrinkage refers to the tendency of the individual unit's intercept or slope to be pulled toward the grand mean (i.e., the mean of all units) during estimation. If we just used OLS regression, for example, unit estimates would tend to be more varied and therefore relatively imprecise. Especially where within-unit samples are small, shrinkage toward the mean is most pronounced—and most needed—to offset the instability of the OLS estimates (Raudenbush, 1988). By pulling each unit's regression equation toward the mean equation, the Bayes estimator smooths the individual-unit equations, generally resulting in a more reliable set of estimates (Raudenbush, 1988).

Shrinkage estimators produced through Bayes estimation will be more accurate than the OLS estimates when the within-unit model is appropriately specified; that is, the underlying assumption of the empirical Bayes approach is that, given the predictors in the between-organizations model, the regression lines for each organizational unit are "conditionally exchangeable" (Bryk & Raudenbush, 1992). Exchangeability means that the researcher has no reason to believe that the deviation of any unit's regression line from its predicted value should be larger or smaller than that of any other unit (Bryk & Raudenbush, 1992). This is functionally equivalent to assuming that the data on organizations constitute a simple random sample (de Finetti, 1964). Under this assumption, exchangeability lays the basis for hypothesis testing, even when no formal sampling mechanism is involved (Raudenbush, 1995).

Where this assumption is not valid, however, unconditional shrinkage becomes indefensible (Bryk & Raudenbush, 1992). In these situations, the researcher may need to make another type of adjustment to the parameter estimates of each unit. For example, in a study of organizations, our theory may tell us that service-oriented organizations should have flatter slopes than product-oriented organizations. Under principles of unconditional shrinkage, a typical service-oriented organization would have its slope increased, or pulled toward the grand mean, which is itself made steeper by the product-oriented organizations in the sample. Conversely, the product-oriented organizations have their slopes flattened because of the existence of the service-oriented organizations.

A remedy for this problem is called *conditional* shrinkage, where instead, each group's slope estimate is pulled toward a *predicted value* based on that group's unit-level characteristics (Bryk & Raudenbush, 1992; Raudenbush, 1988). For example, if our theory tells us that the magnitude of the level-1 regression coefficients in our study ought to depend on level-2 variables, we can use this knowledge to improve the estimates of the level-1 coefficients (e.g., see Strenio, 1981). In the case where the variability of the "true" group parameters was completely explained by their respective level-2 models, the shrinkage would be total, and the predicted values based on the organizational-level model and the empirical Bayes estimates would be the same (Bryk & Raudenbush, 1992). The idea of conditional shrinkage, therefore, greatly expands the cases where shrinkage estimators can be profitably used within multilevel analyses. In this situation, the assumption of exchangeability can be relaxed.

Shrinkage is obviously a phenomenon that must be considered within multilevel modeling. An advantage of taking shrinkage into consideration in the multilevel model is the greater reliability of predictions, whereas a disadvantage is that estimates are often unrealistic for units that have few observations (Kreft & de Leeuw, 1998). It is of interest to note that where there is little variance between organizational units, there is little shrinkage for the individual (within-unit) component and therefore little benefit to using a multilevel model. An individual-level OLS regression analysis would suffice.

In contrast, as we suggested, where almost all of the variance is between units, there is nearly full shrinkage to the grand mean, so that familiar between-unit OLS regression methods can be used (see Bryk & Raudenbush, 1992, pp. 78–82, for further discussion on shrinkage in multilevel modeling). In between these extremes, however, underestimation of between-group variance can often occur (Morris, 1995), due to a variety of factors including, for example, the unreliability of measurement of observed variables (Muthén, 1994), model misspecification that can lead to shrinkage of estimates (Bryk & Raudenbush, 1992; Morris, 1995), and the possible shortcomings of methods of estimation generally used in producing the estimates for different group sample sizes and distributions (Chou & Bentler, 1995; de Leeuw & Kreft, 1995; Morris, 1995).

Estimating Level-2 Parameters

Besides the issue of shrinkage addressed by Bayes estimation, another obvious difficulty in estimating multilevel models is that the outcome variable in the between-unit model is not directly observed. As we have argued, an intercept and slope can be estimated for each level-1 unit using OLS estimation. In this approach, however, efficient estimation requires that the random errors are independent, normally distributed, and have constant variance (Bryk & Raudenbush, 1992). In random coefficients models, we wish to model the differences in unit intercepts and slopes across the sample of units in the study. This requires modeling an error structure that is more complex. In this case, OLS assumptions about error are violated. In the multilevel case, the errors within each level-2 unit are dependent because they are common to all individuals within that unit. The errors also have unequal variances (Bryk & Raudenbush, 1992). Because of this complexity, neither the level-2 coefficients nor the error structures would be estimated appropriately using OLS regression (Bryk & Raudenbush, 1992).

Past use of multilevel modeling was limited by the fact that only in cases of perfectly balanced sampling designs (i.e., equal group sizes) were closed-form mathematical formulas available to estimate the variance and covariance components (Bryk & Raudenbush, 1992). Because variance and covariance components must be estimated, when sampling designs are unbalanced, iterative estimation procedures must be used to obtain efficient estimates. Some of the limitations associated with OLS regression have been addressed through newer, iterative methods of model estimation. Most researchers agree that Dempster et al. (1977) provided a breakthrough for numerical efficiency in using maximum likelihood to estimate variance components in balanced and unbalanced designs (due to missing data).

Presently, maximum likelihood (ML) methods of estimation (i.e., FIML and REML) are most frequently used in multivariate research, but they require assumptions about the nature of the sample chosen from the population. ML estimation is based on characteristics of multivariate normality within the sample covariance matrix in order to produce optimal (i.e., consistent and asymptotically efficient) estimates of the population parameters. Because of this, it requires relatively large sample sizes. Of course, in real-life settings, the sample data may depart from normality and therefore may not represent the population accurately. REML estimation provides similar estimates to FIML where the level-2 sample size is large, and better estimates of variance components than full maximum likelihood under conditions where there are smaller numbers of level-2 units (Bryk & Raudenbush, 1992). In other occasions, however, the sample may only be a crude representation of some population, as in a convenience sample.

By using an iterative fitting function such as ML, the parameter coefficients can be more appropriately weighted by considering the covariance structure among the errors. This affects the precision of the structural coefficients considered across the level-2 units, because the amount of data available in each organization will generally vary (Bryk & Raudenbush, 1992). Similar to Bayes estimation, in estimating the structural parameters with ML, the contribution from each organization is weighted in proportion to its precision of measurement. As Bryk and Raudenbush (1992) suggested, this optimal weighting through ML estimation has the effect of minimizing the effects of unreliability on inferences about the model parameters (i.e., by yielding more accurate estimates of standard errors).

Small Numbers of Level-2 Units

Estimating the model's parameters is more problematic when there are small numbers of level-2 units in the study. One problem concerns the number of level-2 predictors that can be included in the model. Where researchers will often enter many predictors into a single-level regression analysis and remove the nonsignificant ones, this strategy may not work where there are relatively few level-2 units. A common rule of thumb in regression analysis is to have a ratio of at least 10 observations per predictor (Bryk & Raudenbush, 1992). As Bryk and Raudenbush argued, for a single level-2 outcome, the number of observations is the number of level-2 units. With multiple random coefficients (e.g., slopes and intercept), however, it is not as clear how to count the number of level-2 observations against each possible level-2 equation, because of the possibility of correlated outcomes and multicollinearity both within and between equations. Moreover, in the case where the intraclass correlations of fixed level-1 predictors are large, this constrains the number of level-1 predictors that can be added to the model to the number of level-2 units. In contrast, if the intraclass correlations are small, the observations-to-predictor rule can be applied to the total number of individuals at level 1 (Bryk & Raudenbush, 1992).

A second problem concerns the method used to estimate the model. There has been considerable debate among methodologists about the efficiency of ML estimation under less than ideal sampling conditions (e.g., Longford, 1993; Morris, 1995; Muthén, 1994). With smaller numbers of level-2 units, Morris (1995) concluded that the problem of biased variance estimates is diminished somewhat for estimating the structural parameters (i.e., random coefficients), but they can still be understated. More importantly, when the number of level-2 units is small, the error variance is likely to be underestimated, resulting in standard error estimates that are too small, and a greater likelihood of committing Type I errors. This is because confidence intervals and hypothesis tests in both FIML and REML are conditional on the accuracy of the point estimates of the variance and covariance parameters (Bryk & Raudenbush, 1992).

In cases of small (or nonrandom) samples of level-2 units, maximum likelihood methods have a potential weakness that can be corrected by the Bayesian approach to the estimation of variances and covariances (Bryk & Raudenbush, 1992). The Bayesian approach is relatively complicated, however, and the underlying theory is not fully accessible to most researchers (Mason, 1995; Raudenbush, 1995), whereas ML methods are more readily available (Bayesian estimates are available within the HLM software [Bryk et al., 1996], as part of the analysis of a model's residuals). While most current SEM programs were designed primarily for single-level analyses, Bayesian estimates are now available in LISREL 8.30 within the program's multilevel modeling approach and the upcoming multilevel version of EQS (Bentler, personal communication, April 4, 1999).

We dealt with the concept of shrinkage when we wished to consider the random variation of intercepts or slopes across a number of groups. As we suggested, the empirical Bayesian approach yields an estimate of one of these unknown level-1 coefficients that uses not only the data from that unit, but also data from all other similar units. Because the researcher can make inferences about the regression coefficients that are not conditional on specific point estimates as in ML, but rather on posterior distributions in the data, Bayesian estimates appear to do a better job of accounting for uncertainty in the random coefficients estimates in situations where the data are less than ideal (Morris, 1995; Lindley & Smith, 1972; Smith, 1973). Given particular types of samples (e.g., random versus convenience), in the Bayesian perspective probability is viewed as a subjective uncertainty about the process that produces the data, rather than the relative frequency of occurrence in a population (Raudenbush, 1995). Thus, in the Bayesian view, empirical research combines new data with prior information, and therefore replication of results becomes an important part of the investigation. The Bayesian approach can be considered where the number of groups is small (Raudenbush, 1998).

Fortunately, however, a growing body of research (e.g., Chou & Bentler, 1995; Hoyle & Panter, 1995; Raudenbush, 1995) suggests ML yields reasonable estimates under a variety of less than optimal conditions (i.e., small samples, departure from multivariate normality). Raudenbush (1995) argued that ML methods can also be used adequately in a variety of cases where the number of level-2 units is relatively small. A number of empirical studies have investigated these issues related to the estimation of both single-level and multilevel models. For example, Hartley and Rao (1967) provided ML estimation for the mixed linear model. Harville (1977) synthesized alternative procedures for maximum likelihood estimation of variance components. Goldstein (1986) developed the iterative generalized least squares (GLS) approach to maximum likelihood estimation in multilevel linear models.

It is well known that REML, the method of estimation used in HLM, duplicates a variety of mixed-model ANOVA designs for balanced data designs, while facilitating generalization to more complex unbalanced designs (Raudenbush, 1995). For example, Marcoulides (1987) used REML in estimating variance components under various normal and nonnormal sampling conditions and found that REML holds up quite well over the different conditions. Goldstein (1987) demonstrated that multilevel modeling can duplicate standard multivariate results. Fotiu (1989) provided a simulation study comparing REML and Bayes estimation and showed that inferences about regression parameters with maximum likelihood were quite robust, unless there was great imbalance across the level-2 units. Similarly, for multilevel covariance structure models, Muthén (1989) developed a quasi-maximum likelihood estimator (called MUML) to use in cases where the sample sizes of level-2 units differ. Muthén's estimation procedure has been shown to approximate maximum likelihood estimation, especially where sample sizes are not greatly different, and is much easier to implement.

Because the issue of appropriate model estimation under different types of conditions is not settled yet, when choosing a method of model estimation the researcher should consider the nature of the sampling scheme for level-2 and the degree of imbalance within those units. Although individuals may be chosen at random within units, they are seldom assigned at random to their existing units. Although including a number of individual-level background variables helps us adjust for differences within units before making comparisons across units, every variable added to the model also contributes to its complexity. At some point, having too many variables in the model may actually create problems in modeling and interpreting the meaning of the between-unit differences (Longford, 1993). Accurately modeling the distribution of effects across the sample of level-2 units that either may be nonrandom or may depart from normality, therefore, is generally more of a problem in multilevel modeling than problems presented by the number of individuals sampled within each unit (e.g., Morris, 1995). In actual cases where level-2 units are also randomly sampled, the idea of random variation at both levels is very appealing.

When the number of organizational units is large, any consistent method of estimation may be used. However, when the number of units is small, accurate estimation may be more difficult to ensure because of the non-normal features of these units (Morris, 1995). As we have argued, smaller numbers of level-2 units can lead to the underestimation of individual variances and hence level-2 regression coefficients may be misleading (Raudenbush, 1995). Where the purpose of the analysis may be to derive more adequate measures of the level-2 variance uncertainty, with small numbers of level-2 units the analysis could become suspect using ML estimation.

In most other cases, where the level-2 units may not be randomly sampled, or there may only be a small number of units available to study, problems in using the multilevel modeling approach may develop. In these cases, it is quite likely that the level-2 units (e.g., organizations) are not normally distributed. As Goldstein (1995b) argued, when convenience samples are used with level-2 units, it is often because researchers believe that there is a close correspondence between their convenience sample and a real population of interest. This assumed correspondence, however, can be difficult to quantify (Draper, 1995; Goldstein, 1995b), and researchers often do not acknowledge this design weakness. Although the resultant model might fit the data well, the extent to which the results might be replicated in other samples would be uncertain. As Morris (1995) noted, programs are being developed to handle a variety of nonnormal distributions. Of course, replicating findings is one manner in which this limitation can be lessened.

Statistical Power and Model Testing

In designing multilevel studies, researchers also need to give attention to issues surrounding statistical power and the sensitivity of their models to hypothesis testing. Tests of statistical significance were designed to help the researcher assess evidence with respect to the probability of an event having arisen because of sampling error, assuming that the hypothesis being tested is true (Pedhazur & Schmelkin, 1991). The hypothesis being tested is the null hypothesis. Statistical power concerns the probability of rejecting the null hypothesis (e.g., that there is no statistically significant difference between group means) if it is *not* true.

As a practical matter, the evaluation of statistical power within a multilevel context is more complex than in the single-level context. Estimating power requires the researcher to consider the level of significance, the magnitudes (called *effect sizes*) and direction of any anticipated effects, the sample size (i.e, number of clusters or groups needed and their within-group sizes), and the likely within- and between-group variance (intraclass correlation) associated with the observations (see Hoyle & Panter, 1995; Kaplan, 1995; MacCallum, Roznowski, & Necowitz, 1992; Muthén & Satorra, 1995; Saris & Satorra, 1993; Satorra & Saris, 1985 for further discussion). The best time to think about these issues is in the design phase of studies.

One consideration in deciding whether or not to reject the null hypothesis in significance testing is the amount of error we are willing to accept in falsely rejecting or failing to reject the null hypothesis (see Pedhazur & Schmelkin, 1991, for an overview of how error, effect size, sample size, and statistical power are related to decisions to accept or reject the null hypothesis). *Type I error* (α) refers to the error of falsely rejecting the null hypothesis. Researchers often set the α region for rejection of a null hypothesis at .05 or .01. For example, if the researcher set α at .05, the researcher would falsely reject the null hypothesis 5 times in 100.

In contrast, *Type II error* (β) refers the failure to reject the null hypothesis when it should have been rejected. As we lower α to protect against making Type I errors, however, we increase the likelihood that we will make a Type II error. For example, where α is set at .001, we would be far less likely to make a false rejection (Type I error) of the null hypothesis. On the other hand, with α = .001, we might fail to find an important relationship (Type II error) in the data. The balancing of α and β, therefore, becomes the statistical power of the test to reject the null hypothesis when, in fact, it should be rejected.

Because *power* is defined as the probability of finding a significant effect if it indeed exists, power is closely tied to hypothesis testing. A *t*-test is one statistical test that is often used to determine the significance of a parameter, defined as the ratio of the estimate to its standard error (i.e., for a large sample, the required t-ratio is 1.96 at $\alpha = .05$). Because of this, the test of significance depends heavily on the accuracy of the standard error estimate in determining the significance of the parameter in the model. The estimated sampling variance of the parameter determines the power of the regression model. If the standard error is small, therefore, the power to detect the effect is high (Kreft & de Leeuw, 1998) and there is less chance of making a mistake regarding rejection or acceptance of the null hypothesis.

A second issue to consider is the anticipated magnitude of effects (called *effect size*). It is important to note that the larger the effect size (ES) considered meaningful, the greater is the power of the statistical test. This should make sense, because larger effects should be easier to detect in a sample. The researcher can use previous theory as a guide to what the anticipated effect size might be in the proposed study. Characteristics of the anticipated effects in a model being tested should therefore be considered in the sampling strategy.

A third issue is the sample size and the complexity the model. For example, sufficient sample sizes are required to determine whether parameters are indeed significant. With small samples, for example, effects may be hidden, which can lead to a failure to reject the null hypothesis when in fact it should be rejected (a Type II error). Increasing the sample size while holding the ES and significance level (α) constant, therefore, increases the power of the test and the chances of rejecting the null hypothesis when it should be rejected. Of course, there is a certain degree of capitalization on chance when sample data are used for the estimation of population parameters (Pedhazur & Schmelkin, 1991). As we have suggested, this tendency is known as shrinkage, and the larger the ratio of the number of independent variables to sample size, the larger is the estimated shrinkage. Because of the tendency of models to fit better in the sample than in the population, with small sample sizes more complex models may look like they fit the data better than they actually do.

Some have suggested rules of thumb, for example, a minimum of 100 to 150 subjects (Schumacker & Lomax, 1996), or ratios of between 5 to 10 individuals per variable (Bentler & Chou, 1987) for single-level analyses. With small samples (i.e., $N < 400$), therefore, the likelihood of finding a replicable model may be quite low (Hoyle & Panter, 1995; MacCallum et al., 1992).

Different methods of estimation (e.g., OLS regression, maximum likelihood) will also provide different estimates within a particular sample size, depending on whether they incorporate the clustering effects of the sample and its size. For example, maximum likelihood estimation techniques depend on large sample sizes, preferably at both levels, for the estimates to have desirable asymptotic properties. As we have suggested, OLS regression methods ignore the intraclass correlation and thus produce smaller (incorrect) standard errors. Because of this, we might falsely reject the null hypothesis (a Type I error) using OLS regression, especially with small group sizes and high intraclass correlations. Because ML estimation incorporates the intraclass correlation, it generally gives a more accurate estimate of the standard errors in multilevel modeling, which results in less bias in testing hypotheses about the significance of the model's parameters.

These issues and statistical power are so related that a small change in one can have a profound influence on power. With multilevel samples, the situation can get even more complicated. For example, with a sample having a large number of groups, a change in the size of the groups (within-group size) will have minimal impact on power. On the other hand, when the sample is comprised of a small number of groups, a relatively small change in the within-group size can have a substantial impact on statistical power (T. E. Duncan, personal communication, October 5, 1998). Where the power of the test is too low, it suggests that the study was not designed sufficiently to reject the null hypothesis for a given sample size, anticipated effect size, and level of significance. Failure to reject the null hypothesis can be due to a variety of factors including that the power of the test is too low, the null hypothesis is indeed true, the theory is faulty, or the variables have been poorly measured.

We can examine tables of statistical power for given effect sizes, significance levels, and sample size in beginning to plan studies (e.g., Cohen, 1988; Kirk, 1982), remembering that these tables were not designed for the model complexity inherent in many multilevel designs. With these power tables, we can illustrate the basic idea of how power works in a multilevel analysis. The power of the statistical test defined as is $1 - \beta$. Because researchers must balance Type I and Type II error in designing a study, many researchers consider setting power at .80 to be realistic in social scientific studies (i.e., 80% chance of correctly rejecting the null hypothesis). For example, the power tables for classical ANOVA experiments with balanced data (e.g., Kirk, 1982) suggest that holding power and alpha constant at .80 and .05 respectively, with 4 groups the researcher would need 11 subjects per group to detect a medium effect (i.e., a 1.5 standard deviation difference in means) between the highest and lowest groups. At the same power and alpha levels, for 8 groups, 14 subjects per group would be needed, and for 12 groups, 16 subjects per group would be a minimal requirement. The reader can no doubt see that adding groups makes more of a difference to statistical power than adding subjects within groups. The implication is that at some point we would have a sufficient within-group number of subjects.

As we have indicated, in multilevel designs, the required number of level-2 units needed is more problematic and depends on the anticipated effects and the complexity of the model being estimated. We must take into consideration the intraclass correlation when thinking about statistical power. Barcikowski (1981) demonstrated that in most analysis-of-variance studies ignoring intraclass correlations can greatly inflate the chances of making Type I errors. For example, in a study with 10 individuals in each group and an intraclass correlation of .2 (20% of the variance is between groups), the significance level of .05 is raised to .28. This would result in many more findings of significance. Similarly, small intraclass correlations in large groups can also inflate the alpha level.

We can extend the basic approach of analysis-of-variance designs to two-level, clustered samples. For variance components models (without randomly varying slopes), the sample design question of how many subjects and units are needed is analogous to that addressed by Kish (1965) in computing effective sample size in two-stage cluster sampling. Effective sample size considers the effect of the intraclass correlation (i.e., the level-2 variance component) in determining a study's sampling scheme. For a given intraclass correlation, adding numbers of units, for example, going from 20 to 100 (with 20 subjects per unit), produces an effective sample size almost four times as large as a similar study with 20 units and 100 subjects per unit.

In a series of multilevel simulations utilizing Kish's (1965) approach with various types of sampling designs, Mok (1995) found that for smaller samples ($N < 800$) there is less bias in designs involving relatively more level-2 units and fewer subjects per unit, than in sample designs involving fewer units and more subjects per unit. For estimating level-1 coefficients the total number of observations is important. In Mok's study, a total subject sample size of larger than 800 produced estimates of the fixed components of the slope and intercept that were within 1 standard error of the true value, regardless of whether there were relatively more units and fewer subjects per unit, or fewer units and more subjects per unit.

The power of level-2 estimates clearly depends on the number of groups in the study (Kreft & de Leeuw, 1998). In Mok's (1995) study, however, estimating the variance of random slopes required larger numbers of units to provide reliable estimates. Estimates of the level-2 slope variance were all within 1 standard deviation of the true variance in designs where there were relatively more units and fewer subjects per unit, and the total sample size was at least 1200 (see also Busing, 1993). Bassiri (1988) determined that to detect cross-level interactions with sufficient power, one might need at least 30 groups with 30 individuals within each group. Sufficient power to detect cross-level effects, therefore, can be obtained when the number of groups is at least 20 or so, and there are sufficient within-group numbers (Kreft and de Leeuw, 1998). When more groups are present, such as 150 or so, five observations per group (for a total $N = 750$) would suffice to bring power to .90 (Kreft & de Leeuw, 1998). The reader will note that these results are very similar to those found in Mok's (1995) study (see Bassiri, 1988, or Mok, 1995, for further discussion and guidelines for balancing level-1 and level-2 sample sizes).

In the multilevel design, there are many more things that can affect power. Although classical experimental designs utilize balanced data and seldom estimate many parameters in a model, many SEM analyses estimate a large number of parameters (e.g., structural coefficients between latent variables, factor loadings, factor covariances, errors of measurement). Our belief is that researchers will continue to refine methods of testing multilevel models, offering expanded options in the future. Most discussions of sample size and related issues (e.g., shrinkage, effect size) are based on the use of probability samples. When convenience samples are used for level-2 groups, it is unclear what the effects might be. As we have suggested, caution should certainly be exercised, especially in putting strong credibility in results where level-2 sample sizes are small. Similarly, missing data may potentially bias the analysis (Byrne, 1995). Of course, the best data collection procedure is to have large numbers of observations per unit, relatively large numbers of units (Mason, 1995), and little or no missing data. Changes in any one of those conditions affect the completeness of our knowledge. In the real world, however, it is not always possible to utilize optimal sampling methods. Therefore, each individual study must be judged on its strengths and weaknesses, as well as how it contributes (whether flawed or not) to the development of research knowledge.

MULTILEVEL STRUCTURAL EQUATION MODELING

In addition to the regression models developed specifically for multilevel (i.e., clustered sampling) data, other approaches for data analysis are also currently being developed. One approach that can be adapted to the analysis of multilevel data is structural equation modeling (SEM) because of its flexibility in modeling relatively complex theoretical relationships. Although this approach and corresponding computer software have been widely accepted in the analysis of single-level multivariate data, SEM has not been widely applied to multilevel data analysis (Hox, 1995; Muthén, 1994). At present, multilevel data structures are more difficult to analyze properly with existing structural equation modeling (SEM) software. Our initial attempts with programs such as *Mplus* and STREAMS were very encouraging. Because of their relevance to the investigation of social and organizational processes, however, we believe these techniques will continue to be expanded and refined in the near future and therefore should become more accessible.

SEM provides a flexible framework that makes possible the specification and testing of a wide variety of theoretical models including those with latent (unmeasured) variables, multiple dependent variables, measurement errors, and models with mediating, longitudinal, or reciprocal effects. Because organizations have complex structural relationships (e.g., multivariate models with direct and indirect effects, nested effects), SEM techniques are often well suited to studies of leadership, organizational processes, and organizational outcomes. SEM techniques can therefore be used to address the inherent multilevel structure of such data and to provide a means of explicating the relatively complex theoretical models used to explain organizational relationships between and across levels.

In general, SEM represents a synthesis of factor-analytic techniques developed in psychology with simultaneous equation modeling (path analysis) from econometrics and sociology (Kaplan, 1998). Several types of multilevel SEM models have been formulated through the SEM approach (see Kaplan & Elliott, 1997, McArdle & Hamagami, 1996, Muthén, 1994, Muthén & Muthén, 1998, and Willett & Sayer, 1996, for some illustrations). Recently, researchers have attempted to integrate multilevel regression modeling with structural equation modeling to provide a general methodological approach that would account for clustered sampling, population heterogeneity, measurement error, and simultaneous equations (e.g., Kaplan & Elliott, 1997; Hox, 1995; Kaplan, 1998; Muthén, 1989, 1991, 1992, 1994; Raudenbush, Rowan, & Kang, 1991). It turns out that the basic features of the SEM approach can be readily adapted to fitting a variety of multilevel models. As we have also noted, multilevel regression programs such as HLM (Bryk & Raudenbush, 1992) and LISREL 8.30 (Jöreskog & Sörbom, 1999) can also be adapted to provide estimates of measurement errors and models with multiple dependent variables (see chap. 8). This overlap between approaches provides researchers with many options for modeling multilevel relationships.

The general form of a structural equation model actually consists of two interrelated submodels. The first is the measurement model, which relates unobserved (latent) variables to their observed indicators; the second is the structural model, which estimates the relationships between the latent variables. The approach was presented by Jöreskog in 1977. Since then, a great number of technical strides have been made in using structural equation modeling with real-world data, including problems of statistical power, violations of normality, strategies for handling missing data, indices to assess the fit of models, and model modification strategies (Kaplan, 1998). More extended introductions to SEM can be found in Marcoulides and Hershberger (1997), Pedhazur and Schmelkin (1991), and Schumacker and Lomax (1996).

Similar to multilevel regression modeling, multilevel SEM models (or multilevel variance components models) also make use of the variance-de-

composition approach (McArdle & Hamagami, 1996). Within a hierarchical or nested data set (e.g., individuals within organizations), variance is
first decomposed to provide an individual component within each organization and a group component across a set of organizations. Rather than
giving estimates for all separate group mean differences from a grand
mean, however, the approach provides an estimate of the variance of these
mean differences.

We can specify several different types of multilevel theoretical models
within a SEM framework. Some of these basic models include path models
that investigate two-level relationships among observed variables, two-level
factor (measurement) models that focus on the definition of latent (underlying) constructs through their observed indicators, and two-level structural models that focus on the relationships among latent variables. One
important advantage is that multilevel structural models allow the investigation of direct and indirect effects both within and between organizations.
Another use of SEM methods is for modeling individual growth trajectories
with latent variables (e.g., see Duncan & Duncan, 1996, Muthén & Muthén,
1998, Willett & Sayer, 1996, for a thorough discussion of SEM methods in
growth modeling), while also incorporating features of organizations. These
latter methods are relatively complex and, as such, this discussion is outside
of the scope of our introduction to multilevel modeling.

Multilevel Path Models

A first type of multilevel SEM model is the multilevel path model. This is
a simplified model that uses only observed variables instead of latent constructs. Unlike the multilevel regression model, however, the path model
allows researchers to investigate more complex relationships that include
intervening variables and therefore indirect effects (effects through several
paths). This can facilitate specifying separate sets of structural relationships
for each level of the organization. The multilevel path model, however,
does not include separate error terms for the variables in the model (because all variables are observed), which potentially introduces sources of
bias into the analysis of the model's parameters.

This is an important limitation for several reasons. First, the unreliability
of the observed measures affects, to some extent, the variance decomposition of the variables across organizational levels into their within- and
between-organizational components (Muthén, 1991). Second, as Kaplan
(1998) noted, in the multilevel path model, measurement error in an
outcome variable will affect the precision of measurement, whereas measurement error in the input variables will affect the accuracy of the estimates.
Where the specific focus is not on measurement error, path models can
be a useful approach to multilevel modeling of organizational processes.

Multilevel Factor Models

A second type of multilevel SEM analysis is where researchers may wish to investigate underlying constructs through factor analysis. Many social processes are conceived as structural processes operating among unobserved constructs. Factor analysis a useful general approach for investigating the relationships between constructs and their observed indicators because it provides a mathematical model that links the observations, or manifestations, of the underlying processes to the theories and constructs through which we interpret and understand them (Ecob & Cuttance, 1987). One way to define constructs through their observed indicators is referred to in the literature as *confirmatory factor analysis* (CFA), which is the first submodel within the SEM approach. Through CFA, the researcher can assess the reliability and validity of the measurements through the careful specification of constructs and their indicators prior to their actual testing with data. This is often a step that is given little attention in the preliminary stages of investigating theoretical models. The lack of measurement quality in defining constructs can be an important limitation to the credibility of results stemming from the test of a particular theory. We can certainly improve the credibility of our results by paying more attention to the reliability and validity of constructs comprising a theoretical model.

It is relatively easy to conceptualize multilevel factor models having a variety of complex formulations (e.g., latent and observed variables, multiple sources of error). Actually fitting the models, however, has presented sizable problems in the past because of the necessity of estimating the fixed and random coefficients across levels. Cronbach (1976), for example, in the mid 1970s discussed issues of using factor analysis with multilevel data. Despite this attention, the ideas did not have a large impact on factor analysis practice with multilevel data, most likely because the methodology and software lagged behind (Muthén, 1991). Dempster and colleagues' (1977) and Harville's (1977) applications of maximum likelihood to the estimation of variance components provided an initial means to estimate covariance structures for both balanced and unbalanced sampling designs (Dempster et al., 1981; Little & Rubin, 1987). More recently, McDonald and Goldstein (1989) and Muthén (1989, 1991, 1994) provided some of the initial work for multilevel factor analysis.

Because of limited options for analyzing multilevel data, previous investigation of constructs in organizational research was generally limited to defining models at the individual level without reference to the nested nature of the data. As we have suggested, this can have effects on the estimates of the parameters and the stability of the model over the group structures in a study. The larger the number of individuals sampled within each organization, and the more homogeneous those individuals are with respect to what is measured, the larger is the underestimation of the true variance of the estimator when using a variance coefficient based on simple random sampling (Muthén, 1991, 1994). On the other hand, simply aggregating individuals' measurements to the group level may ignore the inherent within-group variability.

In comparison to other single-level SEM analyses, multilevel factor analysis and SEM build on a different set of assumptions. Like the multilevel regression model, multilevel SEM approaches relax the assumption of identically distributed observations. This is analogous to random coefficients in regression models (Muthén, 1994). The general statistical model for multilevel covariance structure analysis is complicated and difficult to implement as a practical matter because of the inherent complexities of having separate covariance matrices for each unit (Hox, 1995; McArdle & Hamagami, 1996). One way to simplify the analysis is to assume that there is one population of individuals that are clustered in groups. Instead of developing a separate covariance matrix for each unit, the population covariance matrix is decomposed into two separate models for the within-groups and between-groups structures. The two models are then analyzed simultaneously through the multiple-group option available with most SEM software programs.

Multilevel covariance structure analysis allows the researcher to consider multiple sources of variance (e.g., individual-related, group-related, measurement error at both levels) in the total observed covariance matrix. Variance at each level may be explained in terms of a separate set of predictor variables. For example, tests of the invariance of the factor model within and between groups may consider the invariance of the factor loadings, the measurement properties of the observed variables, and factor variances and covariances at each level. These tests allow the researcher to consider a number of substantive concerns such as whether the same constructs are being measured across groups, whether the constructs vary in the same manner across groups (called *dispersion* invariance), and whether there is "level" invariance—relative similarities between and across groups (McArdle & Hamagami, 1996). This formulation provides great flexibility in modeling the complexity of organizational phenomena.

Measurement models (i.e., multilevel factor models) that incorporate the nested nature of the data can be of great interest themselves, or as the preliminary part of a multilevel structural equation model. For example, our concern may be with the reliability and validity of several constructs and their interrelationships within and across a number of organizations. A simple linear regression approach would not work, however, because we wish to incorporate measurement error in defining each underlying construct through several observed indicators.

Multilevel factor analysis can also help us examine how differences in intraclass correlations of the observed variables may affect the measurement of the latent variables (i.e., the loadings, the factor variance, the measurement error) in both the within-group and between-group factor models (Muthén, 1994). For example, the intraclass correlations (i.e., the proportion of variance between units) of the observed variables used to define a factor may vary from .05 (5% between-group variance) to .30 or so. This information would be important in assessing the measurement properties of the between-group factor. In this type of multilevel analysis, therefore, both the reliability of the individual measures and the validity of the constructs may be more thoroughly examined.

Multilevel factor analyses provides a revised (i.e., error-free) estimate of the proportion of between-level variance for the variables. This gives a more complete means of comparing the substance of results (e.g., the breakdown of variance components) using a latent measure versus single, observed measures (e.g., through combining items into one scale). To accomplish these analyses, however, we have emphasized that larger sample sizes are needed (especially in the number of organizational units). Although the more sophisticated components of this approach are beyond the scope of this introductory volume, it suggests the significance of structural equation applications such as confirmatory factor analysis to multilevel data.

Multilevel Structural Models With Latent Variables

After examining the reliability and validity of measures defining important organizational processes, the analyst can investigate the interrelationships among these constructs. For example, the researcher may wish to investigate how these organizational processes affect outcomes. Incorporating latent variables into the multilevel analysis can bring several benefits to the measurement of variables in a model and, hence, the accuracy of its structural relations. A second contribution of these models is that they allow the researcher to investigate simultaneously both direct effects and indirect effects (through other paths in the model). Indirect effects would be overlooked within the typical multilevel regression study.

We can also examine multilevel models with multiple dependent variables. Although we could define a series of separate models, an advantage of using a multilevel structural model is that we can specify all of the hypothesized relations within one model. Finally, investigating organizational processes within a full structural model allows the definition of a separate structural model operating at each level. The analyst could specify one model that includes indirect and direct effects for within-organization effects on outcomes and a different one for summarizing the impact of organizational variables on outcomes. This latter type of model can, however, be more difficult to test using currently available software. The SEM framework therefore provides a setting in which a variety of complex relations can be appropriately investigated.

SUMMARY

It is clear that multilevel models can be used to investigate a variety of organizational research problems. They can be an important analytical tool for researchers when they are used to test models guided by strong substantive theory. In the next two chapters we provide more detail about the mathematical models underlying the basic linear regression model (chap. 3) and the multilevel regression model (chap. 4).

Chapter 3

Linear Regression Models

In this chapter we provide some of the basic concepts of the general linear model as a background for our subsequent discussions about multilevel regression and covariance structure models. To gain a perspective from which to view the multilevel regression model and to provide a frame of reference, we develop some of the mathematical principles underlying the general linear regression model. We also consider some of the reasons for its continued widespread use in examining a variety of educational and organizational research problems. Readers desiring a more extended overview of these techniques can consult Pedhazur and Schmelkin (1991) for further discussion.

Linear models have a long tradition in the social sciences and have been used to explore myriad research topics. They have been particularly well suited to experimental, quasi-experimental, and nonexperimental research designs. Historically, researchers in fields such as experimental psychology and animal behavior have often favored analysis of variance (ANOVA) in the analysis of experimental and quasi-experimental designs, because in these cases, the independent variable is usually a treatment comprised of several categorical levels. The researcher's interest is often in examining differences in the outcome means (or variances) across the levels of one or more categorical independent variables.

In the analysis of covariance (ANCOVA), additional continuous variables may be added to the model and treated as covariates—that is, they are used to control for individual differences by equalizing subjects on the covariate before assessing the effects of the treatment variable. This results in a more refined assessment of the adjusted mean outcome for each group. In the past, these formulations of the linear model often worked optimally with balanced data—that is, with equal numbers of subjects assigned to every treatment group to minimize potential distortions due to departures from the assumptions of the tests of significance.

Linear models have also been widely used in nonexperimental research designs, where our concern is explaining an outcome as a function of a set of predictors. In this case, regression has been the method of choice, because in this type of linear model continuous variables can be incorporated directly into to the prediction of outcomes. Categorical variables can also be used in the model if they are appropriately recoded. The reason for this preference is also partly historical; in the social sciences such as sociology or education, researchers must generally study people in their natural settings (e.g., cities and neighborhoods, schools, places of employment), for example, by collecting data about them on a survey. The distinction between the regression and analysis of variance approaches, however, is largely one of terminology; applied to the same design and data, they yield identical results (e.g., see Bashaw & Findley, 1968; Pedhazur & Schmelkin, 1991). We mention this difference in terminology because whether multilevel models are formulated and discussed as "random coefficients" and "variance components" models versus multilevel regression models is partly a result of the historical traditions in the research fields from which the methods are derived.

DEVELOPING THE LINEAR REGRESSION MODEL

Linear regression is used as a formal means of expressing the tendency of a dependent (or outcome) variable, Y, to vary with an independent (or predictor) variable, X, in some systematic fashion. In simple regression, the functional relationship between these two variables is expressed as:

$$Y_i = \beta_0 + \beta_1 X_1 + \varepsilon_i \qquad (1)$$

where Y_i is the predicted value of observation i on the outcome of interest; β_0 is the Y intercept, or value of Y when X_1 is 0; β_1 is the slope, or the average change in Y associated with a one unit increase in X_1; X_1 is a known constant; and ε_i is the random error term.

To better understand the foundation of the simple regression model, consider data from a world in which no error exists. In this perfect world, two variables, Y and X, are presumed to be related according to some theoretical model. Assume, more specifically, this theoretical model posits values of Y are in some way dependent on values of X—that is, Y can be

TABLE 3.1
Heuristic Data Set #1

Y	X
2	0
5	1
8	2
11	3
14	4

expressed as some function of X. Data defining such a theoretical relationship are found in Table 3.1.

The simple regression model employs a linear function to express such relationships. In a perfect world with no error, this function is expressed as:

$$Y = \beta_0 + \beta_1 X \qquad (2)$$

and defines a line that passes through the field of joint Y–X values contained in Table 3.1. This line is determined by β_0, the Y intercept, or the point on the Y axis at which the line crosses when X is equal to 0; and β_1, the slope, or the unit increase in Y associated with a one-unit increase in X. We draw the reader's attention to the meaning of the terms *intercept* and *slope*, because these are key concepts in understanding the expanded research questions that can be asked through the use of the multilevel regression model we present in subsequent chapters.

A mathematically perfect linear relationship exists in the data contained in Table 3.1 and is illustrated by Fig. 3.1. Note that the functional relationship between Y and X is perfectly expressed by Eq. 2.

The scatterplot of Y and X in Fig. 3.1 reveals the linear nature of this relationship. By drawing a line through each of the joint values, we can determine that a one-unit increase in X yields a three-unit increase in Y; that is, the slope is 3. Moreover, Fig. 3.1 shows that the line expressing the relationship between X and Y crosses the Y axis at 2 (its intercept)—that is, when X = 0, Y = 2. Thus, the line determined by the data in Table 3.1 is perfectly expressed by the equation Y = 2 + 3X and in Fig. 3.2.

Perfect relationships such as the one just expressed are rarely found in social science data, however. Nonlinear relationships are often accompanied by multiple Y values at any given level of X—a condition under which no single predicted value will be correct in all cases. In such instances, there will be any number of lines that can be drawn through the joint X–Y values to express the relationship, and any straight line that is drawn will not perfectly fit through each of the data points. The problem in such

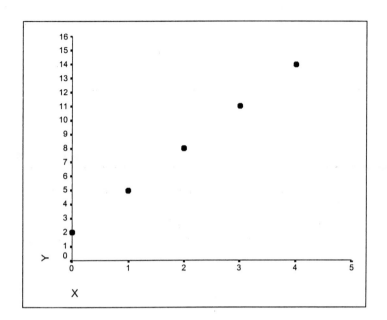

FIG. 3.1. Bivariate plot of perfect linear relationship.

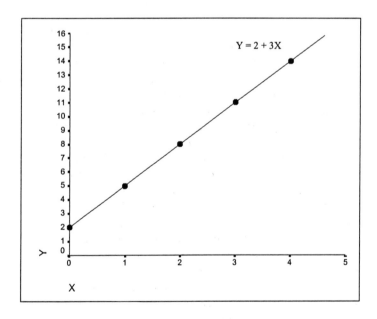

FIG. 3.2. Regression line for perfect linear relationship.

instances becomes the identification of the line that best captures the underlying structural relationship in the data. Moreover, this demands a more realistic model—a model that incorporates error in prediction, as in Eq. 1:

$$Y = \beta_0 + \beta_1 X + \varepsilon_i$$

The sole difference between Eq. 2, capturing a perfect Y–X relationship, and Eq. 1, capturing a more realistic linear, but imperfect Y–X relationship, is ε_i, the error associated with predicting Y based values of X.

Thus, Eq. 1 serves as a tool for defining the functional relationship between two variables where an outcome, Y, is generated by two components. The first component defines the "best" linear relationship between Y and X, $\beta_0 + \beta_1 X_1$. For any given level of X, there is a corresponding "predicted" level of Y, $(E[Y_i] = \beta_0 + \beta_1 X_1)$. The second component is ε_i, the "stochastic" or random source of variation. This "error" term, ε_i, is a random variable for which outcomes are governed by a probability distribution. In the simple regression model, we assume the following about ε_i:

1. It is zero on average, $E[\varepsilon_i] = 0$.
2. It varies independently of X_1, $\sigma_{X_i \varepsilon_i} = 0$.
3. It has constant variance across all levels of X, $E[\varepsilon_i] = \sigma_{\varepsilon \varepsilon}$.
4. In addition it is assumed that ε_i and ε_j are uncorrelated so that the covariance $\{\varepsilon_i, \varepsilon_j\} = 0$ for all i,j where $i \neq j$.

Consider the more complex Y–X relationship contained in Table 3.2.

There exist multiple Y values for any given X and, as a result, a number of different lines can be drawn expressing different relationships between Y and X. This is depicted in Fig. 3.3, where three different lines are proposed. Each line expresses a slightly different relationship between Y and

TABLE 3.2
Heuristic Data Set #2

Y	X	Y	X	Y	X
1	0	7	2	9	2
2	0	7	2	10	3
3	0	8	2	11	3
4	1	8	2	12	3
5	1	8	2	13	4
6	1	9	2	14	4
7	2	9	2	15	4

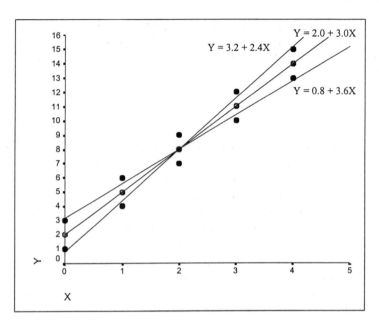

FIG. 3.3. Some possible regression lines and solutions for an imperfect linear relationship.

X, and each results in some amount of prediction error, ε. Of the three lines proposed (out of an infinite set of possible lines), which one best describes the relationship between X and Y? The principle of "least squares" states that the correct line is the one that best "fits" the data points. Fit is assessed by summing the squared distances of each observed value (the actual data point) from its predicted value—that is, the value of Y at point X as determined by the regression line. The line that minimizes the sum of these squared distances is said to best fit the data.

Consider the line $Y = 2.0 + 3.0X$ in Fig. 3.4. It is clear visually that the line drawn through the data does not intersect every data point; that is, prediction error exists. For example, at $X = 3$ there are three observed values of Y—10, 11, and 12. From the line drawn, the predicted value of Y at $X = 3$ is 11. The observed value of 12 at $X = 3$ is 1 point greater than the predicted value of 11 at this value of X. Subtracting the observed value from the predicted value yields a difference of 1 point. Each data point can be analyzed in a similar fashion.

The total prediction error resulting from choosing a particular line can be calculated by summing the squared differences between each of the observed and predicted values. Squared values are used when calculating total error to avoid the differences canceling each other out—similar to calculating the simple univariate variance, the best fitting line will yield as

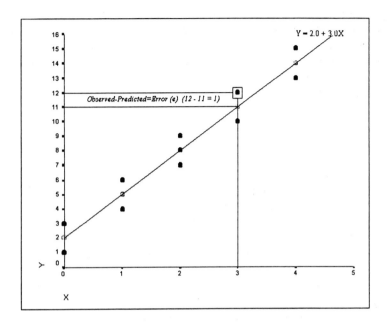

FIG. 3.4. "Best-fitting" regression line and associated error.

many positive as negative values. Formally, total error (or the sum of squared error, SSE) can be expressed as:

$$SSE = \Sigma(Y_i - \hat{Y}_i)^2 \qquad (3)$$

where Y_i is the observed value of Y for individual i and $\hat{Y}$ is the predicted value of Y for individual i. Thus SSE provides a formal gauge for measuring the overall error associated with any particular line. Although the SSE can be calculated for any line, the "best" line is the one that has the lowest SSE value. The least squares principle allows us to calculate estimates for β_1 and β_0 through Eqs. 4 and 5.

$$\beta_1 = \frac{\Sigma(X_i - \bar{X})(Y_i - \bar{Y})}{\Sigma(X_i - \bar{X})^2} \qquad (4)$$

$$\beta_0 = \bar{Y} - \beta_1 \bar{X} \qquad (5)$$

The line defined by these values yields the smallest possible sum of squared errors value; that is, the line determined using Eqs. 4 and 5 is the best fitting of all possible lines—hence the term *least squares* regression.

Let us now turn our attention to an actual example. Consider a model in which we assume the initial earnings of a college graduates are positively affected by their grade performance during college; that is, we assert that postbaccalaureate earnings are a linear function of grade performance. The model is simply that presented in Eq. 1 (with notation corresponding to a sample rather than the larger population):

$$Y = b_0 + b_1 X + e_i$$

where Y is initial earnings in dollars and X is college gradepoint average (GPA) on a scale ranging from 0 to 4, b_0 is the intercept, b_1 is the slope, and e is the error. Figure 3.5 allows visual examination of the relationship between earnings and GPA, suggesting that a positive association exists. The reader may note that the data form a pattern in the scatterplot running up and to the right. The task now is to determine the line best describing the presumed relationship between Y and X. To do this, we need to estimate the values for the slope (b_1) and intercept (b_0) in Eq. 2. This is accomplished using Eqs. 4 and 5.

This line, illustrated in Fig. 3.6, is defined by the following values:

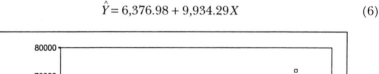

$$\hat{Y} = 6{,}376.98 + 9{,}934.29X \qquad (6)$$

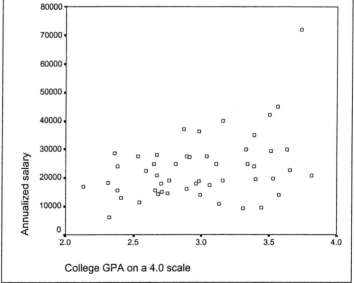

FIG. 3.5. Scatterplot of college GPA and salary.

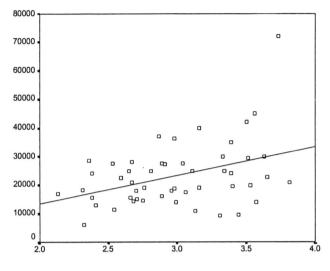

College GPA on a 4.0 scale

FIG. 3.6. "Best-fitting" regression line for college GPA and salary.

where $\hat{Y}$ is the predicted Y, 6,376.98 is the estimated intercept, b_0, and 9,934.29 is the estimated slope, b_1. Note that despite the fact that this is the best fitting line, there exists a considerable amount of error between predicted and observed earnings at any given level of college GPA. This error is attributable to a number of factors including measurement error in Y and the cumulative effects of any unmeasured variables that influence a person's earnings.

Substantively, a return of \$9,934.29 to each full gradepoint difference in GPA average seems significant. One must remember, however, that this is only an estimate of the earnings return on GPA (based on a sample of 50 employed graduates). It is quite likely this value will vary depending on the characteristics of the sample we draw. As in all inferential statistics, we need to find a way to gauge the probability that the value of the statistic of interest is not due solely to sample variation. In other words, we need a way to determine which of the following hypotheses about the population values is correct:

$$H_0: \quad \beta_1 = 0$$
$$H_1: \quad \beta_1 \neq 0$$

The first step in testing this null hypothesis is to find the standard deviation of the slope, b_1. The standard deviation of estimated parameters is usually referred to as the standard error. Once the standard error is calculated, the estimated parameter, b_1 in this instance, can be divided by this value. The resulting ratio is a t-statistic with $N-2$ degrees of freedom. The standard error of any parameter estimate can be found using the following:

$$s_b = \sqrt{\frac{(Y-\hat{Y})^2/(N-2)}{\Sigma(X-\bar{X})^2}} \qquad (7)$$

In the current example, the standard error of b_1 is 3,428.97. The t-statistic used to test the null hypothesis that $\beta_1 = 0$ is calculated by:

$$t_{n-2} = \frac{b_1 - 0}{S_{b_1}}$$

$$= \frac{b_1}{S_{b_1}} \qquad (8)$$

This yields a t-ratio of 2.897 and is far beyond the critical t necessary to reject H_0 (2.021) for the sample size. Therefore, we reject the null hypothesis and conclude that it is highly likely that college GPA and initial earnings are related in the larger population. After determining the correct values for b_0 and b_1 and their significance, predictions of Y, for given values of X, are as straightforward as plugging the appropriate X value into the equation. For example, suppose we want to estimate the earnings of a person who had a college GPA of 3.4:

$$\hat{Y} = -6,376.98 + 9,934.29X$$
$$= -6,376.98 + 9,934.29(3.4)$$
$$= -6,376.98 + 3,3776.59$$
$$= 27,399.61$$

On average, then, we would expect a person with a college GPA of 3.4 to earn $27,399.61. Figure 3.7 illustrates the way the predicted Y is determined from the height of the regression at $X = 3.4$. Notice that none of the cases with GPA = 3.4 have observed earnings equal to the predicted value of $27,399.61. In fact, at GPA = 3.4, there are two observations well below the predicted value and one observation well above. The distance between each of these observed values and the predicted value of $27,399.61 is error.

The adequacy of any particular functional relationship (i.e., a perfect relationship where X determines Y) can be gauged in terms of the degree to which it "fits" the actual statistical relationship found in the data. As in

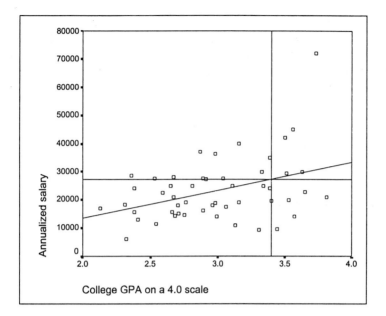

FIG. 3.7.   Regression line and joint means for college GPA and salary.

the preceding example, statistical relationships are generally imperfect relationships, where Y is not perfectly determined by X. This "fit" is often measured by the simple calculation of the variance explained in Y by X, which is the coefficient of determination (r^2) in the case of ordinary least squares (OLS) regression.

The coefficient of determination is a member of the family of measures that define the degree to which knowledge of values of X improve the prediction of Y. The hallmark of r^2 and its larger family of measures, proportionate reduction of error (PRE) measures, is that they are all derived by comparing errors made in predicting the Y, while ignoring X with errors made when making predictions of Y that use information about X. In the case of r^2, we rely on two types of deviation scores to compute a ratio that ranges from 0, indicating the absence of a relationship, to +1, indicating a perfect relationship between X and Y. In the absence of knowledge about X, the best guess of the value of Y will be its mean,

$$\bar{Y}(E[Y] = \bar{Y}).$$

Thus, the first value needed is the total sum of squared deviations (TSS),

$$TSS = \Sigma(Y_i - \bar{Y}_i)^2 \qquad (9)$$

The TSS can then be compared to the total squared deviations when taking into account the independent variable, X. If X and Y are related, knowledge of the value of X will help improve the predictions of Y. Because we know the value of $\hat{Y}$ any level of X, we can calculate the extent of this improvement, the regression sum of squared deviations, using the following:

$$\text{RSS} = \Sigma(\hat{Y}_i - \bar{Y}_i)^2 \qquad (10)$$

In the imperfect world of social science data where the regression line does not perfectly predict each value of Y, error will remain and can be summarized by the error sum of squared deviations or the sum of squared error (Eq. 3):

$$\text{SSE} = \Sigma(Y_i - \hat{Y}_i)^2$$

Then r^2 is simply a ratio of the improvement of the prediction based on knowledge of X over prediction based solely on Y.

$$r^2 = \frac{\text{RSS}}{\text{TSS}} \qquad (11)$$

An alternate measure of goodness of fit is simply the value of the "adjusted average" prediction error, the standard error (SE) of the estimate. The SE is adjusted for degrees of freedom as shown in Eq. 12 and increasingly approximates a true average error as sample size increases.

$$SE = \sqrt{\frac{\Sigma(Y_i - \hat{Y}_i)^2}{N - 2}} \qquad (12)$$

In our example estimating postgraduate earnings as a function of college GPA, the model has a r^2 value of .149. This suggests that GPA explains 14.9% of the total variance in earnings. Similarly, as a PRE measure, r^2 tells us that knowledge of individuals' GPAs improves our prediction of their earnings by 14.9%. This is a small but noteworthy improvement in prediction, although a great deal of prediction error obviously remains. This is confirmed by the value of SE, \$10,430.26, which suggests conservatively that the average prediction error for any individual is about \$10,430.26. Thus, there is much room for improvement in this model.

Multiple Regression

Most likely, the model we just presented is underspecified; that is, we have excluded a number of theoretically important variables that are correlated with the outcome, postgraduate earnings. In addition, it would be desirable to reassess the impact of GPA after taking into account other variables such as years of experience or field of study that may be influencing the relationship. This is accomplished by extending the simple regression model to account for these multiple influences. The model appears as:

$$Y = b_0 + b_1 X_1 + b_2 X_2 + b_3 X_3 + \cdots + b_k X_k + e \qquad (13)$$

where Y is the dependent variable, X_1, X_2, X_3, . . . , X_k are the independent variables, b_0 is the intercept, b_1, b_2, b_3, . . . , b_k are partial slopes, and e is the error term.

Multiple regression is a very powerful analytical tool, in part because it allows for the assessment of effects of an individual X on Y, while statistically controlling for other theoretically important variables. This statistical control, as contrasted with an experimental control, is accomplished by determining the proportion variance of shared by each of the variables in the model and then adjusting the respective coefficients accordingly. Consider the three-variable model:

$$Y = b_0 + b_1 X_1 + b_2 X_2 + e \qquad (14)$$

If X_1 and X_2 are correlated with one another, as they usually are to some degree, we can assess their common variance by regressing X_1 on X_2.

$$X_1 = c_0 + c_2 X_2 + u \qquad (15)$$

Providing X_1 and X_2 are not perfectly correlated, Eq. 15 will yield some amount of prediction error, u. This error, u, represents a part of X_1 that is completely independent of X_2. We can rewrite Eq. 15 to separate its linear and stochastic components in order to isolate this error:

$$u = X_1 - c_0 + c_2 X_2$$
$$u = X_1 - \hat{X_1} \qquad (16)$$

Using the same logic, we can also separate out the portion of the outcome variable that is linearly independent of X_2:

$$Y = d_0 + d_2 X_2 + v$$
$$v = Y - d_0 + d_2 X_2$$
$$v = Y - \hat{Y} \tag{17}$$

Once we have identified the portions of X_1 and Y that are completely independent of X_1, u and v, we join these two components to determine the adjusted or partial value for b_1:

$$b_1 = \frac{\Sigma(u)(v)}{\Sigma u^2} \tag{18a}$$

or, by substitution:

$$b_1 = \frac{\Sigma(X_1 - \hat{X}_1)(Y - \hat{Y})}{\Sigma(X_1 - \hat{X}_1)^2} \tag{18b}$$

In this way, we have determined the effect of X_1 adjusted for any linear influence of X_2. Thus b_1 represents the effect of X_1 net of any common effect of X_2. Again consider our earnings example. It is obvious that a wide variety of factors other than college GPA (e.g., college major, IQ, social capital, etc.) might be associated with earnings. We might even go so far as to propose that the observed effect of GPA is spurious—that is, that the relation between GPA and earnings is really due to some third variable not included in the model.

Suppose someone expert in this area suggested that the GPA–earnings relationship is actually the result of years of experience in the graduates' current positions. This expert contends that the observed bivariate relationship exists largely because older graduates in the sample—those who may have been working for many years before returning to college—have higher GPAs due to their relatively greater focus on the academic requirements of college and more serious commitments to their studies. Therefore, the expert suggests that the GPA–earnings relationship we observed is actually an artifact of a more important theoretical relationship between time on the job and earnings. We can test this proposition directly by examining the GPA–earnings relationship while controlling for graduates' length of time on the job. Upon calculating the new "partial" slopes for X_1 and X_2, we find the following:

$$\hat{Y} = 3,778.54 + 5,207.30 X_1 + 2,195.66 X_2 \tag{19}$$

where X_1 is college GPA, X_2 is years of experience at job, $r^2 = .493$, and SEE = $8,135.59. The t-values for both b_1 ($t = 1.858$) and b_2 ($t = 5.648$) are significant at the .10 level, suggesting that there is only slight chance (less than 1 in 10) that these estimates are the result of sampling error and do not reflect a true structural relationship in the larger population.

The interpretation of the multiple regression coefficients is a straightforward extension of the bivariate case. The intercept, b_0, remains the same as before: the value of Y when each of the X_1, X_2, . . . , X_k is set to 0. The slope coefficients b_1, b_2, . . . , b_k, however, now take on a different interpretation. Each b_k now represents the effects of X net of all other X terms in the model. These b_k values are referred to as *partial slopes* or *partial regression coefficients*. Note also that it is impossible to depict the three-variable relationship with a line as we could in the bivariate case. Rather than fitting a line in two-dimensional space, the three-variable model requires us to conceive of the fitting of a plane in three-dimensional space. Error in this three-dimensional space would be captured as the distance between the observed values and the predicted values defining the plane. Extending this, multiple regression models with k independent variables would require the fitting of a plane through $k + 1$-dimensional space.

Comparing these b_1 values to the bivariate example in Eq. 6, we find that the estimated effect of GPA has been reduced by over 47% ($9,934.29 vs. $5,207.30). This is a direct result of the removal of the common effect of GPA and years experience on earnings. Despite this notable diminishment in magnitude, GPA remains significant at the .10 level. We would conclude that although a large portion of our initial estimate was due to the relationship between GPA and years of experience, a unique GPA–earnings relationship still exists. Therefore, the expert who suggested that the GPA–earnings relationship was spurious was incorrect—although the expert was right in assuming that a strong relationship existed between these two predictors, and that years of experience was a theoretically important variable that should have been included in our model.

Specification Error

Cast in other terms, one thing we learned from the three-variable model is that our initial bivariate model was incorrectly specified. As a result, this incorrect model yields an overstated estimate (by over 47%) of the effect of college GPA on earnings. In essence, in the bivariate model, we mistakenly attributed to GPA part of the effect of time on the job. The lesson here is that when specifying any such statistical model, theory should closely guide the inclusion or exclusion of independent variables.

Recall that many things are subsumed in the error term of the regression model, including the effects of omitted variables. When an omitted variable is correlated with other independent variables in the model, the error term will also be correlated with these other variables—a violation of the assumptions concerning the error term. Moreover, individual slope estimates will be biased to the degree that an omitted variable both influences the dependent variable and is correlated with the other independent variables in the model. This should again reinforce the need to have any statistical model firmly grounded in relevant theory.

TENABILITY OF OLS ASSUMPTIONS

Finally, we provide a few words about regression assumptions beyond those associated with the error term. Although the regression model is unusually robust, failure to meet these assumptions still presents a serious threat to the generalizability of results. There are four basic regression assumptions, including those associated with the properties of the error term, that must be met to ensure that the OLS model yields the best linear unbiased estimates of the population parameters of interest:

1. No specification error.
2. No measurement error.
3. No perfectly correlated independent variables.
4. The error term, e, has the following properties:
   a. It is zero on average, $E[e_i] = 0$.
   b. It varies independently of X_1, $\sigma_{X_i e_i} = 0$.
   c. It has constant variance across all levels of X, $E[e_i^2] = \sigma_{ee}$.
   d. It is assumed that e_i and e_j are uncorrelated so that the covariance $\sigma\{e_i, e_j\} = 0$ for all i, j where $i \neq j$.

The assumptions concerning the distribution of the error term are most realistic when using data collected through a simple random sampling scheme.

More often than not, however, organizational and educational research involves data collection efforts employing more complex sampling schemes that draw on clustered data from multiple levels. Multilevel data structures result when a researcher starts with a random sample of organizations and then obtains another random sample of individuals within those organizations. Such schemes raise questions about the viability of assumptions 4c and 4d. With clustered samples, each of the organizational units sampled may have unequal variances on individual-level characteristics of interest. Moreover, if we presume that a higher level organizational unit has an effect on the individuals within it, we must also presume, as we argued in chapter 2, that individuals will be more homogeneous within organizations than between them. In short, the foundational assumptions about e_i in simple regression are questionable in the context of multilevel data structures.

Multilevel Regression Models

The multilevel regression model is one member of a family of models that we explore in this book—a family of models specifically designed to capitalize on hierarchical data structures. Other members of this family include mixed-effects and random-effects models, random-coefficient models, and covariance-component models. In this chapter, we provide an overview of the mathematical elements of the multilevel model and we illustrate the logic of the development of the model and interpretation of the results.

OVERVIEW OF MULTILEVEL REGRESSION MODELS

As we pointed out in chapter 3, the assumptions necessary for ordinary regression models to yield the best linear unbiased estimates are most realistic when using data collected through a simple random sampling scheme. However, such sampling methodology is rarely used in large-scale organizational and educational research. In addition to the efficient data collection strategies that often involve some form of cluster sampling, conceptual interest in the relationships of variables on a number of different levels requires more complex sampling schemes that capture theoretically important information from each of these levels. Whatever the motivation, the fact is that more often than not, data collected in organizational studies are hierarchically structured. As we argued at the end of chapter 3, multilevel data challenge the least-squares regression assumptions necessary for efficient and unbiased regression estimates.

In contrast to a single-level regression analysis, consider the nature of a multilevel analysis—one that uses data, for example, on j organizations, with N employees nested within each organization. In this example, we have two distinct levels of data—organizational (level 2) and individual (level 1). Fully specified multilevel linear models require one continuously measured outcome variable at the lowest level of data (level 1) and at least one independent variable at each level (i.e., level 1 and level 2 in the two-level example). From these data one can use the multilevel modeling framework to specify a hierarchical system of regression equations that exploit the multilevel data structure.

Multilevel modeling techniques involve first estimating a level-1 model (the individual level in the organizations and individuals example) within each higher (level-2) unit and then estimating a series of between-unit models using the within-unit estimates as dependent variables. At the individual level, we can specify a single-level regression equation that can be estimated within each higher, level-2 unit. In other words, as in traditional regression, the researcher assumes that a single model is appropriate across all level-2 units in the sample. At this stage, the primary difference between ordinary regression and multilevel regression is that in the multilevel case, the researcher conceptualizes the overall data structure differently, acknowledging the existence of higher level units in which lower level units are nested.

Developing the Mathematical Models

In its simplest form, the level-1 model is equivalent to an ordinary regression model. Rather than estimating parameters across all N cases in the data set, however, the level-1 model is used to produce estimates within each level-2 unit, j, in the data. As in ordinary regression, the same model is assumed appropriate for all higher level units. The multilevel approach, however, yields a potentially different set of estimates for each level-2 unit. The level-1 model appears as:

$$Y_{ij} = \beta_{0j} + \beta_{1j}X_{1j} + \varepsilon_{ij} \tag{1}$$

where Y_{ij} is the observation for the ith individual in level-2 unit j, β_{0j} is the level-1 intercept within unit j, β_{1j} is a level-1 slope within unit j, and ε_{ij} is error for individual i in organization j.

If sufficient variation exists within and between the level-2 units, this model will yield a different set of estimates of β_{0j} and β_{1j} for each level-2 unit. Within each level-2 unit, ε_{ij} is assumed to have a mean of 0 and constant variance across all levels of X_j. Each of the j within-unit models is simply an ordinary regression model, where the regression coefficients indicate the effects of level-1 characteristics on a level-1 outcome *within each level-2 unit*. Rather than considering these j models separately, however, we treat them as a system of estimates with an overall mean and variance (averaged across all j level-2 units). The fact that the intercept and slope are allowed to vary across level-2 units enables the researcher to take a next step and try to account for this variation using level-2 variables—that is, the researcher can now treat the level-1 intercept and slope as outcomes of level-2 predictors.

Consider, for example, the relationship between employee morale and level of pay across a sample of 50 organizations. Equation 1 yields 50 separate sets of estimates defining the functional relationship between these two variables. These relationships are illustrated in Fig. 4.1. Again, each level-1 equation gives us the estimated intercept and impact of level-1 variables on the level-1 outcome, within each level-2 unit. The reader will note from Fig. 4.1 that these intercepts and slopes can and will vary across level-2 units.

In ordinary regression, the potential for this variation is ignored and the slope and intercept are understood as being fixed, or common, across any higher level units that are manifest in the data structure. In contrast, the multilevel modeling approach allows the researcher not only to examine such variation across units, but also to test the validity of the assumption that such random variation exists by providing a framework for comparing these estimates across higher level units. The multilevel framework provides the analyst the flexibility to conceptualize these estimates as random, if desired, rather than fixed. This increased flexibility to model intercepts

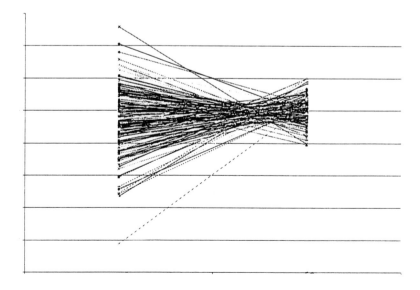

FIG. 4.1. Relationship between morale and pay across 50 organizations.

and slopes as randomly varying across units has led some to refer to multilevel models as *random-coefficient models*.

These varying level-1 slopes and intercepts—expressing the functional relationship between the level-1 outcome and predictor within each level-2 unit—are a distinctive feature of multilevel regression analysis. For each slope and intercept in the level-1 models, the implied between-unit model is:

$$\beta_{kj} = \gamma_{k0} + u_{kj} \quad \text{for } k = 0, 1, 2, \ldots, k \tag{2}$$

where β_{kj} represents the within-unit regression parameters from the level-1 model in Eq. 1 and γ_{k0} is the mean value for each of the within-unit parameters. Across all level-2 units, then, each β_{kj} has a distribution with a mean and variance. Should there exist significant variance in any level-1 coefficient between level-2 units, β_{kj}, multilevel regression gives the researcher the option to model this variance using higher level variables. Alternatively, the researcher may also specify a common or fixed regression slope for any level-1 coefficient, β_{kj}, that is relatively homogeneous across level-2 units.

The determination of how to treat each level-1 slope or intercept, as a random or fixed parameter, depends first on the researcher's theoretical framework, and second, on the amount of variance that exists across level-2 units. Should the researcher, based on these criteria, decide to treat any given β_{kj} as randomly varying across level-2 units, a model to explain the variation in β_{kj} would be developed using explanatory variables from level 2. Assuming a level-1 model with one predictor, X_1, the level-2 models would appear as:

$$\beta_{0j} = \gamma_{00} + \gamma_{01} Z_j + u_{0j} \tag{3}$$

and

$$\beta_{1j} = \gamma_{10} + \gamma_{11} Z_j + u_{1j} \tag{4}$$

where β_{0j} is the level-1 intercept in level-2 unit j; γ_{00} is the mean value of the level-1 outcome, controlling for the level-2 predictor, Z_j; γ_{01} is the slope for the level-2 variable Z_j; u_{0j} is the error for organization j; β_{1j} is the level-1 slope in level-2 unit j; γ_{10} is the mean value of the level-1 slope, controlling for the level-2 predictor, Z_j; γ_{11} is the slope for the level-2 variable Z_j; and u_{1j} is the error for organization j.

In contrast to level-1 outcomes, which are based on N individual-level observations, the level-2 estimates specified in Eqs. 3 and 4 are based on

j unit-level observations. Because the level-2 outcomes β_{0j} and β_{1j} are not observed—they need to be estimated from level-1 data—it is not possible to estimate these level-2 equations directly. By considering the level-1 and level-2 models as a single system of equations, however, all of the information necessary for estimation of parameters at both levels is provided. By substitution, this system of equations is represented in Eq. 6:

$$Y_{ij} = \beta_{0j} + \beta_{1j}X_{1j} + \varepsilon_{ij} \tag{1}$$

$$\beta_{0j} = \gamma_{00} + \gamma_{01}Z_j + u_{0j} \tag{3}$$

$$\beta_{1j} = \gamma_{10} + \gamma_{11}Z_j + u_{1j} \tag{4}$$

$$Y_{ij} = (\gamma_{00} + \gamma_{01}Z_j + u_{0j}) + (\gamma_{10} + \gamma_{11}Z_j + u_{1j})X_{1j} + \varepsilon_{ij} \tag{5}$$

$$Y_{ij} = \gamma_{00} + \gamma_{10}X_{ij} + \gamma_{01}Z_j + \gamma_{11}Z_jX_{1j} + u_{1j}X_{1j} + u_{0j} + \varepsilon_{ij} \tag{6}$$

As with ordinary regression models, Y_{ij} is generated by two components: the linear relationship defined by the model; and stochastic, or probabilistic, error captured by ε_{ij}. This latter error component is comprised largely of measurement and specification error.

Beyond this similarity, two major differences between the ordinary regression model and the multilevel model warrant note. First, in the deterministic component of Eq. 6 is the term $\gamma_{11}Z_jX_{1j}$, which represents a cross-level interaction between level-1 and level-2 variables. Essentially, this can be understood as the moderating effect of a level-2 variable on the relationship between a level-1 predictor and the outcome Y_{ij}. Second, in the stochastic component of Eq. 6 is the more complex error term, $u_{1j}X_{1j} + u_{0j} + \varepsilon_{ij}$. This error term accommodates the relationship between u_{0j} and u_{1j}, which are common to every level-1 observation within each level-2 unit—a dependency that violates the assumption in ordinary regression of independent errors across observations.

The two-level multilevel model can be generalized to three or more levels, depending on the research question being addressed and the structure of a particular set of data. One might, for example, wish to use a two-level model to explore the effects of schools on individual student learning. This is a popular focus in much of the "school-effects" literature in education. This model could be enlarged into a three-level analysis by including classroom effects. The researcher would explore the effects of the structural characteristics of schools on classroom processes that, in turn, have effects on individual student learning. As with the two-level model presented in this section, more complex models allow the researcher increased control over the variation of lower level parameters,[1] and the ability to partition overall variance in the outcome across all levels of analysis.

DEVELOPING A MULTILEVEL REGRESSION MODEL

There is a logical progression common to the development of all multilevel regression analyses. First, the researcher analyzes variance in an outcome, Y_{ij}, with special attention to the distribution of this variance within and between level-2 units. Second, attention is paid to development of a level-1 random-intercept model. Third, slopes of theoretical interest are examined to determine the amount of variation that exists across higher level units. Finally, models are developed using higher level variables in an effort to explain between-unit variation in parameters discovered in previous stages. It will become clear to the reader that, at each stage of this progression, there are a number of decisions that predetermine choices at subsequent stages.

Multilevel models are useful and necessary only to the extent that the data being analyzed provide sufficient variation at each level. "Sufficiency" of variation is relative and depends as much on theoretical concerns as it does on the structure and the quality of data. Accordingly, a good first step in developing a multilevel model is to examine the extent to which variation in a level-1 outcome exists *within* level-2 units relative to its variation *between* level-2 units. A disproportionately small amount of variance within the level-2 units would suggest greater homogeneity among all level-1 observations than exists among level-1 observations from different level-2 groups. In other words, such evidence might suggest that the nesting of level-1 observations is not systematically associated with levels of the outcome, Y. Recall that ordinary regression models assume independence among observations. The partitioning of variance between level-1 and level-2 allows the researcher to test the validity of this assumption and provides important information about the sources of variation in the outcome variable. Multilevel models obviate the assumption of independence and actually allow the research to capitalize on its violation.

Variance in the outcome variable, Y, is partitioned within and between level-2 units by fitting a within-unit one-way analysis of variance (ANOVA) model where only a dependent variable is specified:

$$Y_{ij} = \beta_{0j} + \varepsilon_{ij} \tag{7}$$

where Y_{ij} is the observation for the ith individual in level-2 unit j, β_{0j} is the level-1 intercept within unit j, and ε_{ij} is error for individual i in organization

---

[1] By definition, all intercepts and slopes at the highest level of data are fixed.

j (that is, ε_{ij} represents the deviation from the level-2 unit mean for individual i). Each level-1 error term is assumed to have a mean of 0 and a constant variance, σ^2. Simultaneously, a companion, level-2, equation is fitted to complete the partitioning of variance in the level-1 outcome into its within- and between-unit components:

$$\beta_{0j} = \gamma_{00} + u_{0j} \qquad (8)$$

where β_{0j} is the level-1 intercept in level-2 unit j, γ_{00} is the mean value of the level-1 outcome across all level-2 units, and u_{0j} is the random effect of organization j (that is, u_{0j} is the deviation from the grand mean of Y for level-2 unit j). Each level-2 random effect is assumed to have a mean of 0 and variance τ_{00}. Substituting Eq. 8 into Eq. 7 yields:

$$Y_{ij} = \gamma_{00} + u_{0j} + \varepsilon_{ij} \qquad (9)$$

where ε_{ij} is the level-1 effect and u_{0j} is the level-2 effect, and γ_{00} is the grand mean of Y_{ij}. The model represented by Eq. 9 only partitions variance in Y_{ij} between level 1 and level 2, and does not "explain" any of the total variance. The partitioning creates two variance components, one at level 1 (σ^2) and another at level 2 (τ_{00}). From this, the variance of the outcome, Y_{ij}, can be rewritten as:

$$\text{Var}(Y_{ij}) = \text{Var}(u_{0j} + \varepsilon_{ij}) = \tau_{00} + \sigma^2 \qquad (10)$$

The researcher now has all of the information necessary to determine the proportion, at each level, of variance in the outcome, Y_{ij}. These proportions are determined by calculating the intraclass correlation ρ with knowledge of σ^2 and τ_{00} from Eq. 11:

$$\rho = \tau_{00} / (\tau_{00} + \sigma^2) \qquad (11)$$

The intraclass correlation provides a sense of the degree to which differences in the outcome, Y_{ij}, exist between level-2 units. More specifically, it helps answer the question of the existence or nonexistence of meaningful differences in outcomes between the level-2 units—differences that determine the extent to which the data are hierarchically differentiated and, by extension, encourage the development of helpful level-2 models to explain the variance in Y.

Assuming that sufficient levels of variance in Y exist at each level, warrant is now given to begin exploring the specification of the level-1 model—a model using only variables at the lowest level of analysis:

$$Y_{ij} = \gamma_{00} + \gamma_{10}X_{ij} + u_{0j} + \varepsilon_{ij} \tag{12}$$

Initially, the level-1 variables should be modeled with fixed slopes (i.e., where the variance components for each coefficient are constrained to 0) in order to assess the importance of each in accounting for variance in Y_{ij}. Once a reasonable fixed model has been identified, the researcher can then determine whether any of the level-1 slopes vary significantly across the level-2 units. Although testing of slopes can be purely exploratory, we stress that theory should guide which slopes might be considered random in subsequent models.

$$Y_{ij} = \gamma_{00} + \gamma_{10}X_{ij} + u_{1j}X_{1j} + u_{0j} + \varepsilon_{ij} \tag{13}$$

The overall significance of any level-1 parameter is based on its adjusted mean value across all j groups. From Fig. 4.1, it is clear that such averages can mask potentially significant differences across groups. For this reason, it is often fruitful to carefully reexamine level-1 variables omitted from the fixed model—especially those of theoretical interest that may have appeared suspiciously nonsignificant in earlier specifications.

Once a reasonable level-1 model has been established, a third step is to develop the level-2 model that will help explain variation in level-1 intercepts and slopes across level-2 units.

$$Y_{ij} = \gamma_{00} + \gamma_{10}X_{ij} + \gamma_{01}Z_j + u_{1j}X_{1j} + u_{0j} + \varepsilon_{ij} \tag{14}$$

By modeling the level-1 intercept, β_0, the researcher is testing the degree to which the level-2 predictor variable, Z, contributes to the explanation level-2 variance in Y_{ij}.

Finally, the researcher can now begin to test for hypothesized cross-level interactions. This is accomplished by specifying an appropriate level-2 model for the random slope β_1. In contrast to the random intercepts-as-outcomes model, in which the variation in level-1 intercept was modeled, this random intercepts- and slopes-as-outcomes model enables the development and testing of variation in the level-1 intercept and slopes using level-2 variables. In other words, it is now possible to consider potential level-2 characteristics that might help explain variation in any given level-1 parameter. Of course, modeling the variation in level-1 slopes is best accomplished with regard to theoretical considerations, as opposed to engaging in random "fishing expeditions." The full multilevel model, with both the level-1 intercept and slope modeled, appears as:

$$Y_{ij} = \gamma_{00} + \gamma_{10}X_{ij} + \gamma_{01}Z_{1j} + \gamma_{11}Z_{1j}X_{1j} + u_{1j}X_{1j} + u_{0j} + \varepsilon_{ij} \tag{15}$$

At each major stage in developing the multilevel model, hypotheses are tested on the basis of significance tests for individual parameters, changes in the initial variance components, and changes in the overall fit of the model. We next show, using a 2-level example, how each of these steps is considered and how each step affects the variance components of the multilevel data structure.

Improvement in Reading Skill: An Example

Consider an example in which we examine improvement in reading between the third and sixth grades, after controlling for student gender and socioeconomic status. We are interested in determining the ways in which schools' mean reading scores vary, after controlling for these individual level factors and the degree to which this variation is related to schools' median parental income. The secondary data for this illustration come from a state's Department of Education database. These data include information for the population of sixth-grade students and schools during a particular year. Included in the sample are 9,741 students from 152 schools. Our research question is, how does a school's family wealth affect improvement in reading skills, controlling for student gender and family socioeconomic status?

Creating a Sufficient Statistics Matrices (SSM) File for HLM

A two-level HLM analysis requires separate input files for each level. In our example, we have one data file with "individual-level" characteristics ($N = 9,741$) containing variables describing students' gender, free lunch status, and previous reading test scores. We also have a separate "school-level" data file containing information about the schools ($N = 152$) these students attend. Transferring data to HLM from traditional statistical packages such as SPSS, SAS, or SYSTAT has become remarkably easier in more recent versions (1996 and beyond) of HLM for Windows.[2] There remain, however, a number of issues that demand the analyst's attention. The two main issues involve the identification variable linking level-1 and level-2 files and missing data.

Foreign data files imported into HLM, such as those used in SPSS or SAS, or raw data from ASCII files are linked hierarchically by an identification (ID) variable that is unique to each higher-level unit. In our example, we rely on the school identification number. Each student observation at level 1 must have a school identification number by which that student

---

[2]Although HLM can accept data in ASCII format, for simplicity, we limit our discussion to the transference of data from other statistical packages and refer those interested in ASCII transfers to the exercise at the end of this chapter or to Bryk et al. (1996).

can be linked to school-level data. In the level-1 file then, many students will share the same school identification number. At level 2, the school identification numbers uniquely identify schools. The HLM program matches students with their schools as it creates a *sufficient statistics matrices* (SSM) file—an HLM-specific data file. An important technical note should be made: The ID variable must be converted to a string variable of length n in both files, regardless of its format in the foreign data set, before HLM will recognize the foreign files as eligible for import.

A second data management issue concerns missing data in each of the input files. HLM is only able to handle missing data at level 1. The usual methods for deletion of missing level-1 data are included (listwise and pairwise). Of course, selection of either means of handling missing data will have an impact on the analysis—either in terms of entirely eliminating cases with any missing data (listwise) or by producing estimates based on unclear combinations data from all cases in the data set (pairwise). Both can impact the model's estimates. If data are transferred from an existing statistics package, HLM will automatically recognize any missing values that have been established in that package. If ASCII data are read in, HLM allows the user to specify missing values for each variable.

Data at all higher levels must be complete. This requires restricting the level-2 data set to those observations that have valid data on all variables of interest. Although missing data present problems to the researcher using most statistical procedures, they are particularly problematic in the multilevel environment. This is evidenced by a number of discussions concerning the handling of missing data in various software packages (e.g., Goldstein & Woodhouse, 1996). One simple but helpful strategy to maximize level-2 sample sizes in HLM is to first substitute level-2 cases with missing values with the mean of cases that have valid data. Then one can create a dummy variable corresponding to each variable on which substitutions were made. This dummy variable should be coded 1 for those observations that required substitution (i.e., had missing data) and 0 for all others. When the substituted variable and the dummy variable are included in the analysis, one can determine (by observing the significance or nonsignificance of the dummy variable) if level-2 units that had missing data are significantly different from the observations with complete data. From this information, the analyst can decide to include the cases that had missing data or to remove those cases due to their apparent difference in terms of the outcome.

However missing data are handled, all level-2 units that are omitted due to missing data have a direct impact on the size of the level-1 data set; that is, all individuals associated with the excluded level-2 unit will be omitted from analysis. Before importing foreign level-2 data files into HLM, all cases with missing data must be deleted from the file. No modification to the foreign level-1 file is necessary as HLM matches only those level-1 cases associated with existent level-2 units.

After addressing these data management issues and selecting variables to be included in the hierarchical analysis, HLM then translates and merges the input files into a SSM file. HLM can read SYSTAT files directly into SSM files. The current Windows version of the program uses DBMS/COPY to translate SPSS, SAS, and STATA data sets into SYSTAT files that are recognizable by the HLM program. Data sets from other applications will have to be translated into one of these formats prior to being imported into HLM (see Bryk et al., 1996, for a thorough discussion of how to construct data sets in HLM).

Several files are created by HLM during the import procedure and SSM definition. The user, through the SSM file creation dialog box, specifies the foreign input files to be used, the name of the SSM file to be created, and the name of a response (RSP) file that captures all inputs during this procedure. This response file makes note of all input files, variables chosen at each level, and the SSM file that was created. The RSP file can be used in subsequent sessions in which variables are added to or deleted from a particular SSM file. Also produced is a file, HLM2SSM.STS, containing descriptive statistics. The contents of the STS file should be carefully compared to descriptive output produced from the native statistics package in which the files were originally created. Any discrepancies between descriptive statistics produced by HLM and other programs should be cause for concern.[3] Users should be warned that creating the SSM file for HLM could take quite a bit of time to "debug" all potential problems. Table 4.1 displays the contents of the STS file that summarizes data at both levels.

Variables in the level-1 file include a dummy variable designating gender (FEMALE), another dummy variable designating low socioeconomic status (LOWSES), total score on a third-grade standardized reading test (PREVREAD), and the outcome, total score on a sixth-grade standardized reading test (TOTREAD). The two level-2 variables are MDINC100, capturing the median family income for each school, and NINJ, which captures the number of students nested within each school.

Once the SSM file has been created, we are ready to begin working in a multilevel environment with HLM. As outlined in the first section of this chapter, there are three main steps involved in a hierarchical analysis. In the first step, the variance in the outcome is partitioned into its within- and between-unit components to provide a sense of the proportion of variance at each level and to provide an initial unadjusted estimate of the

---

[3]The analyst should carefully observe the number of observations, at both levels, that are incorporated into the SSM file in HLM. Omission of level-1 data resulting from deletion of missing data at level 2 will impact the comparability of these descriptive statistics.

TABLE 4.1
Descriptive Statistics from the HLM *.STS file

LEVEL-1 DESCRIPTIVE STATISTICS					
VARIABLE NAME	N	MEAN	SD	MINIMUM	MAXIMUM
FEMALE	9741	0.49	0.50	0.00	1.00
TOTREAD	9741	645.75	33.33	564.00	801.00
LOWSES	9741	0.41	0.49	0.00	1.00
PREVREAD	9741	581.07	38.20	484.00	761.00
LEVEL-2 DESCRIPTIVE STATISTICS					
VARIABLE NAME	N	MEAN	SD	MINIMUM	MAXIMUM
MDINC100	152	403.11	131.37	147.01	769.07
NINJ	152	64.77	49.39	3.00	315.00

outcome. A second step involves developing and estimating a level-1 model and testing for any theorized random effects in level-1 parameters across level-2 units. The development and estimation of a level-2 model constitute a third step. Level-2 models may be specified for a random level-1 intercept, as well as any random or nonrandomly varying level-1 parameter in the model.

One-Way ANOVA Model

A first step before developing a full multilevel model is to determine the variation in an outcome that lies within and between levels. This is accomplished through the specification of a one-way ANOVA with random effects model (alternatively referred to as the "no-model" or "null-model") in which no level-1 or level-2 variables are used. This "no-model" was presented earlier in Eq. 9:

$$Y_{ij} = \gamma_{00} + u_{0j} + \varepsilon_{ij}$$

This model yields a number of important pieces of information. First, the no-model yields an estimated mean reading test score for all schools. Second, this model provides a partitioning of total variation in test scores between level 1 (ε_{ij}) and level 2 (u_{0j}). Third, the no-model provides a measure of dependence within each level-2 unit by way of the intraclass correlation. Fourth, a measure of the reliability of each school's mean reading test score is provided. Finally, fifth, the model provides the means for a formal test of the hypothesis that all schools have the same mean test scores. The actual salient HLM output for the "no-model" appears in Table 4.2.

From this output, we have all of the information necessary to determine the proportion of variance at each level of the outcome, Y. The variance

TABLE 4.2
One-Way ANOVA or "No-Model"

```
Random level-1 coefficient    Reliability estimate
-----------------------------------------------------
INTRCPT1, B0                          0.885

The value of the likelihood function at iteration 2 = -4.736123E+004

The outcome variable is  TOTREAD

Final estimation of fixed effects:
------------------------------------------------------------------------
    Fixed Effect      Coefficient   Standard Error   T-ratio   P-value
------------------------------------------------------------------------
For        INTRCPT1, B0
    INTRCPT2, G00     646.835534      1.143287       565.768    0.000


Final estimation of variance components:
------------------------------------------------------------------------
Random Effect            Standard      Variance     df   Chi-square   P-value
                         Deviation     Component
------------------------------------------------------------------------
INTRCPT1,       U0       13.26159      175.86989    151   1893.31762   0.000
level-1,        R        30.71515      943.42024
```

components produced in this step can be used to create a measure of within level-2 unit dependence, which is determined by calculating the intraclass correlation ρ with knowledge of variance components σ^2 and τ_{00} from Eq. 11:

$$\rho = \tau_{00}/(\tau_{00} + \sigma^2)$$

Values for the level-1 variance component, σ^2, and the level-2 variance component, σ^2, come from the Final Estimation of Variance Components table in the HLM output (in this table, τ_{00} is designated by U0 and σ^2 by R). Note that in the output from HLM, there is an initial set of estimates that provide starting values for the iteration process required in maximum likelihood (ML) estimation. The ML method attempts to find the most likely population parameter estimates that could have produced the observed sample covariance matrix. These values change at each successive iteration, and the highest and lowest are reported in the output. Using these final values and Eq. 11, we can determine the within-school dependency, or intraclass correlation:

$$175.86989/(175.86989 + 943.42024) = .15713$$

In our data, the intraclass correlation is .15713, or in other words, roughly 15.7% of the total variance in test scores is associated with schools as opposed to individuals. Of course, the largest proportion of variance in test scores is associated with the individual rather than the school. Although the variance component at level-2 is small (15.7%) relative to the level-1 variance component, the null hypothesis that it is zero is tested using a one-way random ANOVA model. This yields a χ^2 value of 1,893.31762 with $j - 1$, or 151, degrees of freedom. In this case, we reject the null hypothesis that mean test scores of students from all schools are equal and conclude that significant variability in means exists across schools. This is important to note, as it is an indication that there is sufficient variability to proceed with the multilevel analysis.

Another important piece of information provided by HLM is an estimated grand mean of students' test scores, 646.835534. As we have established through the intraclass correlation, mean test scores will vary from school to school. The reliability of the sample mean for any school as an estimate for its population mean can also be assessed with information gleaned from the variance components. Because sample sizes within each j are apt to differ, this reliability will vary across level-2 units. Reliability within any particular unit can be estimated with:

$$\lambda_j = \tau_{00} / [\tau_{00} + (\sigma^2 / n_j)] \tag{16}$$

From the descriptive statistics generated when the SSM file was created (contained in the HLM2SSM.STS file), we see that the within level-2 unit N (N_j) ranges from 3 to 315. Using these within-group N values, we can calculate the range of reliabilities across the 152 schools in the sample. For example, using Eq. 16, we can determine that the within-unit reliability for the school represented by 3 students is:

$$0.35867 = 175.86989 / [175.86989 + (943.42024 / 3)]$$

This is contrasted with the school represented by 315 students, in which the within-unit reliability is much higher:

$$0.98326 = 175.86989 / [175.86989 + (943.42024 / 315)]$$

HLM produces a summary measure of these within-unit reliabilities that is an average of the level-2 unit reliabilities:

$$\lambda = \Sigma \, \lambda_j / j \tag{17}$$

The average within level-2 unit reliability across the 152 schools in our data is $\lambda = 0.885$. This value appears at the top of the HLM output in Table 4.2.

To summarize, the intraclass correlation provides a sense of the degree to which differences in the outcome, Y, exist between level-2 units; that is, it helps answer the question of the existence or nonexistence of meaningful differences in outcomes between the level-2 units. These differences in outcomes determine the extent to which the data are hierarchically differentiated and, by extension, encourage the development of helpful level-2 models to explain the variance in Y. These estimated differences are only helpful if they are accepted as reliable indicators of real differences among schools' population means. Within-school reliability estimates provide the analyst a means by which this assumption can be checked.

The results from the one-way ANOVA model suggest that the development of a multilevel model is warranted. It is important to note also that we have a sufficient number of level-2 units to provide stability in estimation (see our discussion of power in chap. 2).

Level-1 Random-Intercept Model

With substantive theory as a guide, the analyst should now focus on developing a thoughtfully specified level-1 or *unconditional*[4] model. As with developing a model using traditional OLS regression, the analyst's primary concern is whether or not any predictor X_q should be included based on its contribution to explaining variance in the outcome. But unlike OLS, where the intercept and slope coefficients are fixed, multilevel regression using HLM requires the analyst to determine whether coefficients should be specified as fixed, random, or nonrandomly varying.

A good strategy for developing a level-1 model is to begin by testing the impacts of a minimal set of theoretically important predictors with fixed slope coefficients—that is, by assuming the effect of each of these individual-level variables is homogeneous across schools. After specifying a random-intercept level-1 model, hypotheses concerning heterogeneity of individual slope coefficients can be tested. We again stress the importance of theory as a guide for the model development process. Without such a guide, these models can quickly become oversaturated and obscure information necessary for testing hypotheses related to research questions. We call the reader's attention to our discussion in chapter 2 of problems associated with model misspecification (e.g., shrinkage problems). For ex-

---

[4]This level-1 model is often referred to as an unconditional model—that is, a level-1 model unconditional at level 2.

ample, the absence of substantive theory may encourage the use of an overspecified random slopes and intercept model that the data are simply unable to support. Given the data requirements for estimating multilevel models (i.e., HLM first produces OLS regression estimates within each group), parsimony is a highly valued characteristic.

At level 1 in our example, we want to test for relationships between reading test scores, gender, socioeconomic status, and performance on previous reading tests. Our unconditional random-intercept level-1 model is:

$$Y_{ij} = \beta_{0j} + \beta_{1j}(\text{FEMALE}) + \beta_{2j}(\text{LOWSES}) + \beta_{3j}(\text{PREVTEST}) + \varepsilon_{ij}$$

where the implied level-2 model is:

$$\beta_{0j} = \gamma_{00} + u_{0j}$$

As this level-2 model treats the intercept as an outcome, it is very important that the level-1 model yield an interpretable value for β_0. The intercept in traditional OLS models is generally interpreted as the value of the outcome variable when all predictors $(X_1, \ldots, X_q)$ are set to zero (0). This interpretation is adequate when all X terms have a meaningful 0 point, as in the case of dummy variables or continuous measures that have scales bounding 0. Often, however, this condition does not hold, and as a result, the intercepts are of little interpretative value to the analyst. Because multilevel models treat lower level intercepts and slopes as outcomes, it is critical that these variables have realistic numerical meanings. For this reason, level-1 variables are often transformed through various forms of "centering," which yields meaningful 0 values for each variable, and hence each intercept.

In cases where X values of 0 are not meaningful, such as the previous reading test, which ranges from 484 to 761, the two of the most often used transformations are *grand-mean centering* and *group-mean centering*. Grand-mean centering of level-1 variables $(X_{ij} - \bar{X})$ provides an intercept that is interpreted as an "adjusted" mean for group j as in Eq. 3:

$$B_{0j} = u_{yj} + B_{1j}(X_{.j} - \bar{X})$$

The intercept is now understood as the outcome for a subject whose value on X_{ij} is equal to the grand mean of the sample. Grand-mean centering effectively equalizes level-2 units on each X_q at level 1—that is, units are adjusted for the differences on each X_q among individuals.

In contrast, group-mean centering of level-1 variables $(X_{ij} - \bar{X}_{.j})$ yields an intercept that is interpreted as an unadjusted mean for group j as in Eq. 4:

$$\beta_{0j} = u_{yj}$$

The intercept is now the outcome for a subject whose value on X_{ij} is equal to the mean of its respective level-2 unit. This has the effect of emphasizing differences between level-2 units resulting from the composition of the lower level units they contain. We discuss these issues more in chapter 6.

Depending on the goals of the analysis, the researcher might opt to center the level-1 variables at a location other than the group or grand mean. Bryk and Raudenbush (1992) and Kreft, de Leeuw, and Aiken (1995) provided thorough discussions of the various forms and effects of centering level-1 variables.

In the current example, we have chosen to center the level-1 variables on the grand mean of the sample. By doing this, we adjust β_{0j} for differences in schools' distributions of females, students from low socioeconomic backgrounds, and previous test performance. In other words, we can now say, if every school were the same in terms of the level-1 characteristics we have specified, the expected value for the mean test score of any school would be β_{0j}. As we show later, this "equalization" of individual level characteristics across schools substantially impacts the variance in school means. Of course, this would not be the case if we chose to center on school means rather than the grand mean. The relevant output from our level-1 random-intercept model appears in Table 4.3. From the Final Estimation of Fixed Effects portion of the output, we can see that the values for mean test scores, adjusted for all level-1 characteristics in the model, is 646.847076. This value is interpreted as the average of the mean adjusted-school performance—where each school's average has been adjusted for differences in the level-1 variables in the model.

Recall that we specified this model to allow this intercept to vary across schools. The chi-square test reported in the Final Estimation of Variance Components table portion of the output indicates that, even after equalizing schools on the level-1 characteristics specified in our model, significant variation in these mean values still remains across schools ($\chi^2 = 1170.56557$, $p < .0000$). A more precise estimate of the variance remaining can be determined through the intraclass correlation. From Eq. 11 we find that

$$0.09439 = 78.49382/(78.49382 + 753.11245)$$

indicating that the total variance between schools is diminished by 40% relative to the intraclass correlation for the no-model ($\rho = .15713$), when

TABLE 4.3
Random-Intercept Model

```
Random level-1 coefficient    Reliability estimate
-----------------------------------------------------
INTRCPT1, B0                      0.818          [overall reliability of β₀ⱼ]
```
[*overall reliability of* β_{0j}]

```
The value of the likelihood function at iteration 6 = -4.623177E+004

The outcome variable is  TOTREAD

Final estimation of fixed effects:              [estimates of level-1 parameters]
```
[*estimates of level-1 parameters*]

Fixed Effect	Coefficient	Standard Error	T-ratio	P-value
For INTRCPT1, B0				
INTRCPT2, G00	646.847076	0.794739	813.911	0.000
For FEMALE slope, B1				
INTRCPT2, G10	4.874374	0.562299	8.669	0.000
For LOWSES slope, B2				
INTRCPT2, G20	-12.399518	0.617961	-20.065	0.000
For PREVREAD slope, B3				
INTRCPT2, G30	0.153518	0.003619	42.417	0.000

Final estimation of variance components: [*summary of variance components and test of homogeneity*]

Random Effect		Standard Deviation	Variance Component	df	Chi-square	P-value
INTRCPT1,	U0	8.85967	78.49382	151	1170.56557	0.000
level-1,	R	27.44289	753.11245			

we control for the factors included in our model at level 1. In other words, much of the variation in means across schools can be attributed to differences among students in those schools. However, we also find that, even after controlling for these differences, significant variation in means continues to exist across schools. The overall reliability in the random-intercept model (.818) drops compared to the estimated reliability of the no-model (.885). This is a direct function of the reduction in level-2 variance that renders schools more homogeneous in terms of the outcome.

In contrast with the intercept, which we specified as random, the slope coefficients in our level-1 model are fixed—that is, we are initially assuming that the effects of each variable are the same across schools. As in ordinary linear regression, the statistical significance of individual parameters is determined by a *t*-score resulting from dividing the parameter estimate by its standard error. In this case, we have reasonable faith in the standard error estimates because of the number of schools in the sample.

Among our level-1 predictors, several significant effects emerge. Girls, on average, perform at slightly higher levels than boys do ($\beta_{ij} = 4.874374$). Students from families of low socioeconomic status have test scores 12.399518 points lower than their peers of more advantaged backgrounds. Finally, on average, students' reading test scores improved 15.3518% over their third-grade scores. This latter parameter is of special interest to us, and it, along with adjusted mean test scores, becomes the focus of our next model.

Level-1 Random-Intercept and Random-Slopes Model

Our research question concerned a possible association between schools' parental wealth and level of test score improvement from the third to the sixth grades. Implicit in this question is the assumption that test score improvement varies from school to school. We observed in the level-1 model that was just estimated that, on average, students' sixth-grade test scores are 15% higher than their scores in the third grade. We also observed that mean test scores, adjusted for gender, socioeconomic status, and prior performance, varied significantly from school to school. Given these observations, we now want to test the implicit proposition that test score improvement will also vary from school to school.

We next consider the results from this test. The level-1 model remains the same as before, but the level-2 model is now represented by two equations:

$$\beta_{0j} = \gamma_{00} + u_0 \qquad \beta_{3j} = \gamma_{30} + u_3$$

where β_{0j} represents the randomly varying intercept, whereas β_{3j} represents the randomly varying slope parameter for previous test performance (PREVREAD). The HLM output in Table 4.4 contains the relevant output from this specification.

Level-2 Intercept- and Slopes-as-Outcomes Model

The chi-square tests found in the Final Estimation of the Variance Components section of the table indicate that significant variation exists across schools both in terms of the intercept (average test scores) ($\chi^2 = 850.94376$, $df = 151$) and the PREVREAD slope ($\chi^2 = 7006.54329$, $df = 151$). We can therefore reject the null hypothesis that reading improvement is constant across schools.

Having established that variation in these parameters exists across schools, we turn our attention to accounting for this variation. Is a school's parental wealth associated with its average improvement in reading ability? We test this proposition by developing a level-2 intercept- and slopes-as-outcomes model. Again, the level-1 model remains the same as before:

$$Y_{ij} = \beta_{0j} + \beta_{1j}(\text{FEMALE}) + \beta_{2j}(\text{LOWSES}) + \beta_{3j}(\text{PREVTEST}) + \varepsilon_{ij}$$

CHAPTER 4

TABLE 4.4
Random-Intercept and Random-Slopes Model

```
Random level-1 coefficient    Reliability estimate
-----------------------------------------------------
  INTRCPT1, B0                    0.741
  PREVREAD, B1                    0.904

The value of the likelihood function at iteration 6 = -4.540563E+004

<BREAK HERE>
The outcome variable is  TOTREAD

Final estimation of fixed effects:
-----------------------------------------------------------------------
  Fixed Effect      Coefficient   Standard Error   T-ratio    P-value
-----------------------------------------------------------------------

For        INTRCPT1, B0
   INTRCPT2, G00     643.576022      0.640042      1005.522    0.000
For  FEMALE slope, B1
   INTRCPT2, G10       3.321783      0.509883         6.515    0.000
For   LOWSES slope, B2
   INTRCPT2, G20      -9.782038      0.559929       -17.470    0.000
For PREVREAD slope, B3
   INTRCPT2, G30       0.371509      0.023144        16.052    0.000



Final estimation of variance components:
-----------------------------------------------------------------------
Random Effect          Standard      Variance     df   Chi-square   P-value
                       Deviation     Component
-----------------------------------------------------------------------
  INTRCPT1,      U0      6.81274      46.41341     151    850.94376    0.000
  PREVREAD slope, U3     0.27215       0.07407     151   7006.54329    0.000
  level-1,       R      24.65167     607.70473
```

The level-2 models are changed to include the level-2 characteristic of interest to us:

$$\beta_{0j} = \gamma_{00} + \gamma_{01}\text{MDINC100} + u_0$$
$$\beta_{3j} = \gamma_{30} + \gamma_{31}\text{MDINC100} + u_3$$

where MDINC100 represents the median income of parents (divided by 100 for ease of interpretability) at school j. The output from this final, unconditional at level-2, slopes-as-outcomes model appears in Table 4.5.

Focusing first on the estimates for the equation modeling the intercept (β_{0j}), we see that median parental income has a small but positive impact on average reading test scores in each school. On average, a \$10,000 dollar increase in median parental income is associated with a 1.5-point increase in schools' reading scores, after controlling for salient student-level characteristics including individual socioeconomic status. Students in schools educating children of wealthier families perform slightly better than their counterparts in schools representing less affluent families.

TABLE 4.5
Final Intercept- and Slopes-as-Outcomes Model

```
Random level-1 coefficient    Reliability estimate
--------------------------------------------------
INTRCPT1, B0                       0.729
PREVREAD, B1                       0.898

The value of the likelihood function at iteration 6 = -4.540896E+004

<BREAK HERE>
The outcome variable is  TOTREAD

Final estimation of fixed effects:
-----------------------------------------------------------------------
  Fixed Effect      Coefficient   Standard Error  T-ratio   P-value
-----------------------------------------------------------------------
For         INTRCPT1, B0
   INTRCPT2, G00      637.405715     2.090050     304.972    0.000
   MDINC100, G01        0.015040     0.004929       3.051    0.003
For    FEMALE slope, B1
   INTRCPT2, G10        3.334486     0.509866       6.540    0.000
For    LOWSES slope, B2
   INTRCPT2, G20       -9.574940     0.564276     -16.969    0.000
For PREVREAD slope, B3
   INTRCPT2, G30        0.171284     0.073323       2.336    0.020
   MDINC100, G31        0.000488     0.000172       2.829    0.005
```

```
Final estimation of variance components:
-----------------------------------------------------------------------
Random Effect          Standard     Variance     df   Chi-square  P-value
                       Deviation    Component
-----------------------------------------------------------------------
INTRCPT1,       U0      6.57915      43.28525    150    808.29715   0.000
PREVREAD slope, U3      0.26212       0.06871    150   6247.84252   0.000
  level-1,      R      24.65665     607.95020
```

Examining the estimates for the equation modeling the effect previous performance, (β_{3j}), the results indicate that students in schools representing wealthier families realize greater improvement in reading. On average, a \$10,000 increase in median parental income yields a 4% advantage in average reading improvement. Thus, students in schools with more affluent parents tend to enjoy greater improvement in reading skill—at least as measured by the standardized reading test we are using in this example. Again, this is after controlling for the individual characteristics of gender and socioeconomic status.

The chi-square tests in Table 4.3 continue to indicate that significant variation in parameter estimates exists across schools, although the variance components and associated χ^2 values have been diminished. In cases where the analyst is able to specify powerful level-2 models, the chi-square statistics associated with these components are rendered nonsignificant. This would indicate there is little level-2 variance left to be accounted for by further analysis.

Although the χ^2 statistics indicate significant variability in the random parameters remains, it is useful to calculate the proportion of variance explained in each of the variance components of the model. This is accomplished by comparing the initial values of each of the components with those in the final model. From Eq. 15, the proportion of variance explained in mean test scores is $(175.86989 - 43.28525)/175.86989 = .75388$. Our final model accounted for a full three-fourths of the initial between-school variance in test scores.

SUMMARY

Beyond the interpretations we provide here, the HLM program permits a range of other specification and tests (including residual analyses) that can be used to illustrate some of the more complex conceptual elements we introduced in chapter 2. Some of these more complex specifications include multilevel time-series models and nonlinear multilevel models for dichotomous outcomes. We encourage the reader to consult Bryk and Raudenbush (1992) to learn more about the powerful features of these models. In chapter 8, we consider a three-level example demonstrating some of this potential.

We have shown, through the example used in this chapter, the ways in which the multilevel model is simply an extension of ordinary single-level regression. In chapter 2, we called attention to the numerous shortcomings of ordinary regression when faced with a hierarchical data structure (e.g., unit of analysis questions and dependence of observations within units). This chapter has demonstrated some of the advantages of working in a multilevel framework rather than the traditional single-level approach. An exercise is provided at the end of this chapter to allow the reader an opportunity to explore the development and interpretation of a simple two-level model.

Despite the clear advantages of multilevel regression models, limitations still remain. In the following chapters we extend the models we have worked with in chapters 2 and 3 and consider structural equation modeling techniques that permit analysis of broader range of theoretical models and greater refinement of error specification. As we moved from the single-level regression model in chapter 2 to the multilevel regression model in this chapter, we next begin with single-level SEM techniques and then extend these techniques to applications at multiple levels.

We encourage you to try the following multilevel regression exercise. You only need access to the HLM for Windows program. You should be able to develop the necessary SSM file by following the accompanying instructions and using the data found in Appendix A of this chapter.

Although we have provided some guidance in setting up the model in the following exercise, you may still hit a few snags. Persistence is a virtue, and with a little debugging you will be able to replicate some of what we have shown in this chapter.

APPENDIX A
Student-Level Data

100	0	623	0	107	0	654	0
100	1	635	0	107	1	654	0
100	1	700	0	107	1	602	0
100	0	663	0	107	1	679	1
100	1	656	0	107	1	611	0
100	1	695	0	107	1	683	1
100	0	802	0	107	1	664	1
100	0	648	0	107	1	594	1
100	0	594	1	107	1	623	1
100	0	679	0	107	1	626	1
103	0	655	0	108	1	654	0
103	0	674	0	108	1	663	0
103	1	688	0	108	0	658	0
103	0	660	1	108	1	623	0
103	0	665	0	108	0	746	0
103	0	663	0	108	1	673	0
103	1	728	0	108	0	614	0
103	1	665	1	108	0	706	0
103	1	657	0	108	0	676	0
103	1	686	0	108	0	734	0
104	1	628	0	109	0	761	0
104	0	644	0	109	1	695	0
104	1	605	1	109	0	671	0
104	0	631	1	109	0	693	0
104	0	594	1	109	0	625	0
104	1	645	1	109	0	695	0
104	1	663	0	109	0	676	0
104	0	660	1	109	0	731	0
104	1	657	1	109	0	671	0
104	0	663	1	109	0	669	0
105	1	638	1	110	1	731	0
105	1	633	1	110	1	635	1
105	1	607	1	110	0	717	1
105	0	679	0	110	0	631	0
105	1	671	0	110	1	663	1
105	0	580	0	110	1	752	0
105	1	669	1	110	1	650	1
105	0	637	1	110	1	713	0
105	1	686	1	110	1	666	1
105	0	662	0	110	1	685	0
106	1	689	1	111	0	614	1
106	1	706	0	111	1	634	0
106	0	719	0	111	0	717	0

(Continued)

106	1	689	0	111	0	690	1
106	1	669	1	111	0	691	1
106	0	763	0	111	0	611	0
106	1	699	1	111	1	673	0
106	1	655	0	111	1	611	1
106	1	664	0	111	0	619	1
106	1	719	0	111	0	656	0

School-Level Data	
100	.74
103	.70
104	.63
105	.64
106	.78
107	.68
108	.73
109	.78
110	.66
111	.67

Note. Contents of columns explained in Exercise.

EXERCISE

Using a two-level HLM model, a researcher wishes to test of a model designed to assess the effects of principal leadership on math performance in the sixth grade. The school-level "leadership" variable is a preconstructed factor composite of teachers' ratings on six indicators of school leadership: instructional leadership, emphasis on academics, high expectations for student achievement, monitoring of student progress, positive school environment, and positive home–school relations. Student-level variables are female (dummy coded 0 for males and 1 for females) and an indicator of students coming from families of low SES background.

Objective

After constructing an SSM file within HLM, you should first define a "null model" to partition the variance within and between schools. If sufficient variation in math test scores exists between schools, you should develop a random intercept model with the principal leadership factor at level 2.

Constructing the SSM File

Data for this exercise are contained in Appendix A. They are comprised of 100 students from 10 separate schools. To complete this exercise, the reader must enter the data in Appendix A into two separate files—one for student-level data and another for school-level data. The instructions that follow guide the reader through development of the SSM file using ASCII input files. The reader may also enter the data in Appendix A into a standard statistical package such as SPSS or SAS and then transfer the files into HLM to create the SSM file. Either way, the student level file will contain four variables: a school identification number SCHID, a dummy variable indicating student gender (FEMALE), students' sixth-grade reading scores (READ), and a dummy variable indicating family SES background (LOWSES) for 100 observations. The school-level file will contain two variables: a school identification number (SCHID) and (PLEAD) a leadership score for each school's principal.

The ASCII input feature of HLM requires that data be entered in "fixed" format and that you specify the formats of each variable in the raw data files. Therefore, it is crucial that when entering these data, you keep track of the number of columns and decimal points used by each variable. For example, using the "." character to designate spaces, the first three observations in the student file appear as:

```
SCHID  FEMALE  READ  LOWSES
...100.......0...623.......0
...100.......1...635.......0
...100.......1...700.......0
```

The variable SCHID takes up six columns, FEMALE and LOWSES use eight columns, and READ uses six. None of these variables have values to the right of a decimal point.

The first three observations in the school file appear as:

```
SCHID   PLEAD
...100......74
...103......70
...104......63
```

Again, the identification variable, SCHID, takes up six columns. The principal leadership variable takes up eight columns, using two columns to the right of the decimal point.

For purposes of the exercise, it might be helpful to save the student-level data in a text file named student.dat and the school level data in a separate file named school.dat.

Once these data are entered and saved, you can begin constructing a SSM file in HLM. Using the File → SSM → New → ASCII Input menu choices in HLM for Windows (4.01.01), you can specify the characteristics of the data files.

You will first be prompted to indicate whether you wish to specify a 2-level or 3-level model. Choose **2-Level**. You will then be given a **Make**

New SSM File From ASCII Data dialog box that asks for several pieces of information.

If you have opted to create the data files in a package such as SPSS or SAS, you will use the File → SSM → New → Stat Package Input menu choices. With the exception of the data definition step in the ASCII file approach, SSM file construction follows the same logic as that outlined below.

You might work on the **Level-1 Specification** first by entering the name of the data file containing the student level data that you have entered previously into the **Level-1 File Name** box. Specify the **Number of Variables** in the file, excluding the ID variable—in this case that will be 3 (FEMALE, READ, and LOWSES).

There is no missing data so you can ignore the **Missing Data** specification. The contents of the **Data Format** box will depend on the way the level-1 file has been laid out. Assuming you chose to construct the files according to the layout shown here, the data format statement would appear as: (A6, f8.0, f6.0, f8.0). This FORTRAN-style coding simply tells the HLM program that it will be reading four variables. The first will be a string variable appearing in the first six columns of the data file. The second variable will be numeric and will appear in the next eight columns of the data file, and so on.

You should then apply **Labels** to the specified variables. Although the choice of variable names is arbitrary, we suggest you use the names we have provided. The variable SCHID (the first variable in the file) should be designated as the **ID** variable. As there are no weights for this exercise, the **Weighting** function can be ignored.

You should repeat these steps for the **Level-2 Specification**. If the level-2 file has been constructed according to the layout shown here, the **FORTRAN Style Data Format** would appear as (A6, F8.2). The statement indicates that the first variable, SCHID, is a string variable found in the first six columns of the level-2 data file and the principal leadership variable, PLEAD, is found in the next eight columns and is carried out to two decimal points. When applying **Labels** to the variables at level 2, make sure to provide the same name for the ID variable as that used in the level-1 specification. This is the only way HLM will know to link the level-1 and level-2 files on this variable.

After specifying level-1 and level-2 data, you should provide an **SSM File Name**. You might use ch4.ssm (note that you must include the .ssm extension). Finally, you will need to specify a **Response File Name**. The Response File contains all of the information you have entered into the **Make New SSM File From ASCII Data** dialog box and can be reused to alter future SSM specifications. It is helpful to name these after the SSM file. The contents of our RSP file used for this exercise appear as:

```
Contents of ch4.rsp
y
n
1
3
(A6,F8.0,F6.0,F8.0)
C:\STUDENT.DAT
1
(A6,F8.2)
C:\SCHOOL.DAT
FEMALE
MATH
LOWSES
PLEAD
n
n
n
CH4.SSM
y
```

Once all required information has been provided, the **Make SSM** button will illuminate. Clicking on this will create the SSM file and produce descriptive statistics for data at both levels.

If your data files were constructed correctly and your file specification at each level correctly reflect the layout of those files, you will be looking at a DOS screen that contains the following information:

```
format:
Input name of level-2 file:
 Enter 8 character name for level-1 variable number 1:  Enter 8 character name f
or level-1 variable number 2:  Enter 8 character name for level-1 variable numbe
r 3:
 Enter 8 character name for level-2 variable number 1: Is there missing data in
the level-1 file?
Is there a level-1 weighting variable? Is there a level-2 weighting variable?
Enter name of SSM file:
                 LEVEL-1 DESCRIPTIVE STATISTICS
```

VARIABLE NAME	N	MEAN	SD	MINIMUM	MAXIMUM
FEMALE	100	0.53	0.50	0.00	1.00
MATH	100	666.43	41.02	580.00	802.00
LOWSES	100	0.35	0.48	0.00	1.00

```
Do you wish to save these descriptive statistics in a file?
                 LEVEL-2 DESCRIPTIVE STATISTICS
```

VARIABLE NAME	N	MEAN	SD	MINIMUM	MAXIMUM
PLEAD	10	0.70	0.05	0.63	0.78

```
    100 level-1 records have been processed
    10 level-2 records have been processed
```

The last part of this screen, the descriptive statistics, is automatically saved in a file named HLM2SSM.STS. You can open that file in any word processor to examine the statistics.

If the SSM file is not created, it will be necessary to review the layout of the *.dat files as well as the specification you have provided to HLM. This can be a time-consuming process.

Once the SSM file has been created, you can begin constructing models to address the objective stated at the beginning of this exercise. Models are specified in HLM using the File → New File menu choice. You will be prompted for the name of a SSM file and should select the file created in the previous steps. You will specify the HLM models by clicking on the variables on the left of the screen and making the appropriate choices.

Hint

Grand-mean center the level-1 variables FEMALE and LOWSES. Enter the level-2 variable MDINC100 uncentered. Also, remember to constrain variances for each of the level-1 parameters to zero (FEMALE and LOWSES); that is, you are not interested in how they may vary across schools. Only the intercept should be allowed to vary randomly. This is accomplished by removing the error term associated with these parameters (you will see this in the bottom part of your screen).

Solution

The variance components produced by the "null model" show that 17.99% of variance is between schools. This is sufficient to warrant further modeling of the intercept. The next step is to develop a level-1 model controlling for gender and SES.

Pertinent HLM Output From the "Null Model"

```
-----------------------------------------------------
 Random level-1 coefficient   Reliability estimate
-----------------------------------------------------
  INTRCPT1, B0                       0.687

The value of the likelihood function at iteration 2 = -5.076153E+002

The outcome variable is     MATH

Final estimation of fixed effects:
----------------------------------------------------------------------------
  Fixed Effect     Coefficient   Standard Error  T-ratio    P-value
----------------------------------------------------------------------------
For      INTRCPT1, B0
   INTRCPT2, G00   666.430000      6.693878      99.558     0.000

Final estimation of variance components:
----------------------------------------------------------------------------
Random Effect          Standard      Variance     df    Chi-square  P-value
                       Deviation     Component
----------------------------------------------------------------------------
  INTRCPT1,      U0     17.54381      307.78531     9     28.74463    0.001
  level-1,       R      37.45594     1402.94779
```

In the level-1 model, gender has no effect on math test scores, but those with higher SES backgrounds enjoy higher standardized test scores in math. The variance between schools is notably diminished (12%) after the level-1 variables have been controlled. With sufficient variation remaining between schools, a level-2 model should be developed to test for the impact of principal leadership on math test scores and to try to account for the remaining variance.

Pertinent HLM Output From the Level-1 Model

```
-----------------------------------------------------
  Random level-1 coefficient    Reliability estimate
-----------------------------------------------------
  INTRCPT1, B0                        0.577

The value of the likelihood function at iteration 11 = -5.005816E+002

The outcome variable is      MATH

Final estimation of fixed effects:
--------------------------------------------------------------------------
  Fixed Effect      Coefficient    Standard Error  T-ratio    P-value
--------------------------------------------------------------------------
For        INTRCPT1, B0
   INTRCPT2, G00     666.430000      5.732726       116.250     0.000
For    FEMALE slope, B1
   INTRCPT2, G10      -3.606942      8.074033        -0.447     0.665
For    LOWSES slope, B2
   INTRCPT2, G20     -20.196672      8.590850        -2.351     0.043

Final estimation of variance components:
--------------------------------------------------------------------------
  Random Effect          Standard      Variance      df   Chi-square  P-value
                         Deviation     Component
--------------------------------------------------------------------------
  INTRCPT1,     U0       13.76989      189.60983      9     20.72021   0.014
  level-1,      R        37.28679     1390.30480
```

The level-2 model account reveals the important role that principal effectiveness can play in determining math test scores. Not only is the level-2 variable capturing principal leadership positive and significant, but it also explains away the remaining between school variance in math scores—note the χ^2 value of 11.55383 with 8 degrees of freedom. In this case, the full model has accounted for all of the between school variance. It would seem that principal leadership is an important factor in school performance.

Pertinent HLM Output From the Full Model

```
-----------------------------------------------------
  Random level-1 coefficient    Reliability estimate
-----------------------------------------------------
  INTRCPT1, B0                        0.326
```

The value of the likelihood function at iteration 11 = -4.933762E+002

<BREAK HERE>
The outcome variable is   MATH

Final estimation of fixed effects:
```
----------------------------------------------------------------------
  Fixed Effect        Coefficient   Standard Error   T-ratio   P-value
----------------------------------------------------------------------
For         INTRCPT1,  B0
    INTRCPT2, G00      498.748516      66.711644       7.476     0.000
      PLEAD, G01       239.203260     .94.946025       2.519     0.036
For    FEMALE slope,   B1
    INTRCPT2, G10       -1.604808       7.862506      -0.204     0.844
For    LOWSES slope,   B2
    INTRCPT2, G20      -14.750848       8.893210      -1.659     0.135
```

Final estimation of variance components:
```
-----------------------------------------------------------------------
Random Effect            Standard     Variance    df   Chi-square  P-value
                         Deviation    Component
-----------------------------------------------------------------------
INTRCPT1,       U0        8.19713      67.19291     8    11.55383    0.172
level-1,        R        37.23876    1386.72546
```

An Overview of Structural Equation Modeling

The examples presented in the previous two chapters demonstrated the multiple regression approach to single-level and multilevel data. As we have suggested, however, there are some types of theoretical models that cannot be readily analyzed with that basic approach. Structural equation modeling (SEM) techniques are another major component of applied multivariate analysis (Marcoulides & Schumacker, 1996). The term is broadly defined to accommodate the specification and testing of theoretical models that include latent variables, measurement errors, multiple indicators, simultaneity, and complex structural relationships including reciprocal causation. SEM is a generalization of both regression and factor analysis and subsumes most linear modeling methods as special cases (Rigdon, 1998). Structural equation models, therefore, provide researchers with a comprehensive method for the quantification and testing of theories.

SEM techniques are useful in addressing two basic concerns in the analysis of organizational data. First, as we suggested in chapter 2, is the development of underlying (latent) constructs through measuring their hypothesized observed indicators. In SEM logic, this is called defining the *measurement* model because it focuses on the validity and reliability of constructs and their observed indicators. The technique used to define measurement models is referred to in the literature as *confirmatory factor analysis* (CFA), because of the emphasis on proposing a set of theoretical relationships first, and then testing them against the data to "confirm" the existence of the proposed structure. The approach is also referred to as *covariance structure analysis*, which comes from the practice of using a mathematical model to describe the covariance matrix of a set of observed variables from a smaller set of underlying factors (i.e., similar to the use of correlation in multiple regression). Through this analysis, the attempt is made to reproduce the original data matrix of covariances (or correlations) by clustering subsets of the observed variables with a smaller number of underlying factors. The second part of an SEM analysis, the *structural model*, involves investigating the relationships, or paths, between the latent variables in a proposed model.

Because of the relationship of theory in guiding the specification and testing of a structural model, our concern is often first with the model's fit. If the set of theoretical relations implied by the model does not fit the data, it would be necessary to reconceptualize it. For this reason, the reader will note that our presentation of structural equation modeling for multilevel research in the next few chapters rests primarily on model fitting, with the actual substantive meaning of the individual parameter estimates being somewhat deemphasized in our discussions. Of course, in the reader's own research, it is likely that both will take on equal importance.

AN OVERVIEW OF SEM TECHNIQUES

The basic features of the measurement and structural models in SEM can be adapted to the investigation of a variety of multilevel models, although the techniques for doing so have not yet been widely disseminated. In staying with our overall aim to provide an introduction to multilevel methods, we keep our discussion of SEM techniques relatively simple. Our approach is more or less informal, because of the need to use matrix algebra and complex statistical theory (e.g., maximum likelihood) in estimating the parameters of a proposed structural model. Those readers who are unfamiliar with the SEM approach to proposing and testing theoretical models may wish to see Marcoulides and Hershberger (1997), Pedhazur and Schmelkin (1991), or Schumacker and Lomax (1996) for complete overviews.

Defining Constructs Through CFA

As we suggested previously, many social processes are conceived of as structural processes operating among unobserved constructs. Because organizational processes such as leadership, job satisfaction, commitment, and culture cannot be directly observed, however, they must be defined through measuring a set of their observed manifestations. Construct validation takes place when a researcher believes an instrument reflects a particular construct, to which are attached certain meanings. The proposed interpretation generates specific hypotheses that may be tested about the relations among the constructs, which are a means of confirming or disconfirming the claim (Cronbach & Meehl, 1955).

In the CFA approach to construct validation, a smaller set of underlying, or latent, factors are hypothesized to be responsible for the specific pattern of variation and covariation in a set of observed variables. Each of the observed variables is conceptualized as a linear function of one or more factors (Long, 1983). There are two types of factors—common factors that may affect more than one observed variable, and unique or residual factors that may affect only one observed variable. Theoretical constraints postulated on the basis of theory and previous empirical findings are imposed on the set of relationships in a proposed model *before* the model is tested against the data. To define the proposed model adequately, the researcher should already know the number of constructs, the specific construct with which each of the observed variables is to be associated, the particular pattern of correlations between constructs, the relationships among the unique factors (i.e., residuals) and observed variables, and possibly even the relationships among the set of unique factors (see Heck, 1998; Long, 1983).

For example, a researcher may have a number of survey items that the researcher believes should define two underlying constructs. Three of the items are thought to represent one construct, and the other three represent a second construct. The researcher can further hypothesize that a positive correlation exists between the two constructs. The investigator therefore has tremendous control over the specification of the exact set of theoretical relationships to be tested. After specifying this proposed set of relationships, the researcher can test the model against the actual data. Several statistical and practical tests can be used to determine whether the sample data confirm the hypothesized factor model. If the model fits the data well (i.e., it reproduces the observed variation present in the data), the researcher has preliminary evidence of its construct validity.

In practice, however, the researcher may not have only one model in mind, but rather a series of competing models. Testing the adequacy of each proposed model in sequence is known as an alternative-models approach (see Hoyle & Panter, 1995, for further discussion). Through these comparisons, the researcher can determine whether alternative models fit just as well as (called an equivalent model) or better or worse than the primary model (see Rigdon, 1998). Construct validation is therefore an ongoing process of defining and checking to see whether the defined construct is useful within a larger system of theoretical relations among the constructs. Because of the emphasis on theory in using this approach, it is important to begin with clear definitions about constructs, using previous research and theoretical models as guides in their definition. In operationalizing constructs, however, it is important to keep in mind that the observed indicators are not the construct itself, but only a set of possible manifestations of it.

Once a model's preliminary construct validity has been established, researchers often investigate whether the same model fits across other groups (e.g., age, ethnicity, gender), samples, or settings (e.g., organizations). This process is referred to as testing a model's generalizability, and is a second way of investigating its construct validity. The researcher might attempt to determine whether the same factor structure can be confirmed in new samples of subjects. Testing the generalizability of a model helps extend the usefulness of a theory by confirming and, if necessary, modifying a set of proposed relationships in a variety of different settings and groups.

Current SEM software packages provide several means for comparing models across samples or groups. When models are compared across groups, assumptions are generally made that the constructs being measured are similar for all groups examined. Such comparisons yield information about the construct validity of measures as well as potential group or sample differences. These types of investigations using the multigroup approach in SEM are generally undertaken from the standpoint of investigating model invariance. The researcher can question whether the same constructs are being measured across each group, whether the constructs vary in similar manners across the groups (called dispersion invariance), and even whether there is level invariance, or differences between the groups (e.g., comparing their mean structures).

To investigate model invariance, the researcher imposes constraints on particular parameters of interest across the groups and estimates these parameters simultaneously. The same proposed model is fitted to the covariance matrices of different groups. In this way, hypotheses are tested about whether the factor structure is invariant (e.g., number of factors, factor variances and covariances), whether the same pattern of factor loadings exists, and even whether there are invariant measurement errors across the groups examined. The multigroup feature of SEM programs, therefore, allows the researcher to begin to think about ways in which a particular model may be similar or different across a number of different groups.

As the reader can surmise, investigating a model's construct validity across groups can be directly applied to multilevel research. In this situation, we extend the basic premise of fitting the model across several groups or samples to a larger number of organizations. In fact, in the multilevel situation, we can test the measurement properties of a construct (i.e., how well it is defined by its indicators) and its generalizability across groups (e.g., organizations) simultaneously.

An example may help illustrate the basic approach. One application of CFA in organizational settings might be in the investigation of differences in employees' perceptions of their managers' leadership performance within and between organizations. Leadership is obviously an underlying construct. It cannot be directly observed. To investigate leadership, therefore, we must define some possible observed manifestations of it, perhaps through surveying people in organizations. Some observed aspects of leadership are likely to be similar in nature. We could hypothesize that several of these observed indicators might constitute a specific dimension of leadership.

It is also quite likely that leadership is a multidimensional construct; that is, there may be several different dimensions and skills that comprise it. We might have to conceptualize several latent dimensions of leadership, each defined by a set of observed indicators. We would then have to test this conceptualization of leadership against the data and determine whether our proposed model is adequate in accounting for patterns (i.e., variances and covariances) in the data. Of course, we must remember that our preliminary model will be biased if we do not acknowledge the clustered nature of the sample (e.g., employees nested within organizations). A single-level analysis to define leadership constructs, however, provides a necessary starting point for eventually conducting a multilevel analysis. This step can provide some preliminary indications of whether the theoretical model is likely to be supported by the data.

We could extend the basic model to the investigation of factorial invariance across the organizations. If our measurement model of leadership holds across organizations, we would feel somewhat confident that we have succeeded in obtaining valid and reliable measures of leadership. We could then investigate the structural relations between leadership and other organizational processes and outcomes. To the extent that leadership accounts for certain types of organizational processes as hypothesized, we would gain more evidence of our model's construct validity.

We now turn to a discussion of some of the mathematical principles underlying covariance structure analysis. SEM proceeds by assessing whether a sample covariance or correlation matrix is consistent with a hypothetical matrix implied by the specification of a theoretical model (Rigdon, 1998). The basic statistical theory underlying SEM is based on examining the variances and covariances among the observed variables. In many practical applications, however, SEM researchers may analyze a correlation matrix because they are unable to attach substantive meaning to the units of measurement they are using (Jöreskog & Sörbom, 1993a). It is important to note, however, that the chi-square test of model fit and standard errors (used in determining the significance of parameters) are predicated on a covariance matrix being analyzed.

To date, several different mathematical models for SEM have been specified in the literature. Although they can translate data equally well, they differ somewhat in the manner in which they translate the data. Here, we use the general approach presented by Jöreskog and Sörbom (1989), because of the necessity of using a particular programming language in

88   CHAPTER 5

testing models with LISREL. We chose STREAMS as one software program
for multilevel SEM because it uses the LISREL language to specify models.
Mplus uses a similar approach. The input data can be either raw data or
sample moments computed from the data including variances and covariances or correlations, and may also include means and higher order moments (Rigdon, 1998).

Observed variables hypothesized to define the latent constructs are characterized by the covariances among these variables contained in a sample
covariance matrix. This matrix is decomposed by a model that assumes
that unobserved variables (e.g., dimensions of leadership) are generating
the pattern, or structure, among the observed variables. The form of the
covariance structure equation used in specifying relationships between the
observed and latent variables can be represented as

$$\Sigma = \Lambda\Psi\Lambda' + \Theta \tag{1}$$

where Σ is a variance–covariance matrix, Λ is a matrix of factor loadings
(Λ' is the transpose of the matrix), Ψ is a matrix of factor variances and
covariances, and Θ is a variance–covariance matrix of unique factors, or
measurement errors (e.g., Jöreskog & Sörbom, 1989; Long, 1983). Through
a network of proposed equations, the original covariance matrix is recon-
figured into a matrix of factor loadings, a matrix factor variances and
covariances, and a matrix of residuals. Each matrix contains a specific
hypothesized pattern of relationships. By examining the matrices (e.g., the
loadings and residuals), the analyst can determine how well the observed
variables measure the underlying factors. Higher item loadings (and corresponding lower error terms) on the hypothesized factors suggest stronger
measurement properties.

One important distinction between exploratory factor analysis (an approach that the reader may already be familiar with) and CFA, therefore,
is that in the confirmatory approach, the researcher first specifies a particular pattern of observed variable loadings on the factors guided by
theory. This results in many elements in the covariance matrix being fixed
to zero (i.e., not estimated). In contrast, in the exploratory factor method,
every observed variable is free to be identified with, or *load*, on every factor.
Restricting paths to zero is what provides the "test" of a particular hypothesized model and in most cases is needed to identify a unique solution to
the set of equations. The reader should note that this test of the model's
fit using chi-square is actually related to what restricted relationships do
not fit the data; that is, a large discrepancy between the hypothesized
model with the pattern of restricted paths and the data is what constitutes
evidence of poor model fit. In this case, the researcher would have to
reconceptualize at least some aspect of the hypothesized model (e.g., per-

haps by relaxing one of the fixed factor loadings). If the discrepancy between the hypothesized model and the data is small, the researcher has established some initial evidence confirming the model's construct validity.

Another important distinction between the two approaches is that in CFA the error matrix (Θ) is not restricted to being diagonal (i.e., error variance represented in the diagonals and zeros off the diagonals). This greater flexibility permits the specification of covariances between unique terms (i.e., using the off-diagonal elements) within the Θ matrix. It is important to note, however, that this difference makes model identification (i.e., determining whether a unique solution exists) more difficult, because as a result of this flexibility, in the CFA approach there are many more possible parameters that potentially can be estimated.

In the LISREL and *Mplus* approach to CFA, a series of matrices is used to specify the sets of relationships implied in the theoretical model. The model that relates the observed indicators to their underlying (latent) factors is called the measurement model. The general factor equation for a confirmatory factor analysis (for convenience using a "y" specification in LISREL notation) is

$$y = \Lambda_y \eta + \varepsilon \qquad (2)$$

where y is a vector of observed variables, Λ is a matrix of factor loadings of y, η is a vector of latent factors, and ε is a vector of unique factors. We could also define a similar model for a set of "x" variables using similar matrix notation. In LISREL, the "x"specification is used to define exogenous variables (similar to independent variables) and the "y" specification is used to define endogenous (intervening and dependent) variables in more complex models.

Developing a Structural Model

The measurement model (i.e., confirmatory factor analysis) can be extended to the investigation of structural relationships between latent variables. As we noted, defining the measurement model through CFA is often the first part of an SEM analysis. After the constructs are adequately measured, we can investigate relationships between the constructs. The second model, the structural model, specifies the causal relationships among a set of latent variables that have been factored from observed variables through the measurement model.

The variables to be explained in an SEM analysis are called *endogenous variables*. They are explained by specifying that they are causally dependent on other endogenous variables or on exogenous variables. Exogenous variables (similar to independent variables) are determined by causes outside of the model and therefore are not explained by the model. The structural relationships in a model may be written as

$$\eta = \alpha + B\eta + \Gamma\xi + \zeta \qquad (3)$$

where η is a vector of endogenous factors, α is a vector of intercepts, B is a matrix of regression coefficients relating the endogenous factors to other endogenous factors, Γ is a matrix of regression coefficients relating the exogenous variables (ξ) to the endogenous variables, and ζ is a vector of disturbances (or errors in the equations), indicating that the endogenous variables are not perfectly predicted by the structural equations (Long, 1983). As the reader can see from Eq. 2, the observed variables are linked to the underlying factors through their respective factor loading matrices (e.g., Λ_y or Λ_x). The latent variables are connected in a two-equation interdependent system of gamma and beta regression coefficients. Therefore, the general structural model allows the specification of both errors in equations and errors in observed variables.

In cases where all variables are observed (i.e., where there is no specific measurement model linking observed variables to latent variables), the model of structural relationships reduces to a standard path analytic model:

$$y = \alpha + By + \Gamma x + \zeta \qquad (4)$$

In chapter 7, we adapt this general SEM specification to fit multilevel structural models with different sets of predictors at each level.

Proposing and Specifying a Model

Muthén (1994) outlined a general approach to multilevel confirmatory factor analysis (MCFA). The first step is to investigate the theoretical model as a single-level analysis. To illustrate the CFA approach, we use some sample data on employees' perceptions of the effectiveness of managers' leadership practices within and across a sample of organizations. To simplify the presentation, we select six observed indicators of leadership that are hypothesized to define two latent dimensions of leadership.

We propose that three indicators of managers' governance practices (i.e., shared decision making, involving clients in program/planning processes, and using work teams) comprise a first latent dimension of leadership. The second dimension is related to the manager's evaluation of employees and organizational programs, also defined by three observed indicators. The specific indicators are managers' perceived skills in the evaluation of programs and work processes, their use of clear evaluation standards in assessing employees' work, and their use of systematic assess-

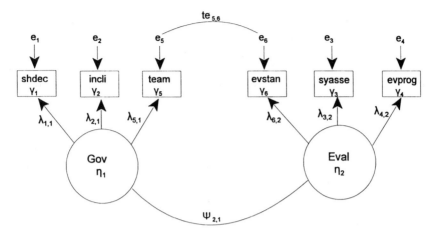

FIG. 5.1. Proposed single-level factor model.

ment practices in evaluating their employees. In the model, we also propose that the two latent dimensions of leadership are positively correlated.

The model is represented visually in Fig. 5.1. It is customary to use ovals or circles for latent variables and rectangles for observed variables. As suggested, one of the advantages of using latent variables within the model is the ability to incorporate residual (error) variance for individual indicators into the model. In the figure, the reader will notice that we can provide an error term (i.e., unique factor) for each observed variable that is associated with a factor. This allows an assessment of the reliability of each indicator.

We can also show this specification $(\mathbf{y} = \Lambda_y\boldsymbol{\eta} + \boldsymbol{\varepsilon})$ written in matrix form as:

$$
\begin{bmatrix} y_1 \\ y_2 \\ y_3 \\ y_4 \\ y_5 \\ y_6 \end{bmatrix} = \begin{bmatrix} \lambda_{1,1} & 0 \\ \lambda_{2,1} & 0 \\ 0 & \lambda_{3,2} \\ 0 & \lambda_{4,2} \\ \lambda_{5,1} & 0 \\ 0 & \lambda_{6,2} \end{bmatrix} \begin{bmatrix} \eta_1 \\ \\ \\ \\ \eta_2 \end{bmatrix} + \begin{bmatrix} e_1 \\ e_2 \\ e_3 \\ e_4 \\ e_5 \\ e_6 \end{bmatrix}
$$

Through examining both Fig. 5.1 and the corresponding matrix specification, the reader can see that each observed variable has been restricted to load on only one common factor, with the loadings on other common factors being specified as equal to zero. Of course, we could decide to have one observed indicator load on both factors if our theory suggested that relationship. Because these restrictions are imposed on the model, the model becomes confirmatory, in that various model fit indices will be used to evaluate how well this particular model fits the data, as opposed to some other model that we might propose.

As we suggested earlier, besides having a unique factor for each observed indicator, through using matrix specification the researcher may also choose whether or not particular residuals are specified to covary (e.g., e_5 and e_6). Similarly, one may also decide which factors are specified to covary (e.g., in this case, only η_1 and η_2). We could actually even specify the strength of the relationships for certain parameters (e.g., loadings, factor variances and covariances) ahead of time and test whether these estimates fit the actual data. Thus, there is great flexibility afforded by this approach or investigating underlying structures.

SPECIFYING A CFA MODEL IN LISREL

There are a number of issues that we need to consider in proposing and testing a theoretical model. First, we must specify the measurement model illustrated in Fig. 5.1 in LISREL terminology. Unlike our presentation of multilevel regression with HLM (in a windows format), using LISREL 8.30 for multilevel models with latent variables requires some special program language. Although this language may appear difficult at first, the time spent in its acquisition pays off in terms of the flexibility of the program in modeling a wide variety of theoretical relationships. The reader can also conduct these analyses with other existing SEM programs (e.g., Amos, EQS). Other software programs are more recently available (e.g., *Mplus*, STREAMS) for multilevel covariance structure analysis that are certain to make the specification and testing of multilevel models easier in the near future.

LISREL, STREAMS, and *Mplus* require a basic understanding of matrices, because this is the form in which the model to be tested is specified. The matrices provide the locations to "store" the necessary information for the proposed model so that the system of equations may be solved. Although it is possible to shortcut the use of this terminology for single-level models (e.g., by using the new SIMPIS language for LISREL), for multilevel models in LISREL the use of the terminology will facilitate model specification. The STREAMS (Gustafsson & Stahl, 1996) computer program for multilevel modeling, which makes use of LISREL programming language, and *Mplus* both provide an easier means for specifying the model; however, one still needs to understand the output generated.

For ease of presentation, we will use an "all y" specification in LISREL terminology, using the *lambda* y (LY) matrix for the factor loadings, the *psi* matrix (PS) for the factor variances and covariances, and the *theta epsilon* (TE) matrix for the unique factors (i.e., errors in the indicators). The reader should consult the *LISREL User's Reference Guide* (Jöreskog & Sörbom, 1989) for further information about these matrices (e.g., the meaning of *full, symmetrical,* and *diagonal* matrix) and other programming language. For an "x" specification, we would use the lambda x (LX), phi matrix (PH), and the theta delta (TD) matrices. The actual LISREL specification we used to test the proposed model is shown in Table 5.1.

There are several required input statements to run the proposed model. Line names consist of two-letter keywords. For any run, the analyst must include a data (DA) statement, a model (MO) statement, and an output (OU) statement. On the data (DA) line we define the number of groups as one (NG = 1) for the time being, the number of input variables (NI = 6), the number of observations (NO = 216), and the type of matrix analyzed (MA), which in this case is a covariance matrix (CM). On the next few lines, we label (LA) the variables. Following the definition of the variables, we list the type of matrix (e.g., covariance) used as input. We could also read the matrix from an external file.

We define the model (MO) on the next line, using several model statements. For example, we have six observed variables (NY) and two latent factors (NE). The lambda y matrix is full (which allows the observed variables to be defined in rows and the factors they are associated with to be

TABLE 5.1
LISREL CFA Model Specification[a]

---

2 Factor Leadership Model (Total Covariance Matrix)
DA NI=6 NO=216 NG=1 MA=CM
LA
sharedec incli syasse evprog team evstan
CM
2.170
.426 .794
.479 .395 .992
.459 .347 .598 .864
.560 .369 .528 .479 1.151
.531 .383 .737 .614 .694 1.294
MO NY=6 NE=2 LY=FU,FI PS=SY,FI TE=SY,FI
VA 1.0 LY(1,1) LY(4,2)
FR LY(2,1) LY(3,2) LY(5,1) LY(6,2)
FR PS(1,1) PS(2,2) PS(2,1)
FR TE(1,1) TE(2,2) TE)(3,3) TE(4,4) TE(5,5) TE(6,6)
FR TE(6,5)
OU ML MI SS

---

[a]With TE(6,5) freed.

defined in columns) and fixed (FI). This means we must free the factor loadings that we wish to have estimated. We also specify the psi (PS) matrix of factor variances and covariances and the theta epsilon (TE) matrix of residuals (errors) for observed variables as symmetrical (SY) and fixed. A symmetrical matrix (i.e., where there the elements are the same above and below the diagonals) allows for the specification of the residual variances in the diagonals and covariances between residuals to be defined as off-diagonal elements in the matrix.

On the next few lines, we then "free" (FR) the specific paths that we wished to have estimated. The reader will notice that the statements used (e.g., FR LY 2,1) correspond to the matrix notation we described previously. It is the specific pattern of freeing paths while allowing others to remain fixed that makes the analysis confirmatory in nature. The reader will notice that the first two observed variables and the fifth are specified to load on the first latent variable (*gov*), and variables three, four, and six are specified to load on the second latent variable (*eval*). We fixed (FI) one observed variable on each latent factor (i.e., LY 1,1 and LY 4,2) to 1.0 to provide a metric scale for each latent variable.

With respect to the theta epsilon matrix, we free the diagonal elements (e.g., TE 1,1) to provide estimates of the variances of the unique factors. If we free an off-diagonal element in the theta epsilon matrix, we could estimate a covariance between two unique factors (e.g., TE 6,5). We next free the elements in the psi matrix (factor variances and covariances). In our example, we also decided to free the path between the two latent factors (PS 2,1). This provides the covariance between the two latent factors.

The final line in our program is the output (OU) statement, requesting maximum likelihood (ML) estimation, modification indices (MI), and a standardized solution (SS). In the standardized solution for a single-level analysis, all latent variables are rescaled to a common metric with a mean of zero and standard deviation (and variance) of 1.0. One advantage of reporting the standardized solution is that the researcher can interpret the relationships among factors as correlations.

Model Estimation

The method of estimating the model's parameters must also be considered. Model estimation involves finding parameter values (i.e., factor loadings, factor variances and covariances, unique factors) such that the predicted covariance matrix is as close as possible to the observed covariances contained in the sample matrix (see Long, 1983, for further discussion of this issue). First, initial parameter estimates (or starting values) are obtained for parameters in the model. Through iteration, these estimates are refined until they are optimal, and there is little difference between the structure implied by the proposed model and the reproduced sample covariance matrix. This should be very close to the original sample matrix. If one considers the sample matrix (**S**) to represent the population matrix Σ, then the difference between the reproduced sample matrix and the sample matrix should be very small if the model is consistent with the data. The evaluation of difference between the observed and reproduced covariance matrices depends on which of several methods of estimating the model's parameters is used.

A function that measures how close a given reproduced covariance matrix is to the sample covariance matrix is called a *fitting function* (see Long, 1983, for further discussion). Several fitting functions are available for estimating the parameters of the model, each with slightly different assumptions. As discussed in previous chapters, maximum likelihood (ML) estimation is the most frequently used method to obtain parameter estimates. The ML method attempts to find the most likely population parameter estimates that produced the observed covariance matrix, assuming that the observed covariance is from a multivariate normal population (see Lawley & Maxwell, 1963). After initial estimates are obtained, in ML the predicted matrix is readjusted at every iteration by assigning greater weight to variables that are more strongly associated with the factor until eventually an optimal solution is reached. Sometimes this process may require a considerable number of iterations, and under some circumstances the program will fail to converge on a solution (e.g., samples under 100 individuals).

ML estimation can be influenced by the relative normality of the data. Extreme departures from normality can especially affect the significance of the model's parameters (e.g., by downwardly biasing the standard errors). With 5-point scales, acceptable solutions can be generated where the data do not depart too much from normality (Boomsma, 1987). Departures from normality can also influence some of the goodness-of-fit indices that would be used in determining whether a proposed model fits the data. For this reason, some have suggested using particular fit indices with this type of data, or have applied modifications to the fit indices (Chou & Bentler, 1995; Hoyle & Panter, 1995).

Similarly, missing data can also be a problem, depending on the extent to which the data are missing and whether or not the data are missing at random. If the researcher has a large sample and the data are missing at random, listwise deletion (if under about 20% missing) is recommended over pairwise deletion (Byrne, 1995; Rigdon, 1998). Listwise deletion, however, can take a toll on sample size and introduce additional biases. Pairwise deletion is inconsistent with some SEM estimation techniques (Rigdon, 1998). Other strategies (e.g., bootstrapping; Arbuckle, 1997) have been developed for dealing with a variety of other missing data situations (see also Stoolmiller, Duncan, & Patterson, 1995). The reader can also consult the *Prelis 2 User's Reference Guide* (Jöreskog & Sörbom, 1993b), which accompanies the LISREL program, for help in dealing with missing data. *Mplus* also has several strategies for models with missing data. Handling missing data in many SEM programs, however, can be difficult.

Assessing the Adequacy of a Model

In testing a structural model against data, we must also make sure that the model has been identified properly. Model identification is a complicated issue that has been widely discussed in the SEM literature (e.g., Bollen, 1989; Bollen & Long, 1993; Jöreskog & Sörbom, 1989; Marcoulides & Hershberger, 1997). Identification has to do with the adequacy of information for parameter estimation. If a model were not identified (called *underidentified*), it would be possible to find an infinite number of values for the parameters, each set of which would be consistent with the covariance equation (Long, 1983). Model estimation assumes that the model has been identified. Either there is just enough information to solve each parameter (called *just-identified*) or there is more than enough information (referred to as an *overidentified* model).

In a general sense, the problem of identification is dealt with by restricting the number of parameters actually estimated from the total number of parameters that could be estimated. As shown in Fig. 5.1, because so many possible paths in our example are fixed to zero (i.e., no hypothesized path), only a small number of paths are estimated out of the total number that could be estimated. In actually testing models, determining whether a model is identified or not can be somewhat challenging, especially when models are more complicated. Thus, overidentified models (with more than enough available variances and covariances than needed to obtain a unique solution) are desired because they will have positive degrees of freedom (*df*) in the model. For this reason, only overidentified models may be tested for their fit against the data. For example, just-identified models (0 *df*) will fit perfectly.

Several pieces of information included in the output can be useful in identifying parts of the model that are not consistent with the data. These include the various goodness-of-fit indices, the modification indices, the parameter estimates, and the residuals and squared multiple correlations. As we noted earlier, in proposing a model, we actually hope to fail to reject the null hypothesis; that is, we wish to accept that the model tested with data does not significantly differ from an ideal model. It is important to keep in mind, however, that failure to reject a particular model does not mean that it is the only correct model. Other models could also be tested that might also fail to be rejected. For this reason, we actually look at quite a bit of information to give us hints about the suitability of a particular model. Part of the "art" of modeling is to look at a variety of information about a model including its fit, possible modifications that could be made, the sensibility of its parameter estimates, and its residuals.

It is often useful to assess the model's preliminary fit first before focusing too much attention on the actual parameter estimates. We can assess the accuracy of the theoretical model in accounting for the variances and covariances present in the data through examining a number of goodness-of-fit tests provided. Remember that with an overidentified model (i.e., more than enough variances and covariances to solve the set of equations), we will have a positive number of degrees of freedom in the model. Positive degrees of freedom are necessary to actually test the model's fit against the data, because with no degrees of freedom the model would fit perfectly. Strictly speaking, therefore, the chi-square test of model fit addresses the lack of fit among the parameters that have been restricted to zero, as opposed to the parameters the researcher has specified to be estimated.

Even with an acceptable model fit, we also need to examine the parameters that have been estimated to determine the model's suitability (e.g., substantive factor loadings, relatively low errors of measurement). On the other hand, without an adequate model fit, it would be necessary to reconceptualize the model. Quite often, some proposed part of the model does not fit the data well. As opposed to blindly searching for the piece of the model that does not fit the data, as we develop in the next section, a sound strategy for making model modifications needs to be developed.

To examine a structural model's fit, the researcher can select several commonly used indices from the more than 30 model fit indices available (see Marcoulides & Hershberger, 1997, for an explanation of fit indices). Not all of the fit indices define goodness of fit in the same way. Most define fit in terms of the discrepancy between the observed and model-implied covariance matrices. Some combine this with a parsimony criterion (i.e., more parsimonious models are preferred). Other fit indices define fit in terms of model complexity (Marcoulides & Hershberger, 1997). While all of these fit indices are available in LISREL 8.3, *Mplus* currently has a more limited set of fit indices for judging model adequacy.

As we suggested, while the chi-square index is probably the most commonly used statistical index of model fit, it does have the undesirable property of being affected by sample size. It is also important to keep in mind that the null hypothesis concerning the fit of the model tested actually only refers to the prespecified, overidentifying constraints. Thus, the chi-square value represents the lack of fit due to the overidentifying constraints in the model, as opposed to the whole model (Hoyle & Panter, 1995). For this reason, we emphasize that it is also important to look at a variety of statistical and practical indices in determining whether or not to reject a particular model.

Other indices that do not provide a specific statistical test of a hypothesis regarding model fit are the goodness-of-fit index (GFI), the adjusted goodness-of-fit index (AGFI), the comparative fit index (CFI), and the nonnormed fit index (NNFI). Although the first three of these fit indices are scaled between 0 and 1, the NNFI is not (e.g., values may be above 1.0). In general, acceptable values on these four indices should be considerably above .9 for a good-fitting model.

GFI and AGFI indicate the degree to which the covariances implied by the pattern of a priori specified fixed and free parameters in the model match the observed covariances from which the free parameters were estimated. GFI and AGFI are also positively associated with sample size—the difference is that AGFI makes an adjustment downward from GFI based on the number of parameters in the model (which is useful where overfitting in a sample is likely). The CFI compares a preferred model to a baseline or null model (defined as a complete absence of a covariance structure; i.e., all off-diagonal elements in the covariance matrix are equal to zero). The NNFI also measures the relative improvement in fit obtained by a proposed model compared to the null model (with a correction for the number of parameters in the model). With maximum likelihood estimation, the NNFI and CFI perform consistently across a variety of modeling conditions including relatively small sample sizes ($50 < n < 250$) and moderate departures from normality (see Hu & Bentler, 1995; Hoyle & Panter, 1995).

In contrast, the root mean squared residual (RMR) is the average of the magnitude of the residuals. Although this coefficient can depend on the scaling of the variables, in most cases an RMR between .05 and zero indicates a good-fitting model. Related to RMR, the root mean squared error of approximation (RMSEA) is another fit index that is widely used because it offers a "close" test of statistical fit for the model, as opposed to the "exact" test of fit for the chi-square statistic. More specifically, the RMSEA index allows for a discrepancy of fit per degree of freedom, which provides a bit more room for acceptance of the model than does the chi-square statistic alone (Marcoulides & Hershberger, 1997). After making this adjustment, it has the desirable property of still using a statistical test that provides a region for rejecting ill-fitting models on statistical, as opposed to practical, grounds.

It is important to mention that the values of these various fit indices are likely to differ (e.g., providing larger or smaller values of chi-square statistic), depending on the method of estimation used to test the model (e.g., maximum likelihood, unweighted least squares, generalized least squares), sample sizes, and the amount of misspecification present in the model (Chou & Bentler, 1995; Hoyle & Panter, 1995; Kaplan, 1995; MacCallum et al., 1992; Saris, den Ronden, & Satorra, 1987). Each method makes slightly different sets of assumptions in minimizing the discrepancy function. These differences can be readily seen in the case of marginal or ill-fitting models. Strong models will be more likely to result in index similarity across methods of estimation used to fit the model to the data. If the model fits the data well, we can examine the unstandardized and standardized estimates for lambda y, psi, and theta epsilon.

Statistical Power

A final issue that we wish to highlight again is statistical power with respect to the estimation of covariance structure models. When estimating the fit of proposed models and considering possible changes, we must also consider statistical power. As the reader will recall from chapter 2, the probability of rejecting an incorrect model is referred to as the power of the test (Saris et al., 1987). In SEM analyses larger sample sizes are required to maintain the accuracy of estimates and to ensure representativeness of the population. What sample size qualifies as large is debatable, but sample sizes of at least 200 or so individuals are viewed as a minimum (e.g., Boomsma, 1987; Hu & Bentler, 1995) for commonly used estimation methods. The need for larger sample sizes is also due to the complexity of the model being tested, such as the multiple observed indicators that are used to define a number of latent variables. From this standpoint, our example data set is sufficient to proceed with our various model tests.

SEM analyses provide estimates of model parameters and a formal test for deciding whether a theoretical model should be rejected. Again, in contrast to many situations where the researcher hopes to reject the null hypothesis (e.g., that the means of a treatment and control group are not different from each other), in SEM analyses, one actually hopes to fail to reject the null hypothesis. Failure to reject the null hypothesis means that the model can be considered a plausible representation of the data. As we have suggested, traditionally the chi-square statistic has been used to test the null hypothesis regarding the proposed model's fit to the data. Because chi-square is sensitive to sample size, however, in large samples good-fitting models may be wrongly rejected as ill-fitting.

Of greater concern in SEM analyses is that with small samples the investigator may rarely reject the null hypothesis, when actually the model does not fit the data very well. Because of this problem, it can be difficult to assess whether a model's fit is due to the hypothesized structure or the sample size (Saris et al., 1987). Assuming that the analyst can rule out other factors that might contribute to model misfit, such as missing data or nonnormality, the difficulty with the chi-square statistic is that in the presence of misfitting models, sample size interacts with the specification error to affect the size of the test statistic.

Power enters into the assessment of structural models in two ways. First, as Kaplan (1995) argued, the analyst may be concerned with rejection of the overall model because of the sensitivity of the chi-square test to sample size. Only when the null hypothesis is false does sample size enter into goodness of fit. If a model fits the data perfectly, there is no chi-square, and the minimum of the fitting function will be zero, so sample size will have no effect. Because models cannot be expected to fit perfectly, however, they will always have some degree of specification error. In these cases, the role of sample size must be assessed against the size of the specification error (e.g., parameters not specified in the model that should be). When a model contains small specification errors, large sample sizes will magnify their effects, leading to rejection of the null hypothesis (see Kaplan, 1995, and Saris & Satorra, 1993, for further discussion on the calculation of power in SEM). In contrast, when a model contains large specification errors, small sample sizes will tend to hide their effects, which would lead the analyst to accept the null hypothesis that the proposed model fits the data.

Second, statistical power enters into attempts to alter structural models that may not fit the data well. If the overall model is rejected, the analyst may assume that the model does not fit the data. The investigator may not know whether there is one large misspecification error in the model or several small ones. The researcher may then examine the modification indices (MI) produced by LISREL or *Mplus*, finding the misspecified parameter that would yield the largest drop in chi-square when the fixed parameter associated with that index is freed. Alternatively, the analyst can also simplify models by removing statistically nonsignificant or substantively unimportant parameters. For example, in LISREL this is often done through examining the t-ratio for that parameter. These individual tests of parameters are also influenced by sample size. However, as Kaplan (1995) argued, making a series of model modifications tends to inflate Type II errors (i.e, falsely accepting that the model is an adequate representation of the data).

To avoid capitalizing on chance, therefore, the analyst should choose model modifications that have maximum power. Kaplan (1995) noted that the outcome of model modifications and corresponding evaluation of power depend on the initial model hypothesized—that is, the pattern of zero (fixed) and nonzero (free) elements in the covariance matrix of the estimates. The pattern is determined once the initial specification of fixed and free parameters is assigned, but can change each time the model is modified. The changes are somewhat difficult to anticipate, suggesting a certain unpredictability in the direction model modifications might take (Kaplan, 1995). Moreover, this new pattern of fixed and free parameters can also interact with such factors as sample size and size of specification errors (Chou & Bentler, 1990; Kaplan, 1995; MacCallum et al., 1992; Silva & MacCallum, 1988).

Adding to the problem of specification error and model modification, relaxing a series of parameter estimates simultaneously (i.e., making several model modifications at once) and relaxing them sequentially (i.e., from largest to smallest chi-square coefficients) may not yield the exact same model results, unless the test statistics used to determine the significance of parameters were mutually asymptotically independent (i.e., where the covariances between the parameters are all zero [Kaplan, 1995]). Since this is unlikely, because test statistics are formed as ratios of parameter estimates to their standard errors, changes in power may result from specification errors elsewhere in the model (Kaplan, 1995). It is therefore more prudent to make sequential changes to models one at a time, with careful attention paid to changes in substantively important parameters and power probabilities.

EXAMINING THE MODEL RESULTS

As a preliminary step in testing the proposed leadership model, it is useful to examine some of the measurement properties of the items comprising the factors. In this model test, we use a subset of data from employees who rated their managers' leadership in several areas. From this larger data set, we randomly selected four individuals within each of 54 organizations to create a balanced design (i.e., same number of individuals in each organization). Of course, this sample is on the small side ($N = 216$), in terms of both the numbers sampled within each organization and the number of organizations, but it will suffice for purposes of demonstration. The use of a balanced sampling design greatly facilitates the specification and testing of the multilevel factor model that we develop from these data in chapter 6.

For the moment, however, we will consider the 216 employees to be independent of their organizations. The items comprising the factors were measured on 5-point scales ranging from 1 (*not implemented*) to 5 (*frequently implemented*). Although there has been considerable discussion about the use of ML estimation with ordinal data (effects on fit indices, parameter estimates), as the number of scale points increases, the data behave more closely to interval level data (Boomsma, 1987; Rigdon, 1998). One should, however, look at the measurement properties of the scale closely before deciding which method of estimation to use.

As summarized in Table 5.2, for the items in this data set, the skewness (−.9 to −.4) and kurtosis (−.5 to +.2) coefficients were judged to be within normal limits. Other methods of estimation can, however, yield somewhat different parameter estimates or perform differently across a variety of sampling conditions (Chou & Bentler, 1995). For example, while the weighted least squares (WLS) fitting function has been suggested for estimating ordinal data (Jöreskog & Sörbom, 1989), it requires large sample

TABLE 5.2
Descriptive Statistics for Leadership CFA ($N = 216$)

Variables	Mean	SD	Skewness	Kurtosis
Shared decisions	3.94	1.07	−.93	.24
Involve clients	4.20	0.81	−.76	−.05
Systematic assessment	3.94	1.00	−.62	−.54
Evaluate programs	3.76	0.92	−.43	−.05
Encouraging teaming	3.50	1.10	−.58	−.20
Using evaluation standards	3.82	1.13	−.80	−.11

sizes that often preclude its use with clustered samples. Fortunately, maximum likelihood appears to perform very well in a variety of less-than-optimal modeling conditions (Arbuckle, 1996; Chou & Bentler, 1995).

Goodness-of-Fit Indices and Possible Modifications

The results of the model proposed in Fig. 5.1 are included in the LISREL output. The program provides a considerable amount of information. In our discussion, we focus only on some of the output information that is provided. Readers can consult the *LISREL User's Reference Guide* (Jöreskog & Sörbom, 1993a) for further information about the meaning of the output provided. For the proposed model, the chi-square (with 8 degrees of freedom) was 10.37 ($p = .24$). This suggests that the model should probably not be rejected on statistical grounds alone. For example, several of the other indices (Table 5.3) provide supporting evidence of the model's fit to the data (GFI = .98, AGFI = .96, CFI = .99, RMSEA = .037, $p = .58$).

We may wish, however, to examine possible changes contained in the model modification indices (MI). These are useful in locating possible ways that the model has been misspecified. The proposed model obviously fits the data pretty well. If model changes are to be made, they should be made sparingly and with respect to theory. If we do make model modifications, it is recommended that only one change be made at a time and that we keep statistical power in mind. The reader will recall that making too many modifications to the model and ones that cannot be theoretically justified can capitalize on idiosyncracies present in the sample and result in a model that cannot be replicated.

There are several strategies for considering other models or making model changes. The preferred strategy is to propose several alternative models based on theory (see Hoyle & Panter, 1995, for more discussion). In this situation, a stronger case can be made for accepting one model over another, because theory can be brought to bear on the examination of each model's fit. Less desirable is a model-generating strategy, which

TABLE 5.3
LISREL Goodness-of-Fit Indices

CHI-SQUARE WITH 8 DEGREES OF FREEDOM = 10.37 (P = 0.24)
ROOT MEAN SQUARE ERROR OF APPROXIMATION (RMSEA) = 0.037
90 PERCENT CONFIDENCE INTERVAL FOR RMSEA = (0.0 ; 0.093)
P-VALUE FOR TEST OF CLOSE FIT (RMSEA < 0.05) = 0.58
ROOT MEAN SQUARE RESIDUAL (RMR) = 0.029
STANDARDIZED RMR = 0.024
GOODNESS OF FIT INDEX (GFI) = 0.98
ADJUSTED GOODNESS OF FIT INDEX (AGFI) = 0.96
NON-NORMED FIT INDEX (NNFI) = 0.99
COMPARATIVE FIT INDEX (CFI) = 0.99

involves making changes to a proposed model based on post hoc criteria in the model modification indices (Hoyle & Panter, 1995). With too many changes, the model may have little substantive meaning and would have little likelihood of being replicated in other samples. Especially problematic are modifications concerning the covariance between error terms on observed indicators, or the covariance between an error term and another substantive variable. In these cases, it is unlikely that there is any real theoretical rationale for freeing the parameters.

The reader will notice in Table 5.4 that we could free one residual parameter (TE 6,5), with a resulting substantial estimated drop in chi-square (χ^2) of 7.86. This is by far the largest modification index in the table. It is likely, however, that this is the source of the problem. From Fig. 5.1, the reader can see this is the covariance between the residuals related to assessing performance with clear evaluation standards (evstan) and encouraging teaming (team). Although there is little theoretical reason to believe these two residuals should be related in our example, there may be other occasions where such a theoretical relationship might be predicted. Because there is an MI associated with each fixed parameter, an assessment of power can be obtained for each fixed parameter (Saris & Satorra, 1993; Satorra, 1989). Saris et al. (1987) developed an index of expected parameter change (EPC) if the parameter were freed. Because power depends on the size of a misspecified parameter (as well as its location in the model and the sample size), one should focus on those modifications where there is a large MI and a large EPC, especially if justified theoretically. Of course, what constitutes a large EPC is a matter of judgment. In our example, the estimated parameter change is not large (.15), but it is more substantial than the other coefficients.

In the event that one wishes to consider modifications by examining the modification indices and expected parameter changes, the drop in chi-square with one degree of freedom (the parameter freed) can be evalu-

TABLE 5.4
Modification Indices

MODIFICATION INDICES AND EXPECTED CHANGE
MODIFICATION INDICES FOR LAMBDA-Y

	ETA 1	ETA 2
sharedec	—	1.49
incli	—	0.11
syasse	2.02	—
evprog	0.04	—
team	—	1.16
evstan	1.55	—

EXPECTED CHANGE FOR LAMBDA-Y

	ETA 1	ETA 2
sharedec	—	−0.94
incli	—	0.19
syasse	−0.59	—
evprog	0.07	—
team	—	1.07
evstan	0.57	—

NO NON-ZERO MODIFICATION INDICES FOR PSI
MODIFICATION INDICES FOR THETA-EPS

	sharedec	incli	syasse	evprog	team	evstan
sharedec	—					
incli	1.16	—				
syasse	0.43	0.78	—			
evprog	0.14	0.46	1.55	—		
team	0.11	1.49	3.01	0.31	—	
evstan	0.38	1.90	0.04	2.02	7.86	—

EXPECTED CHANGE FOR THETA-EPS

	sharedec	incli	syasse	evprog	team	evstan
sharedec	—					
incli	0.08	—				
syasse	−0.04	0.03	—			
evprog	0.02	0.03	0.06	—		
team	0.03	−0.08	−0.08	−0.02	—	
evstan	−0.05	−0.06	0.01	−0.07	0.15	—

MAXIMUM MODIFICATION INDEX IS 7.86 FOR ELEMENT (6,5) OF THETA-EPS

ated for statistical significance (i.e., a drop in χ^2 of 3.84 would indicate a significant improvement at $p = .05$). Based on this statistical criterion, we can conclude that freeing parameters with modification index values under 4 or 5 (i.e., 3.84) will not make any significant improvement in the model. They may be merely capitalizing on chance. If we actually reestimate the model after freeing the covariance indicated (TE 6,5), we should expect a new model chi-square that is substantially lower (roughly $10.37 - 7.86$).

Reestimating the Model

To demonstrate the effects of this change on overall model fit, we decided to free that one error covariance and reestimate the model. We must make one change on the LISREL program statements within the line containing the theta epsilon parameters. We free the covariance between team's residual and evstan's residual (i.e., FR TE 6 5). The fit indices of the reestimated model summarized in Table 5.5 suggest an improved fit to the data. The new χ^2 (with 7 degrees of freedom now because the theta epsilon covariance was freed) is 2.72 ($p = .91$). The other indices are also very strong (GFI = 1.00, AGFI = .99, CFI = 1.0, RMR = .017, RMSEA = .00, $p = .98$). Because the χ^2 is so small, there are no further changes that could be made to improve the model (e.g., by freeing additional parameters identified in the modification indices).

With some models, it may not be as easy to determine where the lack of fit is. There may be several problems with the model (e.g., the wrong number of factors, the wrong items loading on the wrong factors). Some problems may be much more important to the theory one is testing than others. Although better fitting statistical models can be developed by freeing additional parameters, they might make little substantive sense in light of the original model proposed and tested. If caution is not used, the final model might not represent any type of valid test of the proposed theory. Model-generating strategies through extensive use of the modification indices rarely lead to identifying the correct model in practice (MacCallum

TABLE 5.5
Revised CFA Fit Indices

CHI-SQUARE WITH 7 DEGREES OF FREEDOM = 2.72 (P = 0.91)
ROOT MEAN SQUARE ERROR OF APPROXIMATION (RMSEA) = 0.0
90 PERCENT CONFIDENCE INTERVAL FOR RMSEA = (0.0; 0.033)
P-VALUE FOR TEST OF CLOSE FIT (RMSEA < 0.05) = 0.98
ROOT MEAN SQUARE RESIDUAL (RMR) = 0.017
STANDARDIZED RMR = 0.014
GOODNESS OF FIT INDEX (GFI) = 1.00
ADJUSTED GOODNESS OF FIT INDEX (AGFI) = 0.99
NON-NORMED FIT INDEX (NNFI) = 1.02
COMPARATIVE FIT INDEX (CFI) = 1.00

et al., 1992). In such cases where model modification is used, it is also important to replicate the model on new data, or to report the likelihood of its cross-validation from one of the relevant indices provided (see Hoyle & Panter, 1995).

Because the model fits the data well, however, we can also examine the parameter estimates more closely from this reestimated model. In Table 5.6

TABLE 5.6
Unstandardized and Standardized Factor Loadings, Factor Variances and Covariances, Errors, and Squared Multiple Correlations

Confirmatory factor analysis of leadership (Total Covariance Matrix)

Number of Iterations = 5

LISREL Estimates (Maximum Likelihood)

LAMBDA-Y

	ETA 1	ETA 2
sharedec	1.00	—
incli	0.73	—
	(0.13)	
	5.64	
syasse	—	1.17
		(0.10)
		11.53
evprog	—	1.00
team	1.00	—
	(0.17)	
	5.96	
evstan	—	1.20
		(0.11)
		10.73

Covariance Matrix of ETA

	ETA 1	ETA 2
ETA 1	0.54	
ETA 2	0.45	0.52

PSI

	ETA 1	ETA 2
ETA 1	0.54	
	(0.16)	
	3.39	
ETA 2	0.45	0.52
	(0.09)	(0.08)
	5.30	6.25

(Continued)

TABLE 5.6

(Continued)

THETA-EPS

	sharedec	incli	syasse	evprog	team	evstan
sharedec	1.63					
	(0.18)					
	9.29					
incli	—	0.51				
		(0.06)				
		8.43				
syasse	—	—	0.29			
			(0.05)			
			5.83			
evprog	—	—	—	0.35		
				(0.05)		
				7.56		
team	—	—	—	—	0.61	
					(0.08)	
					7.25	
evstan	—	—	—	—	0.14	0.54
					(0.05)	(0.07)
					2.63	7.71

Squared Multiple Correlations for Y-Variables

sharedec	incli	syasse	evprog	team	evstan
0.25	0.36	0.71	0.60	0.47	0.58

Standardized Solution

LAMBDA-Y

	ETA 1	ETA 2
sharedec	0.73	—
incli	0.54	—
syasse	—	0.84
evprog	—	0.72
team	0.74	—
evstan	—	0.87

Correlation Matrix of ETA

	ETA 1	ETA 2
ETA 1	1.00	
ETA 2	0.86	1.00

PSI

	ETA 1	ETA 2
ETA 1	1.00	
ETA 2	0.86	1.00

TABLE 5.7
Mplus Input Instructions for Two-Factor Leadership Model

TITLE:	Example for Leadership Model
DATA:	FILE is A:\ST216pre.txt;
	Format is 5x,6f1.0,2x;
VARIABLE:	Names are shdec incli syasse evprog team evstan;
ANALYSIS:	Estimator is ML;
MODEL:	gov by shdec incli team;
	eval by syasse evprog evstan;
	eval WITH gov;
	team PWITH evstan;
OUTPUT:	SAMPSTAT STANDARDIZED RESIDUAL TECH1;

Selected Fit Indices: Chi-square $(7df)$ = 2.72, p = .91; RMSEA = .000, p = .98

we include the unstandardized factor loadings, factor variances and covariance, unique factors (errors), and the squared multiple correlations (which are another index of how well the observed variables measure the latent factors). The reader can see that the coefficient for the additional error term freed is .14, which is close to what the previous modification index indicated (see Table 5.4). The reader should note differences in factor loadings and factor interrelationships for the unstandardized LISREL estimates and the standardized solution. In the standardized solution, the latent variables are rescaled to a mean of 0 and standard deviation of 1 to facilitate comparisons between latent variables. As some have argued, however, it can be difficult to interpret exactly what this means, as latent variables are unobserved and therefore must be defined through their observed indicators (e.g., see Rigdon, 1998).

This model now appears to be a plausible representation of the data. Notice, however, that not all items measure the factors equally well; that is, certain observed variables are not as strongly associated with their factor (i.e., they have lower loadings, lower squared multiple correlations, and larger residuals). It is also important to remember that the parameter estimates are likely to be biased at least to some extent, because of the violation of independent observations in the single-level analysis of multilevel data. We also estimated this model with *Mplus* and achieved a similar solution. We provide the input file we used in Table 5.7. Notice the slight difference in how the model is specified with *Mplus*.

INVESTIGATING MULTILEVEL CHARACTERISTICS

After estimating a preliminary, single-level CFA model, we can begin to investigate the multilevel characteristics of the data set. A number of ways have been proposed for comparing CFA models across groups. McArdle and

Hamagami (1996) suggested that one way to incorporate multilevel characteristics of data is through the multiple-group SEM perspective. We can specify and test a variety of models through testing their invariance across a number of groups (e.g., comparisons of means, comparisons of regression coefficients, comparisons of variances). For example, testing the invariance of means across groups allows the researcher to more closely mimic an ANOVA model. They can also be approached from the standpoint of a *variance-components* model. In this formulation, rather than investigating the invariance of means across groups, the investigator examines the variance of the mean differences over the groups (McArdle & Hamagami, 1996). More complex formulations allow these basic models to be extended to a variety of *random-coefficients* models that investigate the variation in outcomes in terms of predictors measured on every individual within a group. Even the invariance of within-group regression coefficients could be investigated by holding the parameter invariant across the groups (see McArdle & Hamagami, 1996, for further discussion of these approaches).

A limitation of these multiple-group formulations, however, is that the number of groups is generally small in these types of investigations ($N <$ 10) because of the complexity involved in programing and comparing the models across groups. A separate covariance matrix must be used for each group, so this can become problematic because there may or may not be enough individuals available within groups to develop stable covariance matrices. Estimation of the parameters is also a problem. Although McDonald and Goldstein (1989) demonstrated that full information maximum likelihood can be used for multilevel SEM with latent variables, the difficulty is in estimating the different covariance matrices across groups with unbalanced sample sizes. Moreover, if differences exist between the groups, there is no real means of identifying what between-group variables might account for these differences. This is because organizational-level variables are not considered in the comparison of the individual matrices. Therefore, for large numbers of groups, as is required in multilevel analyses, it is inefficient to fit these models using standard multiple-group methods.

Muthén (1989, 1991, 1994) provided a somewhat different approach to multilevel modeling within the same multiple-group feature available in SEM software programs. Disaggregated modeling approaches take the sampling design into account in formulating the model (Muthén & Satorra, 1995). Muthén (1989) formulated the multilevel covariance structure model to investigate differences in means and intercepts between groups. From a number of individuals nested in a number of groups, two matrices of relations are developed prior to the two-group SEM analysis. Unequal sample sizes are taken into account by weighting. The model is specified within the multiple-group feature of SEM programs as a model for one population, with observations on two levels of aggregation—an individual

TABLE 5.8
Selected STREAMS Output

Number of cases in Group................ 216
Number of different groups found.......... 54
Number of different group sizes found...... 1

Group Size No	No of Groups	Group Size
1	54	4

Ad hoc estimator constant: 4.00000
Square root of constant: 2.00000

Overall Means and Variances and Intraclass Correlations for Y-variables

	Mean	Variance	Intraclass Correlation
grsize	4.000	.000	
shdec	3.944	1.150	.239
incli	4.199	.653	.149
syass	3.944	.992	.216
evprog	3.764	.842	.078
team	3.519	1.218	.223
evstan	3.829	1.287	.205

level and a group level (Gustafsson & Stahl, 1996). We develop this model in detail in chapter 6.

Muthén (1994) also developed a strategy for multilevel covariance structure analysis. Because multilevel factor analysis is rather complex, a sound strategy needs to be followed. At step one, the investigator can formulate and test a single-level model using the sample covariance matrix (S_T). This analysis was provided in the last section and gives a rough sense of the model's adequacy. A second step in a multilevel investigation is to examine the within- and between-level variance components of the observed variables that we are planning to use in our multilevel factor model. If the intraclass correlations of the observed variables are close to zero, it may not really be worthwhile to continue the multilevel factor analysis.

A simple way to investigate the variance components is to compute the intraclass correlation for each observed variable in the model. These can be obtained through random-effects ANOVA (e.g., the variance components procedure in SPSS or SAS, HLM, or from Muthén's computer program, which also provides the pooled within- and between-groups covariance matrices). Muthén's program is incorporated within the STREAMS software program that we use in this book and is also available as *Mplus* (Muthén & Muthén, 1998).

Intraclass Correlations

In Table 5.8, we provide the intraclass correlations obtained via STREAMS for our data set ($N = 216$). We use this information in presenting an example of the multilevel factor model with a balanced sampling design in the next chapter. Within the data set there appear to be substantial between-organization differences in perceptions of leadership (ranging from about 8% to 24%).

As the reader can see, varied information is produced from STREAMS, including the various sizes of the groups (in this case only 1 size), the scaling factor (i.e., an adjustment made to provide proper estimates for differing group sizes) needed for the between-groups matrix, descriptive statistics, and the covariance matrices themselves (which are written to separate files). In the balanced design we presented in this chapter, however, all the group sizes were the same (four individuals).

We did find that the various software programs can produce slightly different estimates of the intraclass correlations, depending on the estimation procedures (e.g., FIML, REML, Muthén's maximum-likelihood based estimator), rounding procedures, and so forth. In general, however, the intraclass correlation estimates produced were very close in size. In the next chapter, we turn our attention to examining our example two-factor model of leadership across the organizations in the data set.

Chapter 6

Multilevel Factor Analysis

The basic confirmatory factor model presented in the previous chapter can be readily adapted for multilevel analysis. Multilevel confirmatory factor analysis (MCFA) allows the researcher to investigate the stability of a proposed factor model across organizations (i.e., one means of investigating its construct validity). Through this approach, the researcher can develop a more refined analysis of construct validity (e.g., the effects of measurement error at different organizational levels).[1]

The overall flexibility of the structural equation modeling (SEM) approach and the increased availability of software make this a viable approach for investigating multilevel models. One such application allows the investigation of the features of measurement models within and across organizational levels. Another application of SEM techniques allows the testing of multilevel models with exogenous (independent) variables, intervening variables that mediate the effects of exogenous variables, and outcome variables. As with multilevel regression models, these models could have different sets of variables at each organizational level. Moreover, SEM also allows the specification of theoretical models with reciprocal causation or longitudinal data collection.

---

[1]For the interested reader, there is an expanding literature on issues surrounding the use of SEM techniques in defining and testing multilevel models (e.g., Cronbach, 1976; Goldstein & McDonald, 1988; Hox, 1995; Kaplan, 1998; Kaplan & Elliott, 1997; McArdle & Hamagami, 1996; Muthén, 1991, 1994, 1997; Muthén & Satorra, 1989; Schmidt, 1969).

OVERVIEW OF THE MCFA APPROACH

As we suggested in chapter 5, confirmatory factor analysis (CFA) can be used to examine the construct validity of models (i.e., their measurement properties, the generalizability of a model across groups). In CFA, the relationships among the observed variables are characterized by the co-variances among these variables contained in a sample covariance matrix. The observations are assumed to be independently and identically distributed.

Of course, where individuals are clustered in organizations, this will no longer be the case. Similar to multilevel regression, where we estimate a separate regression equation for each organization, we could estimate a separate covariance matrix for each organization. It is highly likely, however, that the measurement qualities of the individual matrices would be quite different (e.g., varied sample sizes in each organization). Because the methods of estimating the model parameters in SEM require large numbers of individuals for stability, however, it would be very difficult to fit a factor model across a large number of organizations in this manner.

Fortunately, we can reformulate the testing of separate covariance matrices across the groups as a test of covariance matrices across two groups (Muthén, 1989). This formulation is analogous to random-coefficients regression models (Muthén, 1994). One model is formulated for the individual-level variation and another is formulated for the between-group variation in the parameters of the individual-level model. Through this multilevel formulation of the CFA model, we can examine the characteristics of a within-group and a between-group measurement model.

When models are compared across groups, assumptions are generally made that the constructs being measured are similar across the groups examined. Such comparisons yield not only information about potential group differences, but also additional insight into the construct validity of measures. For example, if a factor model is not similar within and between groups, we can determine to what degree it differs (e.g., its factor structure, patterns of variable loadings on factors, factor relationships, quality of measurement).

In tests of model invariance across groups, the researcher imposes constraints on the parameters of interest across the groups and estimates these parameters simultaneously. For example, in the case of multilevel modeling, we might expect the pattern of fixed and free parameters defined in the single-level model to be similar when examining the within-group and between-group covariance matrices. In other cases, we might propose that a somewhat different factor model exists within and between groups (e.g., a two-factor model at the individual level and a one-factor model at the group level). As suggested previously, confirming these hypothesized relationships helps establish a model's construct validity.

Besides assessing the stability of the factor structure within and between groups, multilevel factor analysis is also well suited to the investigation of psychometric properties of the observed variables and the latent factors. For example, we can examine the amount of measurement error in the observed variables that define latent factors both within and between groups. The unreliability of these measures affects the decomposition of variance, which can affect the intraclass correlations (Muthén, 1991). The within-level variation includes individual-level measurement error variance, which tends to inflate the contribution of within-level variation to the calculation of the intraclass correlation. Multilevel factor analysis, therefore, gives results that correspond to those that would be obtained from perfectly reliable measures (Muthén, 1994). When we look at an error-free variance ratio for the intraclass correlation, we are gaining a more precise estimate of the within- and between-level contributions. Finally, if a model proves to be stable within and between groups, we might further investigate the amount of factor variance that lies at each level, and determine the between-group means of the variables in the model.

Although there is limited software designed for multilevel SEM, Muthén (1991, 1994) demonstrated that current multiple-group SEM software packages such as LISREL (Jöreskog & Sörbom, 1993a), EQS (Bentler, 1989), or AMOS (Arbuckle, 1997) can be modified for multilevel factor analysis. One available software program that facilitates the specification and testing of two-level structural models is STREAMS (Gustaffson & Stahl, 1996). This program allows relatively easy specification of a variety of structural models (i.e., through a Windows environment of pull-down menus). Muthén and Muthén (1998) also developed a software program to specify multilevel SEM models. *Mplus* includes Muthén's earlier software routine to create the necessary within-group and between-group matrices in unbalanced designs (B. O. Muthén, personal communication, October 18, 1998). EQS 6 will feature two different methods of doing multilevel SEM analyses when it is released later in 1999 (Bentler, personal communication, April 25, 1999).

There are number of issues to consider in using currently available SEM programs to conduct multilevel analyses. As a practical matter, one problem that must first be overcome is the proper estimation of the within- and between-group covariance matrices needed to conduct the analysis. Full information maximum likelihood (FIML) can be used with balanced designs (i.e., the same sample size within groups). Where within-group sample sizes differ, Muthén (1991, 1994) developed a quasi-estimator (available with STREAMS or *Mplus*) that can be used, although it still remains untested with some types of data structures.

For multilevel models, STREAMS uses Muthén's quasi-estimator to estimate the within- and between-groups covariance matrices for balanced or unbalanced sampling designs. The matrices are then input into the LISREL program to actually test the models. We demonstrate multilevel factor analysis in this chapter using LISREL, *Mplus*, and STREAMS, with balanced data for the reader who does not have access to the specialized software needed to estimate the covariance matrices with unbalanced data. We emphasize, however, that if the reader develops the proper covariance matrices, most current SEM programs can also be used to estimate the models.

A second concern raised in the multilevel SEM literature is the effect of small sample sizes, especially in level-2 units, on the model's fit indices and parameter estimates. This is because SEM techniques are designed to be used with large, multivariate normal, samples. For example, goodness-of-fit indices can differ somewhat, depending on the particular methods of estimation used (e.g., maximum likelihood, unweighted least squares, generalized least squares) and may interact with sampling conditions.

Finally, the procedures for standardizing parameter estimates in SEM, and therefore their meanings, vary across software programs. We did not have to deal with this problem with multilevel regression program we used in chapter 4 (HLM) because the estimates are unstandardized. Similarly, the single-level CFA in the last chapter presented no particular problems in interpreting the standardized estimates (i.e., latent variables are standardized with a mean of 0 and standard deviation of 1). The interpretation of standardizations in the multilevel SEM situation, however, is a bit more complicated. For example, there are several standardizations available in the multisample feature of LISREL to compare parameter estimates across a number of separate samples or groups. The meanings of each standardized solution are quite different, depending on whether the solution is standardized to a metric within each group or to a metric that is common across all groups (Jöreskog & Sörbom, 1989). In contrast, the STREAMS multilevel standardized solution partitions the variability of each observed variable from a single sample into its within- and between-group variance components (with the total variance of each variable standardized to 1.0). *Mplus* standardizes the between-level parameters by the between-level variances for latent and observed variables and standardizes the within-level parameters by the within-level variances for latent and observed variables. This is useful to examine how much variance is explained at each level (L. Muthén, personal communication, December 17, 1998).

In testing multilevel models through SEM and reporting their parameter estimates (either standardized or unstandardized), therefore, it is important to be clear about how the sample was obtained, what particular methods were used to obtain the parameter estimates, and the criteria by which the overall model and the individual estimates were evaluated (Hoyle & Panter, 1995). Despite these limitations and cautions, the results of initial attempts are promising in addressing a number of important organizational research questions. For the present, however, it is probably best to consider multilevel SEM solutions as tentative, and the replication of results should be encouraged.

MATHEMATICAL REPRESENTATION OF MCFA

Unlike conventional single-level analyses, where independence of observation is assumed over all N observations, in MCFA independence is only assumed over the G groups (Muthén, 1994). In our example factor model, each dimension of leadership is hypothesized to account for the covariation present in a set of observed indicators that define it. We use disaggregated modeling to examine components of variation at different levels (Muthén & Satorra, 1995). The individual-level data, again assuming an "all y" specification, may be held in a p-variate vector $\mathbf{Y}_{gi}$. We may summarize these individual-level relationships as:

$$\mathbf{y}_{gi} = \mathbf{v} + \lambda\eta_{gi} + \varepsilon_{gi} \qquad (1)$$

where $\mathbf{y}$ is a vector of items measuring leadership, for example, $\mathbf{v}$ is a vector of intercepts (means), λ is a vector of factor loadings, η represents a factor, and ε is a vector of residuals.

If only the factor means were assumed to vary across groups, using conventional multigroup SEM, we could interpret this as having G (or $G - 1$) factor means estimated for the number of groups we have sampled. Because the groups are viewed as being randomly sampled, however, we need to specify the factor means[2] as random coefficients (Muthén, 1994). We can express these relationships as:

$$\eta_{gi} = \alpha + \eta_{Bg} + \eta_{Wgi} \qquad (2)$$

where α is the overall expectation (grand mean) for η_{gi}, η_{Bg} is a random-factor component capturing organizational effects, and η_{Wgi} is a random-factor component varying over individuals within their organizations. The between-group component contains the group contribution to the individual's score.

---

[2]It is currently not possible to investigate random slopes using available SEM software (Kaplan, 1998).

Cronbach and Webb's (1975) solution to nested data was to express individuals' scores as deviations from their group's means (called *group mean centering*). In this way, the total variance in an individual's score can be decomposed into a between- and a within-group part ($Y_T = Y_B + Y_W$). The advantage of this technique is that group-centered deviation scores (for the pooled within-group covariance) are uncorrelated with the disaggregated group means used for the between-groups matrix (Hox, 1995). The between-factor component (η_{Bg}) and the within-factor component (η_{Wgi}) are therefore independent, as in conventional random-effects analysis of variance.

Conditional on individual i being in organization g, the mean of factor η_{gi} is $\alpha + \eta_{Bg}$, where η_{Bg} varies across organizations (Muthén, 1994). As Muthén argued, it is therefore possible to specify organizational differences in two parameters; that is, α and the variance of η_{Bg} (which we call Ψ_B). One model is formulated for the individual level, and another is formulated for the between-group variations of the individual-level parameters. The decomposition of variables from the sample data into their component parts can be used to compute a between-groups covariance matrix S_B (the covariance matrix of the disaggregated group means Y_B) and a within-groups covariance matrix S_W (the covariance matrix of the individual deviations from the group means Y_W). The covariance matrices are also orthogonal (i.e., uncorrelated) and additive:

$$S_T = S_B + S_W \tag{3}$$

Similarly, if we wish to examine the variance of the latent factors, which we describe in a psi matrix (Ψ), we can break the total factor variance down into a between-groups variance component and a within-groups variance component. This can be summarized as

$$V(\eta_{gi}) = \Psi_T = \Psi_B + \Psi_W \tag{4}$$

As Muthén (1994) noted, from a substantive point of view, because the observed scores are not independent for individuals in the same group, we can estimate the proportion of the factor variance that is between groups (Ψ_B) relative to the total factor variance (Ψ_T). The latent variable counterpart of an intraclass correlation can therefore be expressed as

$$\Psi_B/(\Psi_B + \Psi_W) \tag{5}$$

Similarly, we can also look at the residual variation ε_{gi} as the sum of a between-group and a within-group component:

$$V(\varepsilon_{gi}) = \Theta_B + \Theta_W \tag{6}$$

We can assume that the same factor structure as the within-group model exists across groups, or we may hypothesize that a different factor model exists at the organizational level. For example, if we assume that the same two-factor model of leadership holds for both the within-group and between-group components, at the individual level, the two factors account for the covariation among the individual-level observed variables that are associated with each underlying dimension. This model addresses the portion of variance in the factors that results from variation among individuals. The between-level model addresses across-group variation rather than across-individual variation (Muthén, 1991). Here, the factors express the variation in leadership that exists between organizations.

Because these models are confirmatory models for a population, we have to investigate what implications there are in the population for the decomposition of individual scores suggested by Cronbach and Webb (1975). To do this, we begin with the assumption that we have a population of individuals in different groups. If we similarly decompose the population data, the population covariance structure for this random effects model would be:

$$V(y_{gi}) = \Sigma_T = \Sigma_B + \Sigma_W \tag{7}$$

We then argue that the population covariance matrices Σ_B and Σ_W can be described by separate models for the between-groups and the within-groups structures (Hox, 1995). As Muthén (1994) demonstrated, a more general formulation with multiple factors in a multilevel model may be specified as:

$$y_{gi} = v + \Lambda_B\eta_{Bg} + \varepsilon_{Bg} + \Lambda_W\eta_{Wgi} + \varepsilon_{Wgi} \tag{8}$$

$$V(y_{gi}) = \Sigma_B + \Sigma_W \tag{9}$$

Following this, the between-groups covariance structure model can be represented as

$$\Sigma_B = \Lambda_B\Psi_B\Lambda_B' + \Theta_B \tag{10}$$

and in a similar fashion, the within-group covariance matrix representing within-unit variation can be represented as

$$\Sigma_W = \Lambda_W\Psi_W\Lambda_W' + \Theta_W \tag{11}$$

The reader will note the similarity of these latter representations (Eqs. 10 and 11) of the between- and within-group models with the initial covariance structure model developed in chapter 5 to illustrate the conventional CFA model (i.e., Eq. 1 in chap. 5).

Unfortunately, as we have suggested, in the MCFA case we cannot just use the sample covariance matrix for arriving at the estimates of the population parameters (i.e., because individuals are nested in groups). We must instead develop two separate matrices. Muthén (1989, 1994) demonstrated that the unbiased estimate of the population within-groups covariance matrix (Σ_W) is given by the pooled within-group sample covariance matrix S_{PW} (instead of S_W). This is calculated in a sample as:

$$S_{PW} = (N - G)^{-1} \sum_{g=1}^{G} \sum_{i=1}^{N_g} (y_{gi} - \bar{y}_g)(y_{gi} - \bar{y}_g)' \tag{12}$$

This equation corresponds to the conventional equation for the covariance matrix of individual deviation scores, with $N - G$ in the denominator instead of the usual $N - 1$ (Hox, 1995; Muthén, 1994). Because the pooled within-group covariance matrix is an unbiased estimate of the population within-groups covariance matrix (Σ_W), we can now estimate the population within-group structure by constructing this matrix. In conventional covariance structure analysis with p variables and r parameters, we have $p(p + 1)/2 - r$ degrees of freedom (because the Σ_B matrix is restricted to zero). In the multilevel case, however, we have $p(p + 1) - r$ parameters (because r is reduced by the number of parameters for the between-groups part).

The between-groups covariance matrix for the disaggregated group means for the sample is given by:

$$S_B = (G - 1)^{-1} \sum_{g=1}^{G} N_g (\bar{y}_g - \bar{y})(\bar{y}_g - \bar{y})' \tag{13}$$

It is important to note, however, that the sample between-groups covariance matrix is not a simple estimator of the population between-groups covariance matrix (Σ_B). It turns out that the sample between-group covariance matrix S_B is a consistent and unbiased estimator of

$$S_B = \Sigma_W + c\Sigma_B \tag{14}$$

where c is a scaling factor based on group size (Hox, 1995; Muthén, 1994). Therefore, the between-groups covariance matrix differs from the total covariance matrix $(\Sigma_W + \Sigma_B)$ by the scalar multiplier c for the between-group part. This means that the between components of the variables have to be scaled by $\sqrt{c}$ (Muthén, 1994). With balanced data, c is the common group size. For unbalanced data, c is similar to the mean of the within-group sample sizes (Muthén, 1994). In studies where there are different group sizes, Muthén's quasi-likelihood estimator (called MUML), available with *Mplus* and STREAMS, can be used produce the necessary within- and between-group covariance matrices with the proper scalar.

Sample Sizes of Groups and Estimation Procedures

Because the between-group covariance matrix is a combination of the within-group and between-group matrices, it requires some special attention in testing the proposed within-group and between-group factor model. As Muthén (1994) argued, for practical purposes one can proceed as if the group sizes were equal and calculate the scaling factor c as a combination of the observed group sizes:

$$c = \left[N^2 - \sum_{g=1}^{G} N_g^2 \right] [N(G-1)]^{-1} \tag{15}$$

McDonald (1994) referred to this as a pseudobalanced solution, which is not a full maximum likelihood solution. With unbalanced group sizes, therefore, it is very difficult, and often not practical, to use conventional SEM estimation techniques (Muthén, 1991). Using FIML with unbalanced group sizes is quite complex, and extreme inequality of within-group sample sizes may distort results (Kaplan, 1998; Muthén, 1994). Muthén (1991) demonstrated that the MUML fitting function is a consistent estimator of the population between-group covariance matrix, where sample sizes are sufficiently large. Where the group sizes are not extremely different, it has produced satisfactory solutions, even though it makes use of less information than FIML (Hox, 1993, 1995; Muthén, 1990, 1994). At this time, however, chi-square values and fit indices should be considered as approximate (see Muthén, 1991, 1994, for further discussion).

The discussion of the scaling factor (c) needed to estimate the between-groups covariance matrix properly returns us to the issue of sample sizes across level-2 units. In general, the SEM approach favors larger samples, especially with respect to the number of groups needed. Researchers have argued that as many as 50 to 100 groups might be required, with preference under budgetary constraints to sampling fewer individuals within groups and more groups (e.g., Cronbach, 1976). Setting aside cost, we provide some general guidelines for determining sample size in multilevel studies. For variance-components models (without randomly varying slopes), the sample design issue for balanced designs is analogous to that addressed by Kish (1965) in computing effective sample size in two-stage cluster sampling. Effective sample size of a two-stage cluster sampling design, n_{eff}, is computed by

$$n_{\text{eff}} = n/[1 + (n_{\text{clus}} - 1)\rho] \tag{16}$$

where n is the total number of individuals in the study, that is, the actual sample size, n_{clus} is the number of individuals in each cluster, and ρ is the intraclass correlation. As the denominator of this equation suggests, for example, the larger the number of individuals sampled within organizations and the larger the homogeneity of individuals with respect to what is measured (ρ), the larger will be the underestimation of the true variance of the estimates when their variance expression is based on simple random sampling. We can make adjustments for these types of measurement problems within multilevel designs.

As the reader will realize, power in examining between structures in multilevel models is influenced by both the number of groups and the number of individuals (Muthén, 1991). In a series of sampling simulations, Mok (1995) found, as expected, that for smaller samples ($N < 800$) there is less bias in designs involving relatively more level-2 units and fewer subjects per unit, than in sample designs involving fewer units and more subjects per unit. For estimating slopes and intercepts, a total subject sample size larger that 800 produced estimates that were within one standard error of the true value, regardless of whether there were more relatively more units and fewer subjects per unit, or fewer units and more subjects per unit (see Mok, 1995, for further discussion and guidelines for balancing level-1 and level-2 sample sizes).

In light of our discussion of sample size, it is important to acknowledge that we had a sufficient number of individuals to develop our factor model at a single level. We should, however, be mindful that our number of organizations ($N = 54$) used to develop our level-2 model is by no means large by SEM standards. For example, with single-level analyses, Boomsma (1987) found that sample sizes under 100 were much more likely to fail to converge during model estimation. On the other hand, Bentler and Chou (1987) suggest that a ratio of as low as 5 subjects per variable should be sufficient for normal and elliptical distributions when the latent variables have multiple indicators, whereas a ratio of at least 10 subjects per variable should be required for other distributions. From that standpoint, our sample of organizations can be seen as at least minimally adequate. As a practical matter, Marcoulides (1993, 1994) suggested that in deciding how to design a study of this nature, one often has to balance statistical power with measurement precision and cost factors.

These arguments surrounding sampling requirements and statistical power (see chap. 2) apply optimally to situations with balanced designs— that is, where the number of individuals in each group is the same. In this case, the scaling factor c is equal to the common group size. Where within-group sample sizes are all the same, and the level-2 sample size is large enough, maximum-likelihood estimation can be used. We demonstrate this case, because this approach will be more readily available to most readers who may not have the special program needed to create the proper between-group covariance matrix for an unbalanced design.

Of course, in cases of unbalanced data, which are more likely in real-world situations, an adjustment needs to be incorporated into the between-group covariance matrix for each group's specific sample size. Obviously, more empirical testing is needed regarding methods of estimating within- and between-group variance–covariance matrices in multilevel SEM. Some issues are the effects of group-size diversity, effects of missing data, and sample sizes needed for desirable asymptotic properties (e.g., Muthén & Satorra, 1995; Woodhouse, Yang, Goldstein, & Rasbash, 1996).

Producing the Necessary Matrices

As the reader may suspect from our previous discussion, producing the pooled within-group and between-group matrices is a somewhat problematic currently, especially for unbalanced sampling designs. We believe, however, that there will be increased access to software that can more easily perform multilevel SEM analyses.

For unbalanced data, Muthén and Muthén's (1998) program *Mplus* can be used. Muthén's MUML estimator is also included with STREAMS, which allows the necessary matrices and intraclass correlations to be estimated directly from the software program. We found that the version of STREAMS we had was not compatible with the particular version of SPSS where we had the data stored, so it was easiest just to write the data out of SPSS into an ASCII (text) file and use that as input into STREAMS.

For balanced group sizes, we can produce the necessary S_{PW} and S_B matrices with LISREL 8.30. For example, in LISREL 8.30, we can use the multilevel modeling procedure to produce the pooled within-group matrix (S_{PW}) and a between-sample covariance matrix. To produce the between-sample covariance matrix and a pooled within-group matrix (S_{PW}), we used the three-level multivariate model specification with a constant intercept value of 1.0 at level 1 (see user's guide for details). Because S_B is not a simple estimator of the population between-group covariance matrix (Σ_B), however, we must make some additional modifications. As we suggested, the sample between-group covariance matrix S_B is a consistent and unbiased estimator of $\Sigma_W + c\Sigma_B$ (Eq. 14). Therefore, we must multiply the between-group coefficients by the scalar multiplier c (the common group size) and add them to the S_{PW} matrix to produce the ML estimate of Σ_B for two-level data. For the proposed leadership model, the scalar c is 4. The between-group matrix is first multiplied by 4 (using symmetrical matrices for ease of presentation):

$$c\Sigma_B$$

$$4\begin{bmatrix} .27 \\ .12 & .09 \\ .10 & .14 & .21 \\ .12 & .06 & .12 & .06 \\ .22 & .10 & .14 & .10 & .26 \\ .18 & .15 & .21 & .14 & .24 & .25 \end{bmatrix} = \begin{bmatrix} 1.08 \\ .48 & .36 \\ .40 & .56 & .84 \\ .48 & .24 & .48 & .24 \\ .88 & .40 & .56 & .40 & 1.04 \\ .72 & .60 & .84 & .56 & .96 & 1.00 \end{bmatrix}$$

Then these matrices can be added together to obtain the ML estimate of Σ_B for two-level data (see Table 6.1) as follows:

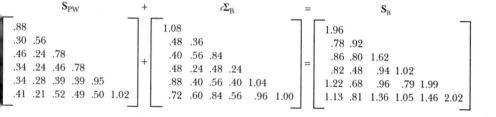

$$S_{PW} \qquad + \qquad c\Sigma_B \qquad = \qquad S_B$$

$$\begin{bmatrix} .88 \\ .30 & .56 \\ .46 & .24 & .78 \\ .34 & .24 & .46 & .78 \\ .34 & .28 & .39 & .39 & .95 \\ .41 & .21 & .52 & .49 & .50 & 1.02 \end{bmatrix} + \begin{bmatrix} 1.08 \\ .48 & .36 \\ .40 & .56 & .84 \\ .48 & .24 & .48 & .24 \\ .88 & .40 & .56 & .40 & 1.04 \\ .72 & .60 & .84 & .56 & .96 & 1.00 \end{bmatrix} = \begin{bmatrix} 1.96 \\ .78 & .92 \\ .86 & .80 & 1.62 \\ .82 & .48 & .94 & 1.02 \\ 1.22 & .68 & .96 & .79 & 1.99 \\ 1.13 & .81 & 1.36 & 1.05 & 1.46 & 2.02 \end{bmatrix}$$

STEPS IN CONDUCTING A MULTILEVEL FACTOR ANALYSIS

Muthén (1994) outlined a series of four steps that are useful in completing a multilevel factor analysis. We presented the first two steps in the last chapter. At the first step, the researcher can propose and test a conventional individual-level factor model using CFA techniques. In our extended example, 216 employees in 54 organizations rated their managers' leadership in 36 areas. Recall that in chapter 5 we developed an example with two leadership factors, with each factor being defined by three observed variables.

Of course, the analysis was to some extent biased (depending on the size of the intraclass correlations) because of its failure to consider the nested effects of the data, but this will likely give some indication of the variables that can be used to serve as indicators of the latent constructs. The S_T matrix is used for this analysis. The tests of fit are likely to give rough estimates of the model's adequacy, however. We may, for example, spot obvious misspecification, such as weak items, or the presence of correlated error.

Once this model fits adequately, we can specify the multilevel factor model and conduct the MCFA. As a second step, Muthén (1994) suggested estimating the between-group variation for the set of observed variables. This is done to check whether $\Sigma_B = 0$. We found in chapter 5 that there was considerable variation in the data set between organizations in the six measures of leadership, ranging from about 8% to 24%.

Specifying the MCFA

Because there was sufficient between-organizational variation in leadership, we can proceed to the third and fourth steps in our analysis. The goal of the multilevel analysis is to summarize the within- and between-group variation in this leadership model and establish whether the same individual-level model holds at the organizational level. It is likely that there may be differences in the quality of measurement of items defining the factors that result from the multilevel nature of the data. For example, we may reasonably expect that employees within each organization differ to some extent in their assessments of a manager's performance with respect to these two leadership dimensions. This is expected within-organization variance.

Similarly, we can expect that there are also differences in managers' leadership performance across the organizations (i.e., between-organization variance). Hence, we hypothesize that the same two-model factor holds across organizations, but that there may be likely differences in the measurement quality of the items used to define the two leadership factors. Some of this difference is also due to the differing amounts of variance contributed by each variable across levels (i.e., differing intraclass correlations). Alternately, we could also hypothesize that a one-factor model (e.g., a general leadership factor) may be sufficient to account for the variation in leadership between organizations. We hope the reader can readily see that there are many additional possibilities to consider when multilevel factor models are conceptualized and tested.

The theoretical model is summarized visually in Fig. 6.1. Similar to Fig. 5.1 in the previous chapter, it shows two latent factors of leadership (enclosed in circles). Each factor is defined by three observed indicators (enclosed in rectangles) and corresponding unique factors (i.e., representing measurement error). To facilitate understanding the meaning of a two-level structural model, it should be considered primarily as a convenient way to obtain the estimates using the available software (Gustafsson & Stahl, 1996). As opposed to the standard multigroup comparison of covariance matrices across a number of populations, the multilevel factor model refers to a total covariance matrix and is therefore a model for one population with observations at two levels of aggregation.

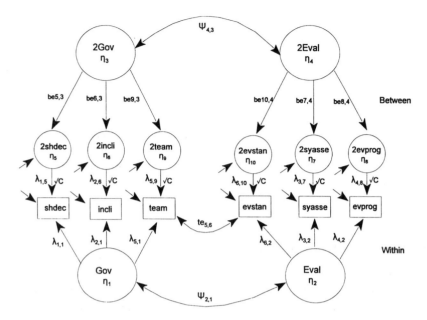

FIG. 6.1.   Proposed multilevel factor model.

In Fig. 6.1 we specify the relationships in the model using the STREAMS terminology to help the reader have a reference point for connecting the output we present back to the proposed model. The basic multilevel factor model suggests that for each observed variable there are four orthogonal sources of variation. The within-group sources of variation are (a) the individual variability common to the variables that load on each common factor, and (b) the individual variability specific to each variable (its residual), shown as an arrow in Fig. 6.1. The between-group sources are (c) the group variability common to the variables (i.e., shown at the group level with 2 as a prefix) that load on each factor, and (d) the group variability specific to each observed variable (also shown as an arrow in Fig. 6.1).

As shown in Fig. 6.1, we can represent the proposed organizational-level model (also consisting of two factors) above the individual-level model. As suggested, this model is used to account for the added between-group sources of variation. The reader will notice that the organizational model is very similar to the individual-level model, except that we need to define the between-group variability common to each of the observed variables in circles. This is because to estimate the model using LISREL or *Mplus*, the between-group variables are specified as latent variables. For each group-level variable, there is also a residual that represents the group-level variability remaining after the latent variables have been taken into account (Gustafsson & Stahl, 1996).

We draw the reader's attention to the paths that connect each of the organizational variables to its counterpart at the individual level, summarizing the between-groups variance for each observed variable. Whether or not the data are unbalanced, it is necessary to set each path to the square root of the constant (c) to ensure proper estimation of the between-group parameters. As we suggested, in the balanced case, this is the square root of the common group size, and in the unbalanced case, it is similar to the square root of the average size of the groups at the organizational level (Muthén, 1994). In the balanced subset of data we present (using four individuals per group), $\sqrt{c}$ is 2. It is important to note that if other SEM programs are used to specify a multilevel model, the reader should consult the specific user's manual to determine exactly how to specify and properly scale the variables across the within- and between-group models.

LISREL Program Specification

To conduct an MCFA using LISREL, we use the program's multigroup feature. The fitting function developed by Muthén (1990, 1991) enables analysis of unbalanced data (available in STREAMS and *Mplus*). Muthén's fitting function is similar to a two-population covariance structure model under the assumption of multivariate normality of the observed variables, where there are G observations for Group 1 and $N - G$ observations for Group 2. This allows us to provide a simultaneous test of the fit of the within- and between-group covariance matrices to the proposed model. Because it is fairly difficult to program even a relatively simple two-factor model, it is necessary to study the program we present in Table 6.1 rather carefully to understand how the various parameters are specified. As the reader may notice, the model setup looks somewhat like the single-level CFA presented in chapter 5, but it has two models stacked together. Remember that the entire model refers to a total covariance matrix for one population, with two levels of aggregation (within-group and between-group), and that as such, each observed variable has four sources of variation.

Group-1 Specification

To facilitate presentation to the reader, we present a subset of a larger data set, using a balanced design. We randomly selected 4 individuals within each of the 54 organizations that had the required number of individuals. For this subsample, therefore, there are 216 individuals in 54 organizations. In contrast to the single-level model in chapter 5, we now must specify two groups in the data (DA) statement (NG = 2). As we suggested, the first covariance matrix used is the between-group (S_B) matrix ($\Sigma_W + c\Sigma_B$). This matrix deviates from the total covariance matrix ($\Sigma_W + \Sigma_B$) by the scalar multiplier c for the between part (Muthén, 1994).

TABLE 6.1
LISREL Program Specifications for Balanced Data

2 Factor Leadership Model (Between Groups) 4 Individuals per Group
DA NI=6 NO=54 NG=2 MA=CM
LA
'shdec' 'incli' 'syasse' 'evprog' 'team' 'evstan'
CM
1.96
0.78   0.92
0.86   0.80   1.62
0.82   0.48   0.94   1.02
1.22   0.68   0.96   0.79   1.99
1.13   0.81   1.36   1.05   1.46   2.02
MO NY=6 NE=10 LY=FU,FI PS=SY,FI TE=SY,FI BE=FU,FI
LE
'gov' 'eval' '2gov' '2eval' '2shdec' '2incli'
'2syasse' '2evprog' '2team' '2evstan'
VA 1.0 LY(1,1) LY(4,2)
FR LY(2,1) LY(3,2) LY(5,1) LY(6,2)
FI LY(1,5) LY(2,6) LY(3,7) LY(4,8) LY(5,9) LY(6,10)
VA 2.0 LY(1,5) LY(2,6) LY(3,7) LY(4,8) LY(5,9) LY(6,10)
FR TE(1,1) TE(2,2) TE(3,3) TE(4,4) TE(5,5)
FR TE(6,5) TE(6,6)
FR PS(1,1) PS(2,1) PS(2,2) PS(3,3) PS(4,3)
FR PS(4,4) PS(5,5) PS(6,6) PS(7,7) PS(8,8)
FR PS(9,9) PS(10,10)
VA 1.000 BE(5,3) BE(8,4)
FR BE(6,3) BE(7,4) BE(9,3) BE(10,4)
VA .7 LY(2,1)
VA 1.13 LY(3,2)
VA .92 LY(5,1)
VA 1.12 LY(6,2)
VA .4 PS(1,1) PS(5,5) PS(2,1)
VA .4 PS(2,2)
VA .1 PS(3,3) PS(4,3) PS(4,4) PS(6,6) PS(7,7) PS(8,8)
VA -.011 PS(9,9)
VA .1 PS(10,10)
VA .5 TE(1,1) TE(2,2) TE(3,3) TE(6,6)
VA .5 TE(4,4)

(Continued)

TABLE 6.1
(Continued)

VA .5 TE(5,5)
VA .1 TE(6,5)
VA .7 BE(6,3) BE(7,4)
VA 1.7 BE(9,3) BE(10,4)
OU
2 Factor Leadership Model (Within Groups)
DA NI=6 NO=162 NG=2 MA=CM
LA
'shdec' 'incli' 'syasse' 'evprog' 'team' 'evstan'
CM
0.88
0.30   0.56
0.46   0.24   0.78
0.34   0.24   0.46   0.78
0.34   0.28   0.39   0.39   0.95
0.41   0.21   0.52   0.49   0.50   1.02
MO NY=6 NE=10 LY=FU,FI PS=SY,FI TE=SY,FI BE=FU,FI
LE
'gov' 'eval' '2gov' '2eval' '2shdec' '2incli'
'2syasse' '2evprog' '2team' '2evstan'
VA 1.0 LY(1,1) LY(4,2)
FR LY(2,1) LY(3,2) LY(5,1) LY(6,2)
FR PS(1,1) PS(2,1) PS(2,2)
FR TE(1,1) TE(2,2) TE(3,3) TE(4,4) TE(5,5)
FR TE(6,5) TE(6,6)
VA .7 LY(2,1)
VA 1.13 LY(3,2)
VA .92 LY(5,1)
VA 1.12 LY(6,2)
VA .4 PS(1,1) PS(2,1)
VA .4 PS(2,2)
VA .5 TE(1,1) TE(2,2) TE(3,3) TE(6,6)
VA .5 TE(4,4)
VA .5 TE(5,5)
VA .1 TE(6,5)
EQ LY(1,2,1) LY(2,2,1)
EQ LY(1,3,2) LY(2,3,2)

(Continued)

TABLE 6.1
(Continued)

EQ LY(1,5,1) LY(2,5,1)
EQ LY(1,6,2) LY(2,6,2)
EQ PS(1,1,1) PS(2,1,1)
EQ PS(1,2,1) PS(2,2,1)
EQ PS(1,2,2) PS(2,2,2)
EQ TE(1,1,1) TE(2,1,1)
EQ TE(1,2,2) TE(2,2,2)
EQ TE(1,3,3) TE(2,3,3)
EQ TE(1,4,4) TE(2,4,4)
EQ TE(1,5,5) TE(2,5,5)
EQ TE(1,6,5) TE(2,6,5)
EQ TE(1,6,6) TE(2,6,6)
OU ML AD=OFF MI VA NS SC

On the data line, we include the number of group-level observations
(NO = 54). It is important to note that within Group 1 we include the
specifications for the entire model to be tested, even though we are estimating the between-group parameters first (with the $\Sigma_W + c\Sigma_B$ matrix). In
Group 2, we use the pooled within-group matrix (S_{PW}) to test the individual-level model. It is possible to reverse the groups to be tested, but the
complete model must be specified within Group 1.

Once again, we use an "all y" specification in LISREL in the model
(MO) statement. At the individual level, this means that the factor loadings
for the 6 observed variables (NY = 6) are contained in the lambda y matrix.
The residual error variances for the individual-level variables are contained
in the theta epsilon (TE) matrix. We specify this matrix as symmetrical
and fixed. We also specify the number of latent variables (NE = 10) that
we will use on the model statement. They can be named with a label
statement (LE). The 10 latent variables include the 2 factors at the individual level for the S_{PW} matrix and the additional 8 variables (6 observed
variables and 2 latent factors) that we use to specify the between-group
model using the S_B matrix.

The between-group factor loadings are contained in the beta (BE) matrix. The psi (PS) matrix will be used to specify the factor variances and
covariances at the individual level, as well as the factor variances and
covariances and the residual variances related to the group-level portion
of the model. We describe the psi matrix as symmetrical (SY) and fixed
(FI).

Within this full model specification, we then free the necessary within-group lambda y, theta epsilon, and psi parameters. First, we free the lambda y matrix of loadings of observed variables on their latent factors. We fix one observed variable at 1.0 to provide a reference metric for each latent leadership factor (i.e., LY 1,1 and LY 4,2). We also free the error terms for each observed variable (TE 1,1 to TE 6,6). The reader will recall from chapter 5 that we decided to free one additional covariance between residuals (see Fig. 6.1), Therefore, on the LISREL model statement the theta epsilon matrix must be specified as symmetric (as opposed to diagonal), and that covariance (TE 6,5) is freed. We also free the variances of the latent variables at the individual level (i.e., the diagonal elements PS 1,1 and PS 2, 2) and the factor covariance (PS 2,1).

We must also define the relationships between each within-group observed variable and its between-group counterpart. These are also defined in the lambda y matrix. The six between-organization variables have fixed effects on their corresponding within-group variables, with each coefficient equal to the square root of the scaling factor c (i.e., in this balanced design, 2.0). Because these are fixed parameters, they do not affect the global fit of the model, but they are needed for the correct interpretation of the model. This is specified in the LISREL model by fixing (FI) each parameter equal to 2.0 (VA = 2.0), which transforms the organizational-level variables to their proper scale. If the reader is running the multilevel model with balanced data, these parameters should be also be set to $\sqrt{c}$ (in this case the common group size) to provide the proper metric. If the reader is using *Mplus*, this scaling is done automatically. The other VA statements are initial starting values to help the program begin the iterations necessary to produce a solution. We discuss these values later.

Next, we focus our attention on the between-group parameters, which are also specified within Group 1. As we suggested previously, the between-group relationships can be confined efficiently within two matrices in LISREL (psi and beta). Because the between-organization S_B matrix is uncorrelated with the within-organization matrix S_{PW}, the covariances between the within-group factors and the between-group factors must be specified as zero in the model specification. The covariances among the factors representing the between-group variables and the factors used to explain them must also be set to zero. This can be done conveniently by fixing matrix psi (the default) in the LISREL model line and then freeing only the variances and covariances that are desired as diagonal and off-diagonal elements. We specify the factor variances for the group-level factors as PS 3,3 and PS 4,4. We will estimate the covariance between the two group-level factors as PS 4,3. This path corresponds to the same relationship between factors at the individual level (PS 2,1). We use psi 5,5 through psi 10,10 to provide estimates of residuals for the between-level observed variables.

We chose not to estimate the extra covariance between residuals at the group level.[3] The relationships connecting the organizational-level observed variables to the organizational-level latent factors may be specified in the beta matrix. Once again, two paths are constrained to 1.0 (BE 5,3 and BE 8,4) to provide a reference metric for each of the group-level

---

[3]The reader will also notice from Fig. 6.1 that we chose not to estimate a group-level covariance between the residuals for team (2team&) and evaluation standards (2evstan&), to match the individual-level covariance between those two residuals. We tested the model with and without this path being estimated and determined that estimating this covariance did not improve the fit of the model. If we wished to estimate an additional path between two residuals for the level-2 observed variables (i.e., to match the relationship at the individual level), we would first have to include them as two additional latent variables (PS 11,11 and PS 12,12). We could then estimate this covariance between the two group-level residuals by freeing PS 12,11. We include this special specification here. The reader should note that this special specification requires the placement of some additional equality constraints across both groups as well. It is much easier to estimate the model without estimating the covariance between these group-level residuals. If it is not a necessary parameter to the model, our advice is not to estimate it.

Partial LISREL Setup (Including Covariance Between Error Terms at Group Level).

```
!Two-factor model of leadership (between group)
DA NI=6 NO=56 NG=2 MA=CM
LA
'shdec' 'incli' 'syasse' 'evprog' 'team' 'evstan'
CM
2.81
0.65      1.29
0.85      1.01      2.49
0.86      0.77      0.91      2.55
1.82      0.91      1.25      1.89      4.37
1.15      1.04      1.84      1.87      2.62      3.50
MO NY=6 NE=12 LY=FU,FI PS=SY,FI TE=SY,FI BE=FU,FI [Change model line NE = 12]
LE
'gov' 'eval' '2gov' '2eval' '2shdec' '2incli'
'2syasse' '2evprog' '2team' '2evstan' '2team&' '2evstan&'      [Add the error terms as
                                                                psi 11 and 12]
VA 1.0 LY(1,1) LY(4,2)
FR LY(2,1) LY(3,2) LY(5,1) LY(6,2)
FI LY(1,5) LY(2,6) LY(3,7) LY(4,8) LY(5,9) LY(6,10)
VA 2.616 LY(1,5) LY(2,6) LY(3,7) LY(4,8) LY(5,9) LY(6,10)
FR TE(1,1) TE(2,2) TE(3,3) TE(4,4) TE(5,5)
FR TE(6,6) TE(6,5)
FR PS(1,1) PS(2,1) PS(2,2) PS(3,3) PS(4,3)
FR PS(4,4) PS(5,5) PS(6,6) PS(7,7) PS(8,8)
FR PS(9,9) PS(10,9) PS(10,10) PS(11,11) PS(12,11) PS(12,12)      [Free the new paths]
EQ PS(9,9) PS(11,11)
EQ PS(10,9) PS(12,11)                                    [Place 3 equality constraints here
EQ PS (10,10) PS(12,12)                                   and place them in Group 2 also.]
```

leadership factors. We simply add the output (OU) line at the end of Group 1 and later discuss how to specify that line more completely at the end of the Group 2 program statements.

Group-2 Specification

Compared to the full model specification in Group 1, the specification of the "limited" within-group model to be tested against full model is a bit easier. As we noted, the within-group (S_{PW}) covariance matrix is used in Group 2. Remember that the pooled within-group matrix represents a "corrected" covariance matrix from our first analysis used within chapter 5 (Step 1), which used the S_T matrix containing information from all of the subjects without regard to their organizations. Therefore, pooled within-group covariance has a smaller sample size of $N - G$ (216 – 54). In the LISREL setup for this model, shown later in Table 6.3, on the data (DA) line, the number of observations (NO) is now 162 because we are analyzing a pooled within-group covariance matrix.

In Group 2, we must respecify the individual-level model that we laid out, including the initial estimates. At the end of this repeated specification of lambda y, psi, and theta epsilon, we must use equality constraints (EQ) for all of the model's within-group parameters. Because the observed S_B matrix is actually a function of both the population between-group and the within-group matrices ($\Sigma_W + c\Sigma_B$), the quality constraints ensure that the same within-group model that we specified in Group 1 is also estimated with the S_{PW} covariance matrix in Group 2 (Muthén, 1994). Of course, when we estimate the individual-level model in Group 2, we do not wish to estimate the between-level paths previously described in Group 1. To ensure that this does not occur, the estimates for the residuals of the organization-level variables (PS 5,5 to PS 10,10), their relationships to the organization-level factors (in the beta matrix) and the variances of the two factors (PS 3,3 and PS 4,4) that we estimated in Group 1 must remain "fixed" in the individual-level model.

We have also added a couple of changes to the output (OU) line. The reader may recall that to estimate the model's parameters, initial estimates must be developed to begin the iterative process needed to converge on a solution. In most circumstances, the LISREL program will determine these initial estimates automatically. In good-fitting models, there is often little discrepancy between the initial estimates and the final solution. In such cases, only a few iterations may be required to obtain a solution. Because of the increased complexity in multilevel models, more iterations will generally be needed to find solutions. It becomes necessary to "help" the computer find these initial estimates (also referred to as starting values).

On the output (OU) line, we must include a statement that we want no automatic starting values (NS).

Because we request no automatic starting values, however, we will have to provide the initial estimates for the lambda y, psi, and theta epsilon parameters necessary to reach a solution. In practice, it can be difficult to determine the initial estimates, as they may be quite varied within any particular matrix. Because of this, sometimes it is necessary to start with a simple model and build its complexity one step at a time. We initially started all the lambda y estimates at .8 (VA .8), the psi estimates at .3, and the theta epsilon estimates at .7. As the reader will notice in Table 6.1, however, we found that we had to adjust quite a few parameters individually. If the reader encounters this problem, we suggest running only the within-groups model first (i.e., as a single-group design). The obtained unstandardized parameter estimates from the output can then be plugged in as the starting values for the needed parameters within the full model specification. We also turn off the model admissibility check (AD = OFF), which allows the computer to continue to solve the set of equations past 20 iterations. Sometimes it also helps to set the number of iterations at a higher number (e.g., IT = 200).

Again, we test the model in LISREL with the ML fitting function. Although we recommend beginning with ML estimation, there may be occasions to use other estimation methods such as unweighted least squares (ULS) or generalized (weighted) least squares (GLS) in order for the model to converge on a solution for the model's parameters. Each method has different distributional assumptions, and a different discrepancy function is used to minimize the difference between the population covariance estimated by the sample covariance matrix and the covariance matrix derived from the hypothesized model (Chou & Bentler, 1995). Parameter values from an initial solution (e.g., ULS) can also be used as starting values in subsequent models then tested with ML. Unfortunately, as a practical matter, it is sometimes difficult to tell whether the problem is only due to poor initial estimates, an unsuitable covariance matrix, or an incorrectly specified model.

Standardizing Variables

On the LISREL model output line for the full model in Table 6.1, we can also specify different standardizations of the parameter estimates. The estimates first produced are the unstandardized estimates in the LISREL solution (i.e., observed variables in original metrics). Where the emphasis is on overall model fit, it may be sufficient (and easiest) to report only the unstandardized solution. Remember that standardizations (e.g., with a mean of 0 and a standard deviation of 1) facilitate making comparisons about the strength of relationships between variables that are measured in different metrics. There are several possible conceptual approaches to standardization that could be considered. These are included in the output if SC is added to the output (OU) line.

Standardizing estimates to within-group variance implies a focus on within-group relations without concern for how big or small is the portion contributed by the within-group variance to the total variance (B. O. Muthén, personal communication, June 28, 1998). LISREL's within-group completely standardized solution standardizes both the latent and observed variables within each group. Hox (1995), for example, reported this solution for his multilevel factor analysis. It is also a convenient solution to use, given that it is readily obtained without specialized multilevel software such as STREAMS. *Mplus* gives a standardization similar to this (i.e., latent and observed variables standardized within each level). Again, we can obtain this standardization with SC on the output line in LISREL. Note, however, that this specification will also produce a common metric, completely standardized solution, the interpretation of which seems unclear within multilevel analysis. It is important to draw these distinctions because the volume of output in LISREL gives a variety of standardized solutions (e.g., within-group standardized, within-group completely standardized, common metric completely standardized), and deciphering them can be very confusing.

A second approach is to standardize an estimate with respect to its total variance (between and within). This puts the results in the perspective of total variance—for example, a between-group parameter may have a substantial standardized estimate, but due to its small intraclass correlation (i.e., small amount of variance between units), this parameter may have a negligible impact in terms of total variance (B. O. Muthén, personal communication, June 28, 1998). This is the approach to standardization used in the STREAMS software. Because the STREAMS standardization is conducted with reference to the total variance in observed variables, it requires that the contributions from both levels are expressed on the same scale; the sums of squares of standardized loadings over both levels sum to 1.0. For latent variables, the standardization is done within each level (see Gustafsson & Stahl, 1996, for further discussion).

A third approach would be standardizing with respect to between-group variance, which would imply a focus on the between-group relations (B. O. Muthén, personal communication, June 28, 1998). All approaches to standardization may therefore be useful to consider. The latter two approaches, however, require special computations. It should be remembered that the reporting of different solutions (e.g., unstandardized, within-group completely standardized solution, between-group completely standardized solution) can lead to somewhat different interpretations of the results. For this analysis, we present the LISREL within-group completely standardized solution (for convenience), the STREAMS total-variance standardization of the parameter estimates, and the *Mplus* standardization.

If Problems Are Encountered Estimating the Entire Model

We again point out that there may be occasions where we are likely to encounter problems if we test the whole model first (e.g., getting the model to converge on a solution). In working with the complexity inherent in multilevel models, therefore, it is sometimes convenient to estimate one level at a time in order to simplify the computations. As Muthén (1994) suggested, we can first test only the within-groups covariance matrix (S_{PW}). This is convenient because most of the observations are in this group, so it will likely be easier to estimate the model. If we only test the individual-level model at this step, we only need to specify one group (NG = 1) on the data (DA) line of the LISREL program. We provide the setup in Table 6.2, if the reader first wishes to estimate that model alone.

EXAMINING THE MCFA OUTPUT

As a preliminary step, we first present the within-group model only (as specified in Table 6.2). We include this step so the reader can see how to develop the necessary starting values (using unstandardized estimates) if they are needed to run the complete between- and within-group model. This should make it easier to achieve a solution that converges, given the added complexity of the multilevel model. The LISREL program produces a great deal of output, most of which is not needed for interpreting the adequacy of the model.

Within-Group Only Model Fit

In Table 6.3 we summarize some of the relevant fit indices of the within-group model only. The table suggests that this model (using S_{PW}) can be considered a plausible representation of the data. The chi-square coefficient (7 degrees of freedom) is 11.09, and nonsignificant ($p = .13$). One can compare this result against the model using the S_T matrix (Table 5.5), which resulted in a chi-square of 2.72 (7 degrees of freedom), which was again nonsignificant.

Other indices also support this as a plausible model. The RMSEA value is .060 ($p = .34$). As suggested in our discussion of fit indices in chapter 5, in this case, the "close" test of RMSEA, which allows an amount of error per degree of freedom, and the "exact" test of chi-square both suggest that the

TABLE 6.2
LISREL Setup for Within-Organizations Model

2 Factor Leadership Model (Within Groups)
DA NI=6 NO=162 NG=1 MA=CM
LA
'shdec' 'incli' 'syasse' 'evprog' 'team' 'evstan'
CM
0.88
0.30   0.56
0.46   0.24   0.78
0.34   0.24   0.46   0.78
0.34   0.28   0.39   0.39   0.95
0.41   0.21   0.52   0.49   0.50   1.02
MO NY=6 NE=10 LY=FU,FI PS=SY,FI TE=SY,FI
LE
'gov' 'eval' '2gov' '2eval' '2shdec' '2incli'
'2syasse' '2evprog' '2team' '2evstan'
VA 1.0 LY(1,1) LY(4,2)
FR LY(2,1) LY(3,2) LY(5,1) LY(6,2)
FR PS(1,1) PS(2,1) PS(2,2)
FR TE(1,1) TE(2,2) TE(3,3) TE(4,4) TE(5,5)
FR TE(6,5) TE(6,6)
OU ML MI SS

TABLE 6.3
Fit Indices for Within-Organizations Model

CHI-SQUARE WITH 7 DEGREES OF FREEDOM = 11.09 (P = 0.13)
ROOT MEAN SQUARE ERROR OF APPROXIMATION (RMSEA) = 0.060
90 PERCENT CONFIDENCE INTERVAL FOR RMSEA = (0.0 ; 0.12)
P-VALUE FOR TEST OF CLOSE FIT (RMSEA < 0.05) = 0.34
ROOT MEAN SQUARE RESIDUAL (RMR) = 0.026
STANDARDIZED RMR = 0.032
GOODNESS OF FIT INDEX (GFI) = 0.98
ADJUSTED GOODNESS OF FIT INDEX (AGFI) = 0.93
NON-NORMED FIT INDEX (NNFI) = 0.97
COMPARATIVE FIT INDEX (CFI) = 0.99

model actually fits relatively well. The other fit indices (Table 6.3) are also sufficiently strong in this model (e.g., GFI = .98, AGFI = .93, CFI = .99, RMR = .026). Of course, we might be able to improve the model by "freeing" additional parameters, but for now we accept the model as it was tested.

Complete MCFA

We now provide the goodness-of-fit output for the full multilevel factor model that we specified in Table 6.1. In actuality, the researcher might have alternative organizational models in mind to account for the organizational-level variation in leadership (e.g., the same two-factor leadership model, or a more general one-factor leadership model). In this case, we first test the two-factor model as hypothesized. Again, we look only at selected output generated by the program. This model also fits the data well. We can conclude that the between-organization model does not result in a diminished fit, because when estimated simultaneously, the chi-square contribution for the Group 1 model is 12.73, representing about 53% of the total chi-square coefficient. For the full model, the chi-square is 24.23 (15 degrees of freedom), and the model is nonsignificant ($p = .06$). Similarly, the RMSEA is .076 and is nonsignificant also ($p = .40$). It is useful to calculate the degrees of freedom associated with each level to make sure the "correct" number of parameters were estimated. Remember that there were seven degrees of freedom in the individual-level model. There are eight degrees of freedom in the group-level model because we chose not to estimate the covariance between the two residuals. The other indices (Table 6.4) are also strong (e.g., GFI = .98, CFI = .98, RMR = .027).

TABLE 6.4
Fit Indices for Full Model (Balanced Data, $N = 216$)

Group 1 Model Only
CONTRIBUTION TO CHI-SQUARE = 12.73
PERCENTAGE CONTRIBUTION TO CHI-SQUARE = 52.56
Both Models
CHI-SQUARE WITH 15 DEGREES OF FREEDOM = 24.23 (P = 0.061)
CONTRIBUTION TO CHI-SQUARE = 47.44
ROOT MEAN SQUARE ERROR OF APPROXIMATION (RMSEA) = 0.076
90 PERCENT CONFIDENCE INTERVAL FOR RMSEA = (0.0 ; 0.13)
P-VALUE FOR TEST OF CLOSE FIT (RMSEA < 0.05) = 0.40
ROOT MEAN SQUARE RESIDUAL (RMR) = 0.027
STANDARDIZED RMR = 0.033
GOODNESS OF FIT INDEX (GFI) = 0.98
NON-NORMED FIT INDEX (NNFI) = 0.96
COMPARATIVE FIT INDEX (CFI) = 0.98
MODEL AIC = 78.23

This analysis of the balanced data subset demonstrates that a multilevel factor analysis can be conducted relatively easily, if the researcher spends a bit of time to develop the data set and proper matrices. Because the model fits the data well, we can next turn our discussion to the parameter estimates.

Unstandardized and Standardized Parameter Estimates

We next examine the parameter estimates for the model. The reader will recall that the unstandardized parameter estimates and fit indices and a within-group completely standardized solution (i.e., where both latent and observed variables in each model are standardized to a mean of 0 and standard deviation of 1) can be obtained from the LISREL output. Because the output produced is extensive and can lead to confusion about what sections to examine, we have reorganized it (e.g., eliminated some sections and moved others around) to facilitate the presentation of these estimates.

Within-Organizations Estimates. In Table 6.5 we present the unstandardized and standardized LISREL estimates. The reader should observe that the unstandardized estimates of the within-organization model can be read out of either the Group 1 or Group 2 output. The unstandardized estimates of the observed variables range from .64 to 1.14 (including the variables needed to be set to 1.0 to provide a metric for each latent variable). Beneath each estimate is its standard error and a t-ratio indicating whether the parameter is significant (the estimate divided by its standard error should equal 2 or greater to be considered significant). The residual variances, which provide one estimate of each variable's reliability in measuring its factor, are also generally low. This suggests that although most items measure the factors quite well, a couple of items could be better measured at the individual level (e.g., team).

The within-group completely standardized estimates for the within-organization portion of the model suggest also that the within-organization variables are good measures of the factors. Estimates range from .57 to .71 on the governance factor (2gov) and from .70 to .83 on the evaluation factor (2eval). In contrast to the unstandardized estimates, note that these must be read out of the within-group (Group 2) portion of the output if they are to be correct. This is because of the different standardization LISREL provides for each group in the multigroup procedure. The residuals are generally low also (.16 to .68). For the within-organization model, we can also see that the leadership factors are correlated at .87.

Between-Organizations Estimates. The unstandardized factor loadings between organizations range from .68 to 2.01. The errors (contained in the psi matrix) are generally low, except that a couple of them are slightly negative. Because the LISREL solution focuses only on the within-group

2 Factor Leadership Model (Between Groups) 4 Sub per Group (N=216)
Number of Iterations = 17
LISREL ESTIMATES (MAXIMUM LIKELIHOOD)

LAMBDA-Y

	gov	eval	2gov	2eval	2shdec	2incli
shdec	1.00	—	—	—	2.00	—
incli	0.64	—	—	—	—	2.00
	(0.10)					
	6.16					
syasse	—	1.14	—	—	—	—
		(0.13)				
		9.01				
evprog	—	1.00	—	—	—	—
team	0.87	—	—	—	—	—
	(0.13)					
	6.44					
evstan	—	1.08	—	—	—	—
		(0.13)				
		8.27				

LAMBDA-Y

	2syasse	2evprog	2team	2evstan
shdec	—	—	—	—
incli	—	—	—	—
syasse	2.00	—	—	—
evprog	—	2.00	—	—
team	—	—	2.00	—
evstan	—	—	—	2.00

BETA

	gov	eval	2gov	2eval	2shdec	2incli
gov	—	—	—	—	—	—
eval	—	—	—	—	—	—
2gov	—	—	—	—	—	—
2eval	—	—	—	—	—	—
2shdec	—	—	1.00	—	—	—
2incli	—	—	0.68	—	—	—
			(0.21)			
			3.17			
2syasse	—	—	—	1.41	—	—
				(0.35)		
				4.03		
2evprog	—	—	—	1.00	—	—

(Continued)

139

TABLE 6.5
(Continued)

BETA

	gov	eval	2gov	2eval	2shdec	2incli
2team	—	—	1.18 (0.34) 3.47	—	—	—
2evstan	—	—	—	2.01 (0.52) 3.86	—	—

PSI

	gov	eval	2gov	2eval	2shdec	2incli
gov	0.45 (0.10) 4.53					
eval	0.38 (0.07) 5.71	0.42 (0.08) 5.02				
2gov	—	—	0.16 (0.09) 1.84			
2eval	—	—	0.10 (0.05) 1.94	0.07 (0.04) 1.67		
2shdec	—	—	—	—	0.10 (0.05) 1.82	
2incli	—	—	—	—	—	0.01 (0.03) 0.42
2syasse	—	—	—	—	—	—
2evprog	—	—	—	—	—	—
2team	—	—	—	—	—	—
2evstan	—	—	—	—	—	—

PSI

	2syasse	2evprog	2team	2evstan
2syasse	0.05 (0.03) 1.65			
2evprog	—	−0.02 (0.02) −0.91		
2team	—	—	0.03 (0.05) 0.61	
2evstan	—	—	—	−0.04 (0.04) −1.08

(Continued)

TABLE 6.5

(Continued)

2 Factor Leadership Model (Within Groups) (N=216)
Number of Iterations = 17
LISREL ESTIMATES (MAXIMUM LIKELIHOOD)

LAMBDA-Y

	gov	eval	2gov	2eval	2shdec	2incli
shdec	1.00	—	—	—	—	—
incli	0.64	—	—	—	—	—
	(0.10)					
	6.16					
syasse	—	1.14	—	—	—	—
		(0.13)				
		9.01				
evprog	—	1.00	—	—	—	—
team	0.87	—	—	—	—	—
	(0.13)					
	6.44					
evstan	—	1.08	—	—	—	—
		(0.13)				
		8.27				

PSI

	gov	eval	2gov	2eval	2shdec	2incli
gov	0.45					
	(0.10)					
	4.53					
eval	0.38	0.42				
	(0.07)	(0.08)				
	5.71	5.02				

THETA-EPS

	shdec	incli	syasse	evpro	team	evstan
shdec	0.44					
	(0.07)					
	6.09					
incli	—	0.38				
		(0.05)				
		7.71				
syasse	—	—	0.24			
			(0.05)			
			4.90			
evprog	—	—	—	0.37		
				(0.05)		
				6.86		

(Continued)

TABLE 6.5
(Continued)

THETA-EPS

	shdec	incli	syasse	evpro	team	evstan
team	—	—	—	—	0.62	
					(0.08)	
					7.64	
evstan	—	—	—	—	0.15	0.50
					(0.05)	(0.07)
					2.97	7.33

SQUARED MULTIPLE CORRELATIONS FOR Y-VARIABLES

shdec	incli	syasse	evprog	team	evstan
0.51	0.32	0.69	0.53	0.36	0.49

2 Factor Leadership Model (Between Groups) 4 Sub per Group (N=216)
WITHIN GROUP COMPLETELY STANDARDIZED SOLUTION

LAMBDA-Y

	gov	eval	2gov	2eval	2shdec	2incli
shdec	0.48	—	—	—	0.74	—
incli	0.45	—	—	—	—	0.62
syasse	—	0.59	—	—	—	—
evprog	—	0.65	—	—	—	—
team	0.41	—	—	—	—	—
evstan	—	0.49	—	—	—	—

LAMBDA-Y

	2syasse	2evprog	2team	2evstan
shdec	—	—	—	—
incli	—	—	—	—
syasse	0.71	—	—	—
evprog	—	0.46	—	—
team	—	—	0.72	—
evstan	—	—	—	0.71

BETA

	gov	eval	2gov	2eval	2shdec	2incli
gov	—	—	—	—	—	—
eval	—	—	—	—	—	—
2gov	—	—	—	—	—	—
2eval	—	—	—	—	—	—
2shdec	—	—	0.79	—	—	—
2incli	—	—	0.93	—	—	—
2syasse	—	—	—	0.86	—	—
2evprog	—	—	—	1.18	—	—
2team	—	—	0.94	—	—	—
2evstan	—	—	—	1.08	—	—

(Continued)

TABLE 6.5
(*Continued*)

PSI

	gov	eval	2gov	2eval	2shdec	2incli
gov	1.00					
eval	0.87	1.00				
2gov	—	—	1.00			
2eval	—	—	0.89	1.00		
2shdec	—	—	—	—	0.38	
2incli	—	—	—	—	—	0.14
2syasse	—	—	—	—	—	—
2evprog	—	—	—	—	—	—
2team	—	—	—	—	—	—
2evstan	—	—	—	—	—	—

PSI

	2syasse	2evpr	2team	2evstan
2syasse	0.25			
2evprog	—	−0.39		
2team	—	—	0.12	
2evstan	—	—	—	−0.17

THETA-EPS

	shdec	incli	syasse	evprog	team	evstan
shdec	0.23					
incli	—	0.42				
syasse	—	—	0.15			
evprog	—	—	—	0.37		
team	—	—	—	—	0.31	
evstan	—	—	—	—	0.08	0.25

2 Factor Leadership Model (Within Groups)
WITHIN GROUP COMPLETELY STANDARDIZED SOLUTION

LAMBDA-Y

	gov	eval	2gov	2eval	2shdec	2incli
shdec	0.71	—	—	—	—	—
incli	0.57	—	—	—	—	—
syasse	—	0.83	—	—	—	—
evprog	—	0.73	—	—	—	—
team	0.60	—	—	—	—	—
evstan	—	0.70	—	—	—	—

PSI

	gov	eval	2gov	2eval	2shdec	2incli
gov	1.00					
eval	0.87	1.00				

(Continued)

143

TABLE 6.5
(Continued)

THETA-EPS

	shdec	incli	syasse	evprog	team	evstan
shdec	0.49					
incli	—	0.68				
syasse	—	—	0.31			
evprog	—	—	—	0.47		
team	—	—	—	—	0.64	
evstan	—	—	—	—	0.16	0.51

standardization as opposed to the total variance standardization as in STREAMS, it is likely that the variables are standardized somewhat inappropriately (i.e., a variable that loads a bit over 1.0 on a factor will produce a slight negative error variance). More specifically, LISREL solution does not take in the different amounts of variance contributed by the group level (i.e., the intraclass correlation) on each of the observed variables (Gustafsson & Stahl, 1996). For example, the intraclass correlations of the observed variables are relatively small in the data set (which could result from the small number of level-2 units). As pessimists, we must be cautious because of the small number of between-group units. As optimists, the fact that the model converged with sample size under 100 is cause for celebration.

The intraclass correlation for the latent variables can be calculated from the unstandardized psi estimates, using the Group 1 (full model) portion of the output. Because of the adjustments for errors of measurement, especially at the individual level, we find that the intraclass correlations of the governance factor is a bit higher (26%) than might be expected $[.16/(.45 + .16)]$, given the separate intraclass correlations of the observed variables (ranging from 12% to 24%). For the evaluation factor, the between-unit variance is about 14% $[.07/(.42 + .07)]$. The separate intraclass correlations for those observed variables ranged from .08 to .22.

Considering Alternative Models

We can use this model to demonstrate one modeling strategy that focuses on the examination of alternative models. Such comparisons should be made on the basis of related theoretical relationships. The researcher may have particular alternative models in mind. For example, the two-factor organizational model could be compared against a simplified model. We might argue that a single-factor model is sufficient to capture the variation in leadership present between organizations. To examine this proposition, we tested the two-factor model against a one-factor model at the organizational level. To make this comparison of alternative models, we would require that all of the between-organization observed variables load on one latent factor instead of two (i.e., we remove one latent factor from the model).

We can use an additional fit index to compare the fit of the alternative models. Akaike's information index (AIC) provides information about the best number of parameters to include in a model (see Marcoulides & Hershberger, 1997, for further discussion of indices that can be used to compare models). The model with the number of parameters that produces the smallest AIC is considered the best model. The two-factor model produced an AIC of 78.23 (see Table 6.4), while the one-factor model produced an AIC of 80.71 (not tabled). Similarly, the other goodness-of-fit indices also indicated that the model with one organizational-level factor did not fit the data as well (e.g., GFI = .97, CFI = .97, RMR = .14). We therefore decided to retain the two-factor model at the organizational level.

As we noted in chapter 5, ideally we should emphasize strategies that compare alternative models, rather than merely making a series of changes in our proposed model through the model modification indices. Again, we emphasize that these model modifications should be made sparingly and with regard to theory and statistical power. Because of the small number of level-2 units available, it would be unlikely that our arbitrary model modifications would replicate in other samples (MacCallum et al., 1992).

STREAMS and *Mplus* Standardizations

The reader will recall that the unstandardized parameter estimates and fit indices and a within-group completely standardized solution (i.e., where both latent and observed variables in each model are standardized to a mean of 0 and standard deviation of 1) can be obtained from the LISREL output. If we wish to standardize the parameter estimates with respect to each observed variable's total variance, we need to use STREAMS software. We present those standardized estimates in Fig. 6.2.

The standardized within-group factor loadings computed with STREAMS range from .53 to .74. The reader can compare the standardized loadings produced with STREAMS with the LISREL within-group completely standardized solution (included in Table 6.5). The residual variances, which provide one estimate of each variable's reliability in measuring its factor, range from .50 to .76 (not shown). This suggests that although most items measure the factors quite well, a couple of items could be better measured at the individual level (e.g., incli). At the individual level, we can also see that the leadership factors were correlated at .58.

The factor loadings between organizations are somewhat lower, ranging from .31 to .49. The reader will notice that at the group level the standardized

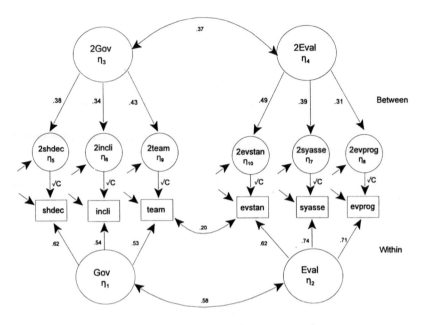

FIG. 6.2. Standardized STREAMS parameter estimates.

loadings produced by LISREL (in Table 6.5) are not the same as the STREAMS estimates. Again, this is because the LISREL solution focuses only on the within-group standardization as opposed to the total variance standardization. More specifically, LISREL solution does not take in the different amounts of variance contributed by the group level on each of observed variables (Gustafsson & Stahl, 1996). The intraclass correlations of the observed variables are relatively small in the data set (which could result from the small number of level-2 units). Therefore, from the STREAMS standpoint, the group-level estimates contribute less to the total variance; hence, their estimates are considerably smaller. The residuals for the level-2 variables are generally low (ranging from .00 to .29). None of them is negative, however. This suggests the reliability of measurement is actually a bit higher at the group level (or less variable because of small intraclass correlations and sample size). Estimates are also provided for the within-group and between-group reliability. The within-group reliability is defined as the ratio of true-score individual variance to observed-score individual variance, and the between-group reliability is the ratio of true group variance to observed group variance. These values are meaningful only when it is reasonable to construct an aggregate score which is the unweighted sum of the observed variables (Gustafsson & Stahl, 1996). Finally, the correlation between the two factors at the organizational level was .37.

We also provide the *Mplus* setup in Table 6.6. The solution was very similar ($\chi^2 = 22.1$, $df = 15$, RMSEA = .047, $p = .51$). The small difference

TABLE 6.6
Mplus Input Instructions for Multilevel CFA
of Leadership and Selected Fit Indices

TITLE: two level confirmatory

DATA: FILE IS A:\St216pre.txt;
          Format is 3x,1f2.0,6f1.0,2x;

VARIABLE: Names are group shdec incli syasse evprog team evstan;
          CLUSTER IS group;

ANALYSIS: TYPE = General Twolevel;
          ESTIMATOR IS ML;

Model:

          %BETWEEN%
          bgov by shdec incli team;
          beval by syasse evprog evstan;
          bgov - evstan*.5;
          bgov WITH beval*.25;

          %WITHIN%
          gov by shdec incli team;
          eval by syasse evprog evstan;
          team PWITH evstan;
          eval WITH gov*.5;

OUTPUT: SAMPSTAT STANDARDIZED RESIDUAL TECH1;

Selected Fit Indices: chi square (15 *df*) = 22.1, *p* = .11, RMSEA = .047, *p* = .51

in fit is the result of slightly different within- and between-group covariance matrices used as input. The *Mplus* standardized estimates are presented in Fig. 6.3. Despite the differences in the LISREL, STREAMS, and *Mplus* standardizations, we can still arrive at a similar conclusion that the observed variables at the group level load well on their factors.

SUMMARIZING THE MCFA

Overall, from our various model tests with the balanced and unbalanced designs, we have determined that our proposed two-factor leadership model fits the data well, both within and between organizations. The confirmation of the proposed model tends to enhance its construct validity; that is, the items define the factors fairly well and the factors are related to each other in a manner that we might expect (i.e., a positive correlation). In most instances we would probably use more items to ensure that we

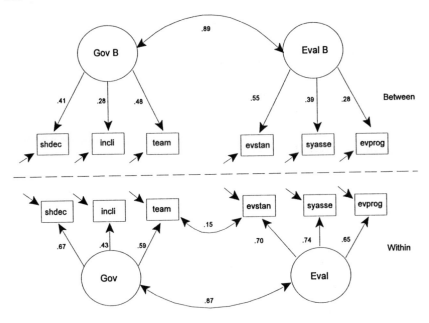

FIG. 6.3. Standardized *Mplus* parameter estimates.

have defined the factors adequately from a theoretical standpoint. The multilevel factor analysis, therefore, has given us valuable information about the psychometric properties of the measures as well as the validity of our proposed model. Of course, unanswered from this part of the analysis is what individual and organizational variables might account for this variation in perceptions about leadership.

When actually estimating multilevel covariance structure models, it is likely that some problems will occur. The between-organization structure can be somewhat difficult to determine or might not be a simple structure (Muthén, 1994). It is quite likely that the full multilevel model estimated with two groups will need more iterations to generate a solution than in other circumstances (Hox, 1995). It also seems that convergence of the model on a unique solution is a problem (depending on widely varying group sizes, total number of groups, etc.). Problems with nonconvergence due to poor choice of starting values also appear to be very common in multilevel factor analysis (Muthén, 1994). Because starting values must be generated so that the program can iterate to a solution, often the solution can be "encouraged" by a careful delineation of start values. One may also proceed from one level to two, or from one or two factors to more complex models.

In the STREAMS program it is possible to estimate a series of models with the starting values used from the previous model estimated. Where maximum likelihood becomes problematic, for example, the investigator may use ULS (unweighted least squares) or GLS (generalized least squares) estimation, keep the start values from previous models, and eventually develop adequate starting values, so that the final model can be made with maximum likelihood. We found the model easy to specify and estimate with *Mplus* after a few starting values were specified (see Table 6.6).

We encourage you to try the following exercise, or to try your own model using a balanced design. You only need access to an SEM program with multiple-group option. You should be able to develop the necessary between-group matrix by following our example calculations presented in the chapter. We have provided some guidance in setting up the model in the following exercise, but you may hit a few snags anyway. It is sometimes difficult to determine exactly where the problem lies, so remember that patience is a virtue!

EXERCISE

A researcher wishes to test a model of how leaders responded to an organizational improvement process within and between organizations. The "process" factor has four indicators concerned with assessing needs, developing goals, conceptualizing professional development activities, and implementing the training. There are 384 individuals in 56 organizations who rate their supervisors on the four items (another sample from the data used in chap. 6). Define and test the model. The between-groups matrix (with labels) to be used in Group 1 is:

```
LA
'needs' 'goals' 'prodev' 'train'
CM
2.17
1.21   1.37
1.83   1.27   2.41
1.66   1.37   1.55   2.83
```

The pooled within-group matrix for Group 2 is:

```
LA
'needs' 'goals' 'prodev' 'train'
CM
1.23
0.29   0.51
0.41   0.25   0.89
0.45   0.26   0.57   1.37
```

You can use the following labels to define the latent variables if you wish to help you set up the psi matrix and the beta matrix in the model:

LE
'tasks' '2tasks' '2needs' '2goals' '2prodev' '2train'

Hints. Group 1 contains the program specifications for the entire model (between and within groups). Remember, you will need to fix one observed variable at each level to 1.0 (e.g., LY 1,1 and beta 3,2) to create a reference variable for the factor. In Group 1, free the individual-level parameters, fix the scaling parameters, and free the diagonals of the entire psi matrix and the theta epsilon matrix for the residuals. Then free the loadings of the between-level variables on their latent factor (the betas). Remember that finding a set of initial estimates (starting values) can be challenging. Because the group sample sizes differ, in this case we must use 2.616 (the square root of *c*) as the metric for the between-group relations (VA = 2.616). You might try the following start values: lambda y (.8), psi (.2), beta (.8), theta epsilon (.7).

In Group 2, don't forget equality constraints on all the individual-level parameters that you specified in Group 1 when you set up the individual model within Group 2. This ensures the same individual-level model is estimated. After the first model solution, you may wish to free an additional error term in the individual-level model. You will want to look at the unstandardized estimates and the within-group completely standardized solution in LISREL (SC on output line).

You may want to find out how well the final model fits the data, how well the items load on the factor at each level, and what percentage of the factor variance is between organizations.

Output

Fit indices (with the largest TE freed from previous MI):

CHI-SQUARE WITH 3 DEGREES OF FREEDOM = 9.63 (P = 0.022)
ROOT MEAN SQUARE ERROR OF APPROXIMATION (RMSEA) = 0.11
90 PERCENT CONFIDENCE INTERVAL FOR RMSEA = (0.036 ; 0.19)
P-VALUE FOR TEST OF CLOSE FIT (RMSEA < 0.05) = 0.17
ROOT MEAN SQUARE RESIDUAL (RMR) = 0.010
GOODNESS OF FIT INDEX (GFI) = 1.00
COMPARATIVE FIT INDEX (CFI) = 0.98

Parameter estimates:

Example One Factor Model (between group)
LISREL ESTIMATES (MAXIMUM LIKELIHOOD)

LAMBDA-Y

	tasks	2tasks	2needs	2goals	2prodev	2train
needs	1.00	—	2.62	—	—	—
goals	0.60	—	—	2.62	—	—
	(0.09)					
	6.74					
prodev	0.91	—	—	—	2.62	—
	(0.15)					
	6.22					
train	0.98	—	—	—	—	2.62
	(0.17)					
	5.80					

BETA

	tasks	2tasks	2needs	2goals	2prodev	2train
tasks	—	—	—	—	—	—
2tasks	—	—	—	—	—	—
2needs	—	1.00	—	—	—	—
2goals	—	0.73	—	—	—	—
		(0.13)				
		5.62				
2prodev	—	1.02	—	—	—	—
		(0.17)				
		6.18				
2train	—	0.91	—	—	—	—
		(0.19)				
		4.73				

PSI (Factor Variance)

tasks	2tasks
0.46	0.19
(0.10)	(0.06)
4.60	3.08

WITHIN GROUP COMPLETELY STANDARDIZED SOLUTION

LAMBDA-Y

	tasks	2tasks	2needs	2goals	2prodev	2train	Streams Standardization
needs	0.46	—	0.66				0.58
goals	0.35	—	—	0.79			0.51
prodev	0.39	—	—	—	0.80		0.58
train	0.39	—	—	—	—	0.73	0.53

BETA

	tasks	2tasks	Streams Standardization
tasks	—	—	
2tasks	—	—	
2needs	—	1.19	0.38
2goals	—	0.92	0.41
2prodev	—	0.94	0.43
2train	—	0.83	0.32

THETA-EPS

	needs	goals	prodev	train
needs	0.35			
goals	—	0.25		
prodev	—	—	0.20	
train	—	—	0.05	0.31

LISREL Statements for Example

Example One Factor Model (between group)
DA NI=4 NO=56 NG=2 MA=CM
LA
'needs' 'goals' 'prodev' 'train'
CM
2.17
1.21   1.37
1.83   1.27   2.41
1.66   1.37   1.55   2.83
MO NY=4 NE=6 LY=FU,FI PS=SY,FI TE=SY,FI BE=FU,FI
LE
'tasks' '2tasks' '2needs' '2goals' '2prodev' '2train'
VA 1.0 LY(1,1)
FR LY(2,1) LY(3,1) LY(4,1)
FI LY(1,3) LY(2,4) LY(3,5) LY(4,6)
VA 2.616 LY(1,3) LY(2,4) LY(3,5) LY(4,6)
FR PS(1,1) PS(2,2) PS(3,3) PS(4,4) PS(5,5)
FR PS(6,6)
FR TE(1,1) TE(2,2) TE(3,3) TE(4,3) TE(4,4)
VA 1.0 BE(3,2)
FR BE(4,2) BE(5,2) BE(6,2)
VA .8 LY(2,1) LY(3,1) LY(4,1)
VA .2 PS(1,1) PS(2,2)
VA .05 PS(3,3) PS(4,4) PS(5,5) PS(6,6)
VA .7 TE(1,1) TE(2,2) TE(3,3) TE(4,4)
VA .1 TE(4,3)
VA .8 BE(4,2) BE(5,2) BE(6,2)
OU ME=ML AD=OFF MI SC NS

one factor model (within group)
DA NI=4 NO=328 NG=2 MA=CM
LA
'needs' 'goals' 'prodev' 'train'
CM
1.23
0.29 0.51
0.41 0.25 0.89
0.45 0.26 0.57 1.37
MO NY=4 NE=6 LY=FU,FI PS=SY,FI TE=SY,FI BE=FU,FI
LE
'tasks' '2tasks' '2needs' '2goals' '2prodev' '2train'
VA 1.0 LY(1,1)
FR LY(2,1) LY(3,1) LY(4,1)
FR PS(1,1)
FR TE(1,1) TE(2,2) TE(3,3) TE(4,3) TE(4,4)
VA .8 LY(2,1) LY(3,1) LY(4,1)
VA .2 PS(1,1) PS(2,2)
VA .05 PS(3,3) PS(4,4) PS(5,5) PS(6,6)
VA .7 TE(1,1) TE(2,2) TE(3,3) TE(4,4)
VA .1 TE(4,3)
VA .8 BE(4,2) BE(5,2) BE(6,2)
EQ LY(1,2,1) LY(2,2,1)
EQ LY(1,3,1) LY(2,3,1)
EQ LY(1,4,1) LY(2,4,1)
EQ PS(1,1,1) PS(2,1,1)
EQ TE(1,1,1) TE(2,1,1)
EQ TE(1,2,2) TE(2,2,2)
EQ TE(1,3,3) TE(2,3,3)
EQ TE(1,4,3) TE(2,4,3)
EQ TE(1,4,4) TE(2,4,4)
OU ME=ML AD=OFF MI SC NS

Multilevel Structural
Equation Models

Multilevel covariance structure analysis (e.g., multilevel factor models) can
be extended to include sets of predictors (multilevel structural models) at
both the individual and group levels. In this chapter we present an overview
of multilevel structural equation modeling (SEM) techniques and an example. Muthén (e.g., 1989, 1994), Hox (1995), Kaplan (1998), and Kaplan
and Elliott (1997) provided some of the necessary theoretical work to allow
the specification of these models and provided empirical demonstrations.
These allow us to investigate a variety of multilevel, multivariate relationships. The models can range from observed variables only (i.e., path models) to models where there are combinations of observed and latent
variables, mean structures, and a variety of direct and indirect effects. The
methods of analysis can also be readily adapted to the multilevel analysis
of dichotomous and ordinal data, longitudinal analyses of effects, and
growth models (e.g., see Hershberger, Molenaar, & Corneal, 1996; McArdle
& Hamagami, 1996; Muthén & Muthén, 1998; Willett & Sayer, 1996).

It must be emphasized, however, that at present it is not practically
feasible to specify and test multilevel structural models that are relatively
complicated. The various multilevel models we describe in this chapter
can be estimated in the same way as we outlined in chapter 6—by decom-
posing the population covariance matrix into separate within-group and
between-group covariance matrices. It is important to remember that the
two-group specification of a multilevel structural model is just a convenient
way to account for the latent sources of variation in the total observed
variation (Gustafsson & Stahl, 1996).

Recall from chapter 6 that in a multilevel covariance structure analysis, we can model four sources of variation in the observed variables. These sources include individual variability shared with a common factor, individual variability specific to each observed variable (its residual), group variability shared with the observed variables (resulting from a group-level factor), and group variability that is specific to each observed variable (its level-2 residual). We assume that variation in the parameters of the within-group model (e.g., factor means) can be accounted for by variation in the organizational-level variables. Explanatory variables (z) can be added at the group level, referred to as "group-level" manifest variables, to account for the between-group portion of the variability in factor means (Kaplan, 1998; Muthén, 1990). Moreover, the group-level manifest variables could also be used to define a group-level latent variable that might account for some of the variability in factor means.

MATHEMATICAL REPRESENTATION OF MULTILEVEL SEM

Currently, it is possible to formulate and test multilevel structural models for variation in intercepts, but not for variation in regression coefficients (i.e., slopes). A recent formulation by Chou, Bentler, and Pentz (1998) opens this possibility, however, using a "two-stage" estimation method that draws on the slopes-as-outcomes approach (Burstein, 1980). The slope estimates are first computed within each unit based on the independent observations within that unit. These estimates are then placed in a new data matrix that can be analyzed through SEM.

In chapter 6, we developed a general covariance structure model used to disaggregate a covariance matrix into its within-group and between-group component matrices. This model was used to develop a multilevel latent variable (factor) model (see Eqs. 8–11 in chap. 6). To extend the model to include predictors at each level, we first focus on defining the level-1 and level-2 predictors and structural relationships. To demonstrate where the within- and between-groups predictors can be contained within a set of structural equations in more detail, we follow Kaplan's (1998) discussion of a multilevel *path* model (i.e., having no latent variables). This simplifies the presentation, because if we do not have latent variables in the model, we do not have to specify a measurement model. Recall from chapter 5 that a structural model without latent variables may be expressed as:

$$\mathbf{y} = \boldsymbol{\alpha} + \mathbf{B}\mathbf{y} + \boldsymbol{\Gamma}\mathbf{x} + \boldsymbol{\zeta} \qquad (1)$$

From this general structural model formulation, we can write a within-groups model as

$$y_{gi} = \alpha_g + B_y y_{gi} + \varepsilon_{gi} \qquad (2)$$

where y_{gi} is a vector of within-group observed variables, α_g is a vector of intercepts or means of the individual-level variables, which are assumed to vary over groups, B_y is a matrix of regression coefficients relating the individual-level variables to each other, and ε_{gi} is the residual term for the within-group equation, with $E(\varepsilon_{gi}) = 0$. To include latent variables, as in the last chapter, we would need to add a vector of latent variables (η) that link the observed measures through measurement models within and between groups (see Muthén & Muthén, 1998).

As in chapter 6 the within-group model is referred to as an "all y" model in LISREL notation. With this specification, all of the variables (i.e., predictors, intervening and outcome variables) are treated as endogenous to simplify the notation. This model may be referred to as the *structural* form of the within-group model (Kaplan, 1998; Kaplan & Elliott, 1997). The direct effects in the B_y matrix are what would be found in a typical path model. If our particular purpose is to model variation in the means of the individual-level variables we may reexpress the equation as

$$y_{gi} = (I - B_y)^{-1}\alpha_g + (I - B_y)^{-1}\varepsilon_{gi} \qquad (3)$$

where it is assumed the inverse of $(I - B_y)$ exists (Muthén, 1994). This is referred to in econometrics as the "reduced form" of the model (Kaplan, 1998).

Next, we assume that the levels of the individual-level variables in α_g vary across the G groups and this can be explained by a set of organizational-level variables. The between-organization model can be written as

$$\alpha_g = \alpha + B_\alpha z_g + \delta_g \qquad (4)$$

where, assuming z_g is centered around the grand mean, α is the grand mean vector across the G organizations, z_g are the organizational variables (e.g., organizational effectiveness, size), B_α is a matrix of regression coefficients relating z_g to the intercepts of the individual-level variables, and δ_g is a vector of residuals for the intercept equation.

The within-group and between-group equations of the model previously developed allow the intercepts to be expressed as a function of the organizational variables (Kaplan, 1998; Muthén, 1990). It is important to emphasize that this model, as demonstrated by Kaplan and Elliott (1997), allows the between-organization variables $\mathbf{z}_g$ to have a separate between-organization simultaneous equation model that can be written as

$$\mathbf{z}_g = \tau + \mathbf{B}_z \mathbf{z}_g + \mathbf{u}_g \tag{5}$$

which, assuming that the inverse of $(\mathbf{I} - \mathbf{B}_z)$ is nonsingular, can be expressed in reduced form as

$$\mathbf{z}_g = (\mathbf{I} - \mathbf{B}_z)^{-1} \tau + (\mathbf{I} - \mathbf{B}_z)^{-1} \mathbf{u}_g \tag{6}$$

In this latter equation, τ is a vector of intercepts and means for the organizational-level equations, $\mathbf{B}_z$ is a matrix of coefficients relating the organizational-level variables to each other, and $\mathbf{u}_g$ is a vector of residuals for the organizational-level equation (Kaplan, 1998; Kaplan & Elliott, 1997).

After a series of substitutions, Kaplan and Elliott (1997) summarized the expression for the ith individual's score in the gth organization, taking into account the structural relationships within and between organizations. This final model can be written as

$$\mathbf{y}_{gi} = (\mathbf{I} - \mathbf{B}_y)^{-1}\alpha + \Pi\tau + \Pi\mathbf{u}_g + (\mathbf{I} - \mathbf{B}_y)^{-1}\delta_g + (\mathbf{I} - \mathbf{B}_y)^{-1}\varepsilon_{gi} \tag{7}$$

where $\Pi = (\mathbf{I} - \mathbf{B}_y)^{-1}\mathbf{B}_\alpha(\mathbf{I} - \mathbf{B}_z)^{-1}$. Kaplan and Elliott referred to Π as a *multilevel total effects* matrix, where the total effects of changes in between-group endogenous variables on within-group endogenous variables are manifested through other between- and within-group variables (see Muthén, 1994; Kaplan & Elliott, 1997).

The multilevel path model can next be extended to include latent variables. We can represent the multilevel model with latent variables using slightly different matrix notation from the general single-level model presented in chapter 5. Following Muthén and Muthén's (1998) discussion, two-level SEM considers a vector of observed variables containing cluster-specific, level-2 variables $\mathbf{z}_c$ ($c = 1, 2, \ldots, C$) and individual-specific, level-1 variables ($\mathbf{y}_{ci}$ and $\mathbf{x}'_{ci}$) for individual i in cluster c, where

$$\mathbf{v}_{ci} = \begin{bmatrix} \mathbf{z}_c \\ \mathbf{y}_{ci} \\ \mathbf{x}_{ci} \end{bmatrix} = \mathbf{v}^*_c + \mathbf{v}^*_{ci} = \begin{bmatrix} \mathbf{v}^*_{zc} \\ \mathbf{v}^*_{yc} \\ \mathbf{v}^*_{xc} \end{bmatrix} + \begin{bmatrix} 0 \\ \mathbf{v}^*_{yci} \\ \mathbf{v}^*_{xci} \end{bmatrix}$$

The asterisked components are independent between and within components of the respective variable vector (Muthén & Satorra, 1995). The between-group matrix contains the between-group predictors ($\mathbf{z}_c$), group-level variation in intercepts ($\mathbf{y}_c$), and group-level variation in the individual-level predictors $(\mathbf{x}_c)$. Note that the individual-level matrix contains the intercepts and individual-level predictors and has zeros (0) for the group-level variables.

This multilevel model can be translated into a between-cluster model with latent variables written as

$$\mathbf{v}^*_c = \mathbf{v}_B + \mathbf{\Lambda}_B \mathbf{\eta}_{Bc} + \mathbf{\varepsilon}_{Bc}, \tag{8}$$

$$\mathbf{\eta}_{Bc} = \mathbf{\alpha}_B + \mathbf{B}_B \mathbf{\eta}_{Bc} + \mathbf{\zeta}_{Bc}, \tag{9}$$

and a within-cluster model with latent variables, which can be written as

$$\begin{bmatrix} \mathbf{0} \\ \mathbf{v}^*_{yci} \\ \mathbf{v}^*_{xci} \end{bmatrix} = \mathbf{\Lambda}_W \mathbf{\eta}_{Wci} + \mathbf{\varepsilon}_{Wci}, \tag{10}$$

$$\mathbf{\eta}_{Wci} = \mathbf{B}_W \mathbf{\eta}_{Wci} + \mathbf{\zeta}_{Wci}. \tag{11}$$

Equations 8 and 10 represent the measurement models linking observed variables to underlying factors for each level, and Equations 9 and 11 represent the latent variable structural models at each level (i.e., similar to our discussion of the multilevel path model formulated in Equations 2 to 7). Using the between-group and within-group models results in the general mean and covariance structure model for multilevel data (Muthén & Muthén, 1998) given in Equations 12 to 14 (see also chap. 6, Equations 8 through 11, for multilevel factor analysis)

$$\mathbf{\mu} = \mathbf{v}_B + \mathbf{\Lambda}_B (\mathbf{I} - \mathbf{B}_B)^{-1} \mathbf{\alpha}_B, \tag{12}$$

$$\mathbf{\Sigma}_B = \mathbf{\Lambda}_B (\mathbf{I} - \mathbf{B}_B)^{-1} \mathbf{\Psi}_B (\mathbf{I} - \mathbf{B}_B)^{\prime -1} \mathbf{\Lambda}'_B + \mathbf{\Theta}_B, \tag{13}$$

$$\mathbf{\Sigma}_W = \mathbf{\Lambda}_W (\mathbf{I} - \mathbf{B}_W)^{-1} \mathbf{\Psi}_W (\mathbf{I} - \mathbf{B}_W)^{\prime -1} \mathbf{\Lambda}'_W + \mathbf{\Theta}_W. \tag{14}$$

For the interested reader, structural equation models that are more general are also formulated in Schmidt and Wisenbaker (1986), McDonald and Goldstein (1989), and Muthén (1989, 1990).

A MULTILEVEL SEM

In this section, we turn our attention to proposing and testing a basic multilevel structural equation model. For this example, we use the complete data set on organizational leadership ($N = 384$) that we presented in chapter 6, where the sampling design is unbalanced. To simplify the presentation, let us assume that we have three leadership scales (i.e., each scale comprised of several survey items). We believe that these three scales can define a single leadership latent variable. The three observed indicators are *governance practices* (e.g., shared decision making, client involvement, team-oriented work environment), *organizational culture and climate* (e.g., two-way communication, morale, high work standards, support for risk-taking), and *task organization* (e.g., effective assessment and evaluation procedures, staff development, utilization of employee skills, effective allocation of resources).

In Fig. 7.1, we hypothesize that the leadership factor varies across organizations and we wish to examine the variance as a result of other explanatory variables in the model. Remember that in the SEM approach, we can define separate structural models at the individual and group levels to account for the variation in leadership practices. The proposed structural model may be conceptualized in manner that is very similar to the multi-

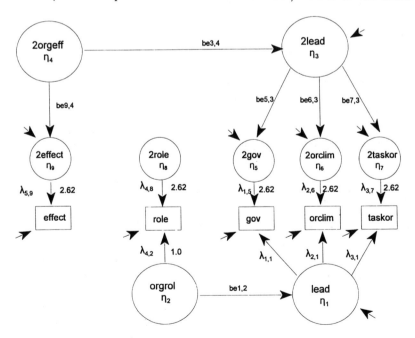

FIG. 7.1. Proposed multilevel structural model.

level factor model presented in chapter 6. One model is formulated for the individual-level variation and another is developed for the between-group variation in the individual parameters. For the within-group model, *leadership* may be affected by one or more predictor variables. In this case, we hypothesize that the individual's *organizational role* (orgrol), which is defined by one observed variable (role), affects leadership. For example, we can ask managers to complete a self-report of their leadership, and we can ask employees to complete a performance assessment of their immediate supervisor. We suspect that managers (coded 1) will systematically rate their leadership skills and activities more favorably than their employees (coded 0) will rate their managers' leadership.

As in the multilevel factor model, the intercepts of the observed variables comprising leadership are hypothesized to vary across organizations. We must define a corresponding between-groups latent variable for each of the within-group observed variables. These variables must be scaled to $\sqrt{c}$ to ensure proper estimation. The group-level variation is modeled in terms of a latent leadership factor (2lead), which accounts for variance in the three indicators (2gov, 2orgclim, 2task). We must also define a group-level latent variable for *role* (2role). This is required because, as the reader will recall, both the pooled within-group covariance matrix and the scaled between-group matrix are used in the Group 1 specification of the whole model. Because of this, all of the observed variables in the model must appear in that matrix. Role is actually a fixed variable within the individual-level model, however, as it has no between-group variability. Similar to the MCFA example we presented, for each group-level variable, there is also a residual that represents the group-level variability remaining after the latent variables have been taken into account (Gustafsson & Stahl, 1996).

We can also introduce a group-level manifest variable (z) to explain variation in the factor mean across groups. In this example, the group-level variable is *organizational effectiveness*. In the between-group model, organizations are referred to as either ineffective (coded 0) or effective (coded 1) according to the levels of outputs they produce. The between-groups variable or variables must be related to a latent factor. We refer to this group-level latent factor as 2effect. We hypothesize that managers in effective organizations will be rated as implementing higher quality leadership (e.g., supervising tasks more effectively, involving others in governance processes) than managers in marginal or poor organizations.

The proposed model presented in Fig. 7.1 provides a simple illustration of how separate structural models (i.e., with different predictors) at both levels may be used to account for variance in leadership ratings (see Eqs. 8 to 11). The usefulness of the SEM approach is that we can account for measurement error at both levels, and we could also model separate sets of intervening variables (and, hence, provide indirect effects) between groups and within groups if we wished. Other examples of multilevel structural models are available in the *Mplus* user's guide (Muthén & Muthén, 1998).

STEPS IN CONDUCTING A MULTILEVEL SEM ANALYSIS

We use the same approach to investigating multilevel covariance structures (Muthén, 1994) that we did in chapters 5 and 6. We cannot run a single-level analysis using the S_T covariance matrix because there is a between-groups variable that does not appear in the within-groups model. So we begin with Step 2, examining whether there is variance in the intercepts of the observed variables across levels.

Examining Between-Organization Variance

In Table 7.1 we summarize the descriptive statistics and intraclass correlations for the observed variables. The variables appear to be normally distributed. For the variables comprising leadership, the intraclass correlations are .17 for governance, .22 for climate, and .25 for task organization (calculated with *Mplus*). It appears, therefore, that there is sufficient variance in our measures of leadership at the organizational level to proceed with a multilevel analysis. Role, of course, has no organizational-level variance, since it is a within-group variable only.

Specifying the Model in LISREL

As before, we must first decompose the population covariance matrix into a pooled within-groups covariance matrix and a between-groups covariance matrix. In this case, we can use STREAMS or *Mplus* to develop the necessary covariance matrices because of the unbalanced sampling design. Of course, the matrices could be developed with balanced data also.

TABLE 7.1
Descriptive Statistics and Intraclass Correlations for the Structural Model

Variables	Mean	SD	Skewness	Kurtosis	ICC[a]
Governance	3.94	1.07	−.91	.17	.17
Climate	4.23	.79	−.76	−.07	.23
Task organization	3.51	1.13	−.48	−.50	.25
Role	.13	NA	NA	NA	.00

[a]Computed with *Mplus*.

The organizational-level variables and within-organization variables are both contained in the between-group sample matrix $(\mathbf{S}_B)$ used in Group 1. As highlighted previously, we define the group-level variability in the observed variables with separate latent factors, each fixed to $\sqrt{c}$ (i.e., 2.62 for this data set). This ensures the correct interpretation of the estimates. Group-level manifest variables must also be connected to separate group-level latent variables (2effect) and have their paths fixed to the $\sqrt{c}$.

Accounting for group-level explanatory (z) variables in the within-group portion of the Group 1 model is more problematic (Hox, 1995). To compare models across groups (using the multiple-group feature) we must have the same number of variables in each matrix being compared. We must therefore include the group-level variable in the within-group covariance matrix. We can "include" a group variable in the within-group model by placing in the $\mathbf{S}_{PW}$ covariance matrix a row and a column with all zeros (i.e., to indicate that the variable has no covariance with any other variable in the within-level model) and a 1 in the diagonal (see Table 7.3). To model this group-level variable, we specify no factor loadings in the lambda y matrix (zeros) and leave its residual error variance in theta-epsilon free (which will be estimated as 1). This specification allows us to have the same number of variables in each covariance matrix and to ignore the group-level variable's presence in the within-group model (see Eq. 10).

It is actually fairly easy to implement this requirement if we specify the lambda y matrix as fixed (FI) on the model (MO) line and then just free the lambda y variables that we wish to have estimated. In our example covariance matrix defined in Group 2, this variable can be included last (see Table 7.3). Since LISREL will count the group-level variable as an observed variable, however, the program will calculate the degrees of freedom in the model incorrectly. One solution is to make the necessary corrections by hand. Because of these complications, the model will be diagnosed as inadmissible, so the analyst must set the "admissibility check" on the output (OU) line to off (AD = OFF). The reader may recall from the discussion in chapter 6 that including the observed variable means (i.e., intercepts) for multilevel models in LISREL would also produce an incorrect calculation of the degrees of freedom. The STREAMS (Gustafsson & Stahl, 1996) solution to this problem is a preestimation program that corrects the degrees of freedoms and writes the necessary correction to the output line (e.g., DF = −5).

If using LISREL to estimate the model, an easier solution than adjusting the fit indices by hand is to figure the discrepancy in the degrees of freedom and place this correction in the output line of the LISREL program. The degrees of freedom will be off by the number of variables in the individual-level matrix, so with five variables in the sample matrix, the degrees of freedom for the within model will be off by 5. For example, using the formula for calculating the degrees of freedom for a conventional, one-level (e.g., considering only the individual-level model) covariance structure analysis of $p(p + 1)/2 - r$ for this model we get $30/2 - 8$ parameters = 7 degrees of freedom. With the organizational-level variable not in the matrix, however, we would have $20/2 - 8$ parameters = 2 degrees of freedom.

We can verify this result empirically by examining the pooled within-group model with and without this missing variable included in the S_{PW} matrix. It turns out in running the pooled within-groups model alone that χ^2 is unaffected by this variable's presence. For example, in Table 7.2, the χ^2 is 3.21 (with 7 df, $p = .87$, GFI = 1.0, AGFI = .99, and RMSEA = .00, $p = .98$). Without organizational effectiveness (2effect) in the matrix, χ^2 is also 3.21 (with 2 df, $p = .20$, GFI = 1.0, AGFI = .97, and RMSEA = .043, $p = .44$). The reader can see the differences in the "corrected" goodness-of-fit indices, however (Table 7.2).

Mplus produces the correct degrees of freedom for multilevel models. Moreover, it is important to note that in cases with unbalanced group sizes, the chi-square values and standard errors obtained with conventional two-group SEM are not correct (Muthén & Muthén, 1998). Another ad-

TABLE 7.2
Goodness of Fit for Within-Group Model
(With and Without Proper Degrees of Freedom)

With incorrect degrees of freedom

CHI-SQUARE WITH 7 DEGREES OF FREEDOM = 3.21 (P = 0.87)
ROOT MEAN SQUARE ERROR OF APPROXIMATION (RMSEA) = 0.0
90 PERCENT CONFIDENCE INTERVAL FOR RMSEA = (0.0 ; 0.036)
P-VALUE FOR TEST OF CLOSE FIT (RMSEA < 0.05) = 0.98
ROOT MEAN SQUARE RESIDUAL (RMR) = 0.0032
STANDARDIZED RMR = 0.015
GOODNESS OF FIT INDEX (GFI) = 1.00
ADJUSTED GOODNESS OF FIT INDEX (AGFI) = 0.99
COMPARATIVE FIT INDEX (CFI) = 1.00

With correct degrees of freedom

CHI-SQUARE WITH 2 DEGREES OF FREEDOM = 3.21 (P = 0.20)
ROOT MEAN SQUARE ERROR OF APPROXIMATION (RMSEA) = 0.043
90 PERCENT CONFIDENCE INTERVAL FOR RMSEA = (0.0 ; 0.13)
P-VALUE FOR TEST OF CLOSE FIT (RMSEA < 0.05) = 0.44
ROOT MEAN SQUARE RESIDUAL (RMR) = 0.0032
STANDARDIZED RMR = 0.015
GOODNESS OF FIT INDEX (GFI) = 1.00
ADJUSTED GOODNESS OF FIT INDEX (AGFI) = 0.97
COMPARATIVE FIT INDEX (CFI) = 1.00

vantage of *Mplus* is that it computes correct χ^2 values and standard errors in the unbalanced case (Muthén & Muthén, 1998).

Group 1: Between-Group and Within-Group Models

The LISREL program statements for the complete model are provided in Table 7.3. We must specify two groups on the data line (NG = 2) and the number of organizational units (NO = 56).

As a practical matter, using an "all y" specification in LISREL (see Jöreskog & Sörbom, 1989) simplifies the necessary programming language required. On the model (MO) line, we identify the lambda y matrix for factor loadings, the psi matrix for factor variances and covariances, the beta matrix for structural relationships between latent variables, and the theta epsilon matrix for residuals for observed variables. All are defined as fixed (FI). There are a total of five observed variables in the model (NY = 5), and we define nine latent variables (NE = 9). These can be verified by looking at Fig. 7.1.

For the within-groups portion of the model in Group 1, we free the paths connecting the observed variables to the leadership factor (LY 1,1, LY 2,1) and fix one path to 1.0 (LY 3,1) to provide a metric necessary to define the leadership factor. We also free the residuals for the observed variables comprising the leadership factor (TE 1,1, TE 2,2, and TE 3,3). The observed variable *role* is used to measure the latent factor *organizational role* (LY 4,2). Because *role* is the only variable measuring the latent factor, we must fix its loading coefficient at 1.0, and its residual variance (TE 4,4) is fixed to 0.0. This is because there is only one indicator of the latent variable, so we must accept it to be measured without error (Jöreskog & Sörbom, 1993a). To describe the structural relationship between the latent variables, we free the path between *organizational role* and *leadership* (beta 1,2). We must also account for the presence of the group-level manifest variable (organizational effectiveness) in the within-groups portion of the model (see Eq. 10). Therefore, we leave it fixed at zero and free its unique factor (TE 5,5), which is estimated as 1.0, in order for the program to analyze the model.

Recall from chapter 6 that because the between-group covariance matrix is orthogonal to the within-group matrix, the covariances between the within-group factors and the between-group factors must be specified as zero (by specifying the psi matrix as fixed on the model line). We can then free the individual factor variances (PS 1,1 and PS 2,2) but leave the factor covariance fixed (PS 2,1) because there is already a beta path defined for that relationship.

The group-level variation in the observed variables is represented by latent variables. The latent variables are related to the corresponding ob-

TABLE 7.3
LISREL Setup for the Within- and Between-Organization Model

Model for Full SEM (Between Groups)
DA NI=5 NO=56 NG=2 MA=CM
LA
'gov' 'orclim' 'taskor' 'role' 'effect'
CM
0.841245
0.870453   1.24732
0.880265   1.20164   1.46499
0.034825   0.030645   0.059923   0.0220053
0.554497   0.644307   0.638800   0.0127616   1.74075
MO NY=5 NE=9 LY=FU,FI PS=SY,FI TE=SY,FI BE=FU,FI
LE
'lead' 'orgrol' '2lead' '2orgeff' '2gov' '2orclim'
'2taskor' '2role' '2effect'
VA 1.000 LY(3,1)
FR LY(1,1) LY(2,1)
FI LY(1,5) LY(2,6) LY(3,7) LY(4,8) LY(5,9)
VA 2.616 LY(1,5) LY(2,6) LY(3,7) LY(4,8) LY(5,9)
FI LY(4,2)
VA 1.0 LY(4,2)
FR PS(1,1) PS(2,2) PS(3,3) PS(4,4) PS(5,5)
FR PS(6,6) PS(7,7) PS(8,8) PS(9,8)
FI PS(9,9)
VA .000 PS(9,9)
FR TE(1,1) TE(2,2) TE(3,3)
FI TE(4,4)
VA .000 TE(4,4)
FR BE(1,2)
VA 1.000 BE(6,3)
FR BE(3,4) BE(5,3) BE(7,3)
FI BE(9,4)
VA 1.0 BE(9,4)
VA .8 LY(1,1) LY(2,1)
VA .3 PS(1,1) PS(2,2) PS(3,3) PS(4,4)
VA .02 PS(5,5) PS(6,6) PS(7,7)
VA −.016 PS(8,8)
VA .1 TE(1,1) TE(2,2) TE(3,3)
VA .4 BE(1,2) BE(3,4)
VA .8 BE(5,3) BE(7,3)
OU
DA NI=5 NO=328 NG=2 MA=CM
LA
'gov' 'orclim' 'taskor' 'role' 'effect'
CM
0.354697
0.281169   0.413307
0.28202   0.365575   0.457480
0.0343621   0.0608538   0.0639287   0.131548
0.0000000   0.0000000   0.0000000   0.0000000   1.00

(Continued)

TABLE 7.3
(Continued)

MO NY=5 NE=9 LY=FU,FI PS=SY,FI TE=SY,FI BE=FU,FI
LE
'lead' 'orgrol' '2lead' '2orgeff' '2gov' '2orclim'
'2taskor' '2role' '2effect'
VA 1.000 LY(3,1)
FR LY(1,1) LY(2,1)
FI LY(4,2)
VA 1.0 LY(4,2)
FR PS(1,1) PS(2,2)
FR TE(1,1) TE(2,2) TE(3,3)
FI TE(4,4)
VA .000 TE(4,4)
VA 1.000 TE(5,5)
FR BE(1,2)
VA .8 LY(1,1) LY(2,1)
VA .3 PS(1,1) PS(2,2)
VA .14 TE(1,1) TE(2,2) TE(3,3)
VA .4 BE(1,2)
EQ LY(1,1,1) LY(2,1,1)
EQ LY(1,2,1) LY(2,2,1)
EQ LY(1,4,2) LY(2,4,2)
EQ PS(1,1,1) PS(2,1,1)
EQ PS(1,2,2) PS(2,2,2)
EQ TE(1,1,1) TE(2,1,1)
EQ TE(1,2,2) TE(2,2,2)
EQ TE(1,3,3) TE(2,3,3)
EQ TE(1,4,4) TE(2,4,4)
EQ BE(1,1,2) BE(2,1,2)
OU ME=ML AD=OFF MI SC IT=200 XM NS DF=−5

---

served variables by freeing the lambda y paths (LY 1,5, LY 2,6, LY 3,7, LY 4,8, and LY 5,9) and then assigning them a value fixed to the square root of c (2.616) that allows them to be interpreted properly. Note that the group-level manifest variable must also be assigned the same fixed value. A group-level latent variable (2lead) is hypothesized to account for variance in the group-level leadership variables. We free the necessary beta parameters (BE 5,3 and BE 7,3) and must set one of the beta paths to 1.0 (BE 6,3) to provide a metric for this latent variable. We also must specify the relationship between 2effect and its latent variable orgeff by fixing the path (BE 9,4) to 1.0. It is then necessary to fix the variance of the residual for 2effect to 0.0 (PS 9,9). We then free the necessary psi diagonals (PS 3,3 to PS 8,8) and the covariance between 2role and 2effect (PS 9,8).

The reader can also see that the initial estimates for the free parameters in Group 1 were set to several different values (VA). For example, the initial estimates in the psi matrix are quite varied. In practice, these can be difficult to obtain. As in chapter 6, we also had to experiment with these estimates. For the lambda y parameters we used .8 (figuring that the observed variables should have high loadings on the factor). For psi we used .3, for theta epsilon we used .14, and for beta we used .2 (i.e., hypothesizing a weak effect between orgrol and lead). In practice, we got the model to converge by estimating the individual model alone (see next section). These estimates were then placed as initial estimates in the full model.

Group 2: Within-Group Model

The Group 2 specification is relatively easy because the required paths for the within-group model have already been defined previously in Group 1. We just "copy" the necessary within-group parameters from the Group 1 specification (i.e., the within-group lambda y, beta, psi, and theta epsilon parameters). Because the S_B matrix in Group 1 contains both a within-group and a between-group component, we must only add the necessary equality constraints to ensure the same within-group model is tested in Group 2.

On the output line we correct for the degrees of freedom (DF = −5) and remove the automatic start values (NS). We also add a statement to provide the set of standardized solutions (SC) in LISREL. Because we removed the automatic start values, we must provide initial estimates to help the computer converge on a solution. As noted previously, this is often a somewhat challenging task for multilevel modeling with SEM software. Setting starting values was facilitated by using STREAMS and incorporating the start values from each previous model estimated until a suitable solution was obtained.

We actually had to begin by estimating a within-group model using ULS to obtain some initial estimates. We then used those estimates and switched to maximum likelihood (ML) estimation. The fit of the within-group ML model was presented previously in Table 7.3 (with the corrected degrees of freedom). To help convergence we can also set the iterations to a higher number (IT = 200). Finally, because of the group-level variable's presence in the within-group model, the "admissibility check" must also be turned off (AD = OFF) on the output line.

Output From the Complete Multilevel SEM

Once again, there is a huge amount of output produced by this model specification—most of it not relevant to the analysis that we conduct. If the STREAMS program is used, there is no need to obtain the standardized output (using the SC statement) in LISREL, as STREAMS will calculate the standardized estimates and summarize them with a couple of pages of output. We highlight some of the necessary program output. The combined model appears to fit the data quite well, as shown in Table 7.4. The overall fit of the model with "corrected" degrees of freedom is good (χ^2 = 12.87, df = 7, p = .075, GFI = 1.0, CFI = .99, RMSEA = .060, p = .45). Remember, however, that these indices are approximate only.

It is important to note that one typical characteristic of multilevel SEM is that there are differing amounts of information available on the two levels. For example, we have 328 individuals contributing to the calculation of the within-group model estimates, and only 56 groups in the between-groups model. Such sample size differences can potentially cause difficulty in interpreting the goodness-of-fit indices. For example, from Table 7.4, the between-groups model contributes almost 71% of the overall model error (χ^2 = 9.35), whereas the within-group model only contributes about 29% (χ^2 = 3.53).

In Fig. 7.2 we summarize the total variance standardization produced with the STREAMS program. We can see that the items load substantially on the within-group and between-group leadership factor. This suggests that the factor accounts for substantial within- and between-group variability in the observed variables. Moreover, we see that organizational role has a small, but statistically significant, effect on leadership ratings (.26), suggesting that managers do rate their leadership higher than their employees rate it. At the organizational level, organizational effectiveness also has a substantial effect on between-group variability in leadership ratings (.50).

TABLE 7.4
Goodness-of-Fit Indices

For the Group 1 Model Only

GOODNESS OF FIT STATISTICS
CONTRIBUTION TO CHI-SQUARE = 9.35
PERCENTAGE CONTRIBUTION TO CHI-SQUARE = 70.65

For Both Models

GOODNESS OF FIT STATISTICS
CHI-SQUARE WITH 7 DEGREES OF FREEDOM = 12.87 (P = 0.075)
CONTRIBUTION TO CHI-SQUARE = 3.53
PERCENTAGE CONTRIBUTION TO CHI-SQUARE = 29.35
ROOT MEAN SQUARE ERROR OF APPROXIMATION (RMSEA) = 0.060
90 PERCENT CONFIDENCE INTERVAL FOR RMSEA = (0.0 ; 0.12)
P-VALUE FOR TEST OF CLOSE FIT (RMSEA < 0.05) = 0.45
ROOT MEAN SQUARE RESIDUAL (RMR) = 0.0040
STANDARDIZED RMR = 0.015
GOODNESS OF FIT INDEX (GFI) = 1.00
COMPARATIVE FIT INDEX (CFI) = 0.99

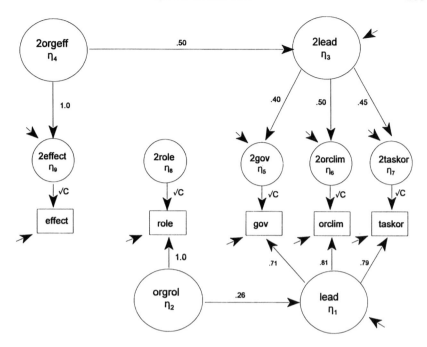

FIG. 7.2.   Standardized STREAMS parameter estimates.

In Table 7.5 we also present the LISREL unstandardized estimates and the within-group completely standardized solution. As in chapter 6, the reader will note that this standardization is quite different from the STREAMS standardization in Fig. 7.2 (i.e., factor loadings and errors), but the standardized structural parameters are the same. For example, in the LISREL standardization the within-group loadings range from .49 to .51. We can also note that organizational role has a weak relationship to leadership (.26) and accounts for 7% of the variance in leadership that exists within organizations (i.e., determined by looking at the squared multiple correlation for the structural relations).

At the organizational level, we also see that the between-level indicators load well on the latent leadership factor. Remember that the LISREL standardized loadings do not reflect the variance contributed at the group level by the observed variables. Organizational effectiveness is moderately related to leadership (.50) and accounts for 25% of its variation at the organizational level. Given the variety of information and the sensibility of the estimates, therefore, we can accept the model as a plausible representation of the data.

We can also determine how much of the factor variance is between levels. The unstandardized psi matrix provides this information. The within-group variance for leadership (lead) is .35. The between-level variance for

TABLE 7.5
Selected LISREL Output

Group: Between
Number of Iterations = 18

LISREL ESTIMATES (MAXIMUM LIKELIHOOD)

    LAMBDA-Y

	lead	orgrol	2lead	2orgeff	2gov	2orclim
gov	0.76	—	—	—	2.62	—
	(0.04)					
	18.42					
orclim	0.98	—	—	—	—	2.62
	(0.04)					
	23.63					
taskor	1.00	—	—	—	—	—
role	—	1.00	—	—	—	—
effect	—	—	—	—	—	—

    LAMBDA-Y

	2taskor	2role	2effect
gov	—	—	—
orclim	—	—	—
taskor	2.62	—	—
role	—	2.62	—
effect	—	—	2.62

    BETA

	lead	orgrol	2lead	2orgeff	2gov	2orclim
lead	—	0.43	—	—	—	—
		(0.08)				
		5.13				
orgrol	—	—	—	—	—	—
2lead	—	—	—	0.36	—	—
				(0.10)		
				3.56		
2orgeff	—	—	—	—	—	—
2gov	—	—	0.71	—	—	—
			(0.08)			
			8.66			
2orclim	—	—	1.00	—	—	—
2taskor	—	—	0.95	—	—	—
			(0.10)			
			9.80			
2role	—	—	—	—	—	—
2effect	—	—	—	1.00	—	—

(Continued)

TABLE 7.5
(Continued)

PSI

lead	orgrol	2lead	2orgeff	2gov	2orclim
0.35	0.13	0.10	0.25	0.01	0.00
(0.03)	(0.01)	(0.03)	(0.05)	(0.01)	(0.01)
10.13	12.97	3.48	5.24	1.22	0.37

PSI

2taskor	2role	2effect
0.02	−0.02	—
(0.01)	(0.00)	
2.34	−10.13	

SQUARED MULTIPLE CORRELATIONS FOR STRUCTURAL EQUATIONS

lead	orgrol	2lead	2orgeff	2gov	2orclim
0.07	—	0.25	—	0.89	0.98

SQUARED MULTIPLE CORRELATIONS FOR STRUCTURAL EQUATIONS

2taskor	2role	2effect
0.85	—	1.00

THETA-EPS

gov	orclim	taskor	role	effect
0.14	0.05	0.09	—	—
(0.01)	(0.01)	(0.01)		
11.09	4.77	6.93		

SQUARED MULTIPLE CORRELATIONS FOR Y-VARIABLES

gov	orclim	taskor	role	effect
0.84	0.96	0.94	1.00	1.00

TI Project: lead. Categorization variable: None   . Group: Between
WITHIN GROUP COMPLETELY STANDARDIZED SOLUTION

LAMBDA-Y

	lead	orgrol	2lead	2orgeff	2gov	2orclim
gov	0.49	—	—	—	0.77	—
orclim	0.51	—	—	—	—	0.84
taskor	0.51	—	—	—	—	—
role	—	2.36	—	—	—	—
effect	—	—	—	—	—	—

(Continued)

TABLE 7.5
(*Continued*)

LAMBDA-Y

	2taskor	2role	2effect
gov	—	—	—
orclim	—	—	—
taskor	0.83	—	—
role	—	17.11	—
effect	—	—	1.00

BETA

	lead	orgrol	2lead	2orgeff	2gov	2orclim
lead	—	0.26	—	—	—	—
orgrol	—	—	—	—	—	—
2lead	—	—	—	0.50	—	—
2orgeff	—	—	—	—	—	—
2gov	—	—	0.94	—	—	—
2orclim	—	—	0.99	—	—	—
2taskor	—	—	0.92	—	—	—
2role	—	—	—	—	—	—
2effect	—	—	—	1.00	—	—

THETA-EPS

gov	orclim	taskor	role	effect
0.16	0.04	0.06	—	—

TI Project: lead. Categorization variable: None   . Group: Within
Number of Iterations = 18
LISREL ESTIMATES (MAXIMUM LIKELIHOOD)

LAMBDA-Y

	lead	orgrol	2lead	2orgeff	2gov	2orclim
gov	0.76	—	—	—	—	—
	(0.04)					
	18.42					
orclim	0.98	—	—	—	—	—
	(0.04)					
	23.63					
taskor	1.00	—	—	—	—	—
role	—	1.00	—	—	—	—
effect	—	—	—	—	—	—

LAMBDA-Y

	2taskor	2role	2effect
gov	—	—	—
orclim	—	—	—
taskor	—	—	—
role	—	—	—
effect	—	—	—

TABLE 7.5
(*Continued*)

BETA

	lead	orgrol	2lead	2orgeff	2gov	2orclim
lead	—	0.43	—	—	—	—
		(0.08)				
		5.13				

PSI

	lead	orgrol	2lead	2orgeff	2gov	2orclim
	0.35	0.13	—	—	—	—
	(0.03)	(0.01)				
	10.13	12.97				

PSI

2taskor	2role	2effect
—	—	—

SQUARED MULTIPLE CORRELATIONS FOR STRUCTURAL EQUATIONS

lead	orgrol	2lead	2orgeff	2gov	2orclim
0.07	—	—	—	—	—

THETA-EPS

gov	orclim	taskor	role	effect
0.14	0.05	0.09	—	1.00
(0.01)	(0.01)	(0.01)		
11.09	4.77	6.93		

SQUARED MULTIPLE CORRELATIONS FOR Y-VARIABLES

gov	orclim	taskor	role	effect
0.61	0.87	0.81	1.00	—

Group: allW
WITHIN GROUP COMPLETELY STANDARDIZED SOLUTION

LAMBDA-Y

	lead	orgrol	2lead	2orgeff	2gov	2orclim
gov	0.78	—	—	—	—	—
orclim	0.93	—	—	—	—	—
taskor	0.90	—	—	—	—	—
role	—	1.00	—	—	—	—
effect	—	—	—	—	—	—

(*Continued*)

TABLE 7.5
(Continued)

BETA

	lead	orgrol	2lead	2orgeff	2gov	2orclim
lead	—	0.26	—	—	—	—
orgrol	—	—	—	—	—	—
2lead	—	—	—	—	—	—
2orgeff	—	—	—	—	—	—
2gov	—	—	—	—	—	—
2orclim	—	—	—	—	—	—
2taskor	—	—	—	—	—	—
2role	—	—	—	—	—	—
2effect	—	—	—	—	—	—

leadership (2lead) is .10. The factor intraclass correlation is $(.10/[.10 + .35])$, or about 22%. Once again, because of the relatively small amount of measurement error, especially at the within-organization level, the factor intraclass correlation is about the same as the intraclass correlations of the observed variables (.17 to .25) in Table 7.1.

We also estimated the model with *Mplus*. The input statements are provided in Table 7.6, along with the χ^2 value (12.93, $p = .074$, for 7 df). Similar to our previous analysis, the variance accounted for in leadership at the organizational level was 26%, and the variance in leadership accounted for at the individual level was 7%. It should be noted that this model was estimated with Muthén's quasimaximum likelihood estimator because of the unbalanced group sizes.

Despite the considerable problems that must be encountered in setting up and running the model, the multilevel SEM provides some interesting information about relationships at each level, as well as information about the measurement of the leadership factor that could not be gleaned from a simple multilevel regression analysis. For example, to run this model as a multilevel regression (e.g., see Heck & Marcoulides, 1996), we would have to use three separate models (i.e., one for each variable that comprises the leadership factor) if employing only a two-level model.

As we demonstrate in chapter 8, however, it is also possible to specify this particular model as a three-level multivariate model, using the level-1 model to estimate the individual "true score" variability on the leadership measures. In the three-level multivariate model and the multilevel SEM, all of these interrelationships are captured in a simultaneous analysis. The advantage of the multilevel SEM analysis is that it gives us a bit more information about how well each observed variable contributes to defining

TABLE 7.6
Mplus Input Instructions and Chi-Square
Fit Index for Multilevel Structural Model

TITLE:	Two-level SEM example
DATA:	FILE IS C:\Mplus\book\semmod7.txt;
VARIABLE:	Names are group effect gov orgclim taskorg role; CLUSTER IS group; BETWEEN = effect;
ANALYSIS:	TYPE = General Twolevel; ESTIMATOR IS MLM;
Model:	%BETWEEN% blead by gov*1 orgclim*.8 taskorg*.8; blead on effect*.4; blead@.1; %WITHIN% lead by gov*1 orgclim*.8 taskorg*.8; lead on role*.4; lead@.3;
OUTPUT:	SAMPSTAT STANDARDIZED RESIDUAL TECH1;

Fit Index: chi-square (7 df) = 12.93, p = .074

leadership effectiveness, both within and across groups. In this manner, it gives us another powerful tool with which to test theoretical models.

EXERCISE

In this exercise we wish to add an organizational-level predictor to our model of leaders' roles in defining organizational improvement processes from the example at the end of chapter 6. We add the variable *organizational effectiveness* as a level-2 predictor of leadership. The new between-groups covariance matrix for Group 1 and labels are:

LA
'needs' 'goals' 'prodev' 'train' 'effect'
CM
2.17
1.21 1.37

```
1.83   1.27   2.41
1.66   1.37   1.55   2.83
0.50   0.28   0.47   0.45   1.75
```

The corresponding pooled within-groups matrix for Group 2 and labels are:

```
LA
'needs' 'goals' 'prodev' 'train' 'effect'
CM
1.23
0.29   0.51
0.41   0.25   0.89
0.45   0.26   0.57   1.37
0.00   0.00   0.00   0.00   1.00
```

You may wish to use the following labels for the latent variables:

```
LE
'tasks' '2tasks' '2needs' '2goals' '2prodev' '2train' '2effect'
```

Specify and test the new model. Notice that you can add 2effect to the model as a seventh latent variable (its residual is psi 7,7). This means the rest of the model can be specified as before. You should be able to use those estimates from the output as start values to get the program running. The model should be set up as before. You will have to define *effect* as loading on 2effect (with its loading set to 2.616 also). Further, you will define the path between the two latent variables at the organizational level.

Other than these changes, the rest of the model should stay the same as the example in the previous chapter. The starting values may be a little trickier this time. You may have to look at the unstandardized estimates in the factor model and use those as starting values for each parameter. Because *effect* exists only at the organizational level, however, remember how it must be defined in the Group 2 matrix. Also, note that the degrees of freedom calculated by LISREL will be incorrect. As there are five variables in the matrix, the degrees of freedom should be off by 5 (similar to the example earlier in chap. 7). You can correct this by putting DF = −5 on the output line. Note that if you calculated the five organizational-level means, too (i.e., designated as "AL" in LISREL), the degrees of freedom will be off by 10.

You may wish to determine to what extent organizational effectiveness determines whether supervisors were rated as implementing the changes.

Output

Parameter Estimates

WITHIN GROUP COMPLETELY STANDARDIZED SOLUTION (Read from Group 1 and Group 2)

LAMBDA-Y (within groups)

	tasks	2tasks	2needs	2goals	2prodev	2train	STREAMS STANDARDIZATION
needs	0.61	—	—	—	—	—	.58
goals	0.58	—	—	—	—	—	.51
prodev	0.66	—	—	—	—	—	.58
train	0.57	—	—	—	—	—	.53
effect	—	—	—	—	—	—	

LAMBDA-Y

	2effect
needs	—
goals	—
prodev	—
train	—
effect	—

BETA (between groups)

	tasks	2tasks	2needs	2goals	2prodev	2train	STREAMS STANDARDIZATION
tasks	—	—	—	—	—	—	
2tasks	—	—	—	—	—	—	
2needs	—	1.20	—	—	—	—	.38
2goals	—	0.91	—	—	—	—	.40
2prodev	—	0.94	—	—	—	—	.43
2train	—	0.83	—	—	—	—	.32
2effect	—	—	—	—	—	—	

BETA

	2effect
tasks	—
2tasks	0.30
2needs	—
2goals	—
2prodev	—
2train	—
2effect	—

THETA-EPS (within groups)

	needs	goals	prodev	train	effect
needs	0.63				
goals	—	0.67			
prodev	—	—	0.57		
train	—	—	0.12	0.67	
effect	—	—	—	—	—

PSI

tasks	2tasks
0.46	0.18
(0.10)	(0.06)
4.61	3.06

GOODNESS OF FIT INDICES
CHI-SQUARE WITH 6 DEGREES OF FREEDOM = 10.01 (P = 0.12)
ROOT MEAN SQUARE ERROR OF APPROXIMATION (RMSEA) = 0.059
90 PERCENT CONFIDENCE INTERVAL FOR RMSEA = (0.0 ; 0.12)
P-VALUE FOR TEST OF CLOSE FIT (RMSEA < 0.05) = 0.56
ROOT MEAN SQUARE RESIDUAL (RMR) = 0.0084
GOODNESS OF FIT INDEX (GFI) = 1.00
COMPARATIVE FIT INDEX (CFI) = 0.99

LISREL Model Statements

One factor model (between)
DA NI=5 NO=56 NG=2 MA=CM
LA
'needs' 'goals' 'prodev' 'train' 'effect'
CM
2.17
1.21   1.37
1.83   1.27   2.41
1.66   1.37   1.55   2.83
0.50   0.28   0.47   0.45   1.75
MO NY=5 NE=7 LY=FU,FI PS=SY,FI TE=SY,FI BE=FU,FI
LE
'tasks' '2tasks' '2needs' '2goals' '2prodev' '2train' '2effect'
VA 1.000 LY(1,1)
FR LY(2,1) LY(3,1) LY(4,1)
FI LY(1,3)
VA 2.616 LY(1,3)
FI LY(2,4)
VA 2.616 LY(2,4)
FI LY(3,5)
VA 2.616 LY(3,5)

```
FI LY(4,6)
VA 2.616 LY(4,6)
FI LY(5,7)
VA 2.616 LY(5,7)
FR PS(1,1) PS(2,2) PS(3,3) PS(4,4) PS(5,5)
FR PS(6,6) PS(7,7)
FR TE(1,1) TE(2,2) TE(3,3) TE(4,3) TE(4,4)
VA 1.000 BE(3,2)
FR BE(2,7) BE(4,2) BE(5,2) BE(6,2)
VA .596 LY(2,1)
VA .909 LY(3,1)
VA .991 LY(4,1)
VA .460 PS(1,1)
VA .193 PS(2,2)
VA -.056 PS(3,3)
VA .019 PS(4,4)
VA .027 PS(5,5)
VA .069 PS(6,6)
VA .700 PS(7,7)
VA .771 TE(1,1)
VA .347 TE(2,2)
VA .502 TE(3,3)
VA .132 TE(4,3)
VA .911 TE(4,4)
VA .700 BE(2,7)
VA .739 BE(4,2)
VA 1.028 BE(5,2)
VA .911 BE(6,2)
OU ME=ML AD=OFF MI SC NS DF=-5
one factor model (within)
DA NI=5 NO=328 NG=2 MA=CM
LA
'needs' 'goals' 'prodev' 'train' 'effect'
CM
1.23
0.29   0.51
0.41   0.25   0.89
0.45   0.26   0.57   1.37
0.00   0.00   0.00   0.00   1.00
MO NY=5 NE=7 LY=FU,FI PS=SY,FI TE=SY,FI BE=FU,FI
LE
'tasks' '2tasks' '2needs' '2goals' '2prodev' '2train' '2effect'
VA 1.000 LY(1,1)
FR LY(2,1) LY(3,1) LY(4,1)
FR PS(1,1)
FR TE(1,1) TE(2,2) TE(3,3) TE(4,3) TE(4,4)
VA 1.000 TE(5,5)
```

```
VA .596 LY(2,1)
VA .909 LY(3,1)
VA .991 LY(4,1)
VA .460 PS(1,1)
VA .771 TE(1,1)
VA .347 TE(2,2)
VA .502 TE(3,3)
VA .132 TE(4,3)
VA .911 TE(4,4)
EQ LY(1,2,1) LY(2,2,1)
EQ LY(1,3,1) LY(2,3,1)
EQ LY(1,4,1) LY(2,4,1)
EQ PS(1,1,1) PS(2,1,1)
EQ TE(1,1,1) TE(2,1,1)
EQ TE(1,2,2) TE(2,2,2)
EQ TE(1,3,3) TE(2,3,3)
EQ TE(1,4,3) TE(2,4,3)
EQ TE(1,4,4) TE(2,4,4)
OU ME=ML AD=OFF MI SC NS DF=−5
```

Chapter 8

Extending Multilevel Techniques

In this final chapter, we give some consideration of how multilevel techniques might be applied to the multivariate investigation of level-1 outcomes using HLM. We could also estimate this type of model using the new multilevel regression program in LISREL 8.30. We then tie up a few loose ends from our presentation of multilevel regression and multilevel covariance structure models. First, we present a brief overview of the multivariate form of HLM, focusing specifically on our previous leadership effectiveness model presented in chapter 7. Next, in the context of the organizational research problems that we have presented in this book, we comment on the usefulness and shortcomings of multilevel regression models, multilevel factor analysis, and multilevel structural equation models. Finally, we offer some brief comments about likely future applications of these techniques in educational and organizational research.

FROM SINGLE OUTCOME TO MULTIVARIATE OUTCOME

Our previous examples have examined two-level multilevel models. These models have focused on individuals nested in organizations. These analyses help us address a variety of methodological problems and research interests including multiple units of analysis, the investigation of the differential impact of important predictors across units (i.e., slopes-as-outcomes models), and the incorporation of measurement error into the model. We can extend the two-level model to a three-level model, which might be useful in examining individuals (level 1) nested in groups (level 2) nested in organizations (level 3). The three-level model partitions the total variability in the outcome into its three components: individuals within groups; groups within organizations; and among organizations. From this, we can determine the proportion of variation that is within subunits, among subunits within organizations, and among organizations (see Bryk & Raudenbush, 1992, or Jöreskog & Sörbom, 1999, for a detailed description of how to specify three-level models) and then develop a multilevel model of within-level and cross-level predictors that accounts for this variance.

A second use of the three-level model is longitudinal studies of individual processes within organizational settings that change over time. For example, to examine the growth or change of individuals who are nested in organizations, we can include three or more measures of individuals over time (called growth trajectories) at level 1, the variation in growth parameters among individuals within an organization at level 2, and the variation among organizations at level 3 (for further discussions of growth models see Bryk & Raudenbush, 1992; Goldstein, 1995a; McArdle, 1998; McArdle & Hamagami, 1996; Rogosa & Saner, 1995; Willett & Sayer, 1996).

We focus our attention on a third useful application of the three-level regression framework. This is the situation where an investigator wishes to examine several organizational or educational variables simultaneously. This is an example of a multilevel, multivariate model. Instead of only one outcome measure, as developed in chapter 4, there could be several outcomes of interest. These could be several different measures of organizational climate, productivity, or several student achievement outcomes (e.g., reading, math, and language test scores). Previously, organizational measures such as climate or culture were often constructed by combining several survey items to create scales. These measures will likely have different measurement properties, however. For example, correlations between the scales will be attenuated by measurement error to varying degrees across levels of the analysis. Besides measurement error, several outcome measures will likely be correlated.

As we suggested in the last chapter, one alternative way to examine clusters of items is to create a latent variable (i.e., construct) consisting of several observed indicators. This approach was demonstrated in chapter 6 through using multilevel factor analysis. In chapter 7, we further examined the within-group and between-group variability in a construct as a function of different sets of explanatory variables.

We can incorporate the investigation of multiple outcome measures into a three-level multivariate regression model. At level 1, we can combine several items to make a construct. At this level a measurement model is defined, which incorporates estimates of the *true score* variance for the constructs—that is, variance remaining after error variance has been removed. The individual-specific error term for each construct allows us to make more refined comparisons of effects across groups. This is important, for example, in assessing outcomes such as student learning accurately, because we would expect errors of measurement in these types of scores. In single-outcome models, such as those presented in chapter 4, we do not have the ability to incorporate such estimates of measurement error.

Another reason for using this type of model is that many organizational outcomes that we might be interested in investigating are not independent of one another (e.g., math, reading, and language outcomes, ratings of various dimensions of leadership). We therefore need to develop models that can incorporate the correlation between such outcomes by providing a test of regression coefficients from dependent samples of scores, as opposed to running a series of separate multilevel regression models.

We keep this introduction to the use of multivariate outcome models in HLM relatively simple, in order to focus on the usefulness of the technique in doing educational and organizational research. More extended treatments can be found in Supovitz and Brennan (1997), Barnett, Marshall, Raudenbush, and Brennan (1993), and Raudenbush, Rowan, and Kang (1991).

MATHEMATICAL RELATIONSHIPS UNDERLYING A THREE-LEVEL MODEL

It is customary to use slightly different notation in developing three-level models with multivariate outcomes and measurement error. We develop the model used in the last chapter for a three-level multivariate regression model. At level 1, we define the measurement model for the leadership latent variable consisting of three indicators (*governance, climate/culture,* and *task organization*). We could actually model several latent variables if we wished (see Bryk & Raudenbush, 1992, for further discussion). The level-1 model represents variation among the item scores within each individual. The general level-1 model may be written as

$$Y_{ijk} = \sum_{p} \pi_{pjk} a_{pijk} + e_{ijk} \qquad (1)$$

where Y_{ijk} is the observed score for the multivariate leadership outcome i for employee j in organization k, and π_{pjk} is the latent true score for individual j in organization k on construct p (i.e., leadership). Note that a_{pijk} takes on a value of 1 if item i measures construct p and 0 otherwise, for constructs $p = 1, \ldots, n$ (which allows the researcher to define several constructs). The error term e_{ijk} represents the error for individual j in organization k for the leadership outcome i.

At level 2, we specify a model that has individual-level variables that are hypothesized to affect the assessment of leadership. These could be variables like gender, experience, or organizational role. In this case, we use only organizational role. As the reader will recall, this is a dichotomous variable, coded 0 (employee) and 1 (manager). The level-2 model describes the distribution of the true scores (π_p) across individuals within organizations. In this case, we have only one leadership construct, so the model can be written as:

$$\pi_{1jk} = B_{10k} + B_{11k}X_{1jk} + r_{1jk} \qquad (2)$$

where B_{10k} is the true score mean on construct p for organization k, B_{11k} is a level-2 coefficient predicting the true score estimate, X_{1jk} is the level-2 predictor (role) for individual j in organization k, and r_{1jk} is the level-2 random coefficient for individual j in organization k.

At level 3, we represent organizational-level variables. In this example, we use one organizational-level predictor, organizational effectiveness, coded 0 (not effective) and 1 (effective). Of course, we could have other variables including size, structure, and so forth. We could model any of the level-2 intercepts and slopes, using the level-3 predictors, but in this case we are only interested in modeling the intercept of the level-2 equation. The level-3 equation for the leadership intercept is represented as

$$B_{10k} = \gamma_{100} + \gamma_{101}W_{1K} + u_{10k} \qquad (3)$$

where γ_{100} is a level-3 intercept, γ_{101} is a coefficient predicting the level-2 intercept (B_{10k}) for the organization-level predictor *effectiveness* (W_{1K}), and u_{10k} is the level-3 random effect. As suggested, this basic model could be modified to include additional predictors at the individual and group levels.

Setting Up and Estimating the Model

Files needed for the creation of the three-level SSM file in HLM differ slightly from those used to create the two-level SSM file. Three input files are needed, one for each level of analysis. The structure of the level-1 file is quite different from that used in the two-level example in chapter 4. Rather than array the three leadership variables for each individual across columns in the level-1 file, each individual-level observation is represented by three rows. For each observation, the rows will consist of an alphanumeric organizational identification number, an alphanumeric subject identification number, and one of the three leadership variables. The number of records in this level-1 input file will equal three times the number of observations (i.e., individuals).

The level-2 input file contains identifiers and the individual-level predictor *role*. The file is structured very much like the level-1 file in the two-level example presented in chapter 4. Each observation is represented by one row, which is comprised of an alphanumeric organizational identification number, an alphanumeric subject identification number, and *role*.

At level-3, the input file defines the organizations in the sample. Each organization is represented by one row in this file. Each row is comprised of an alphanumeric organizational identification number and the organizational-level predictor *organizational effectiveness* (see Bryk et al., 1996, for further information about defining these input files). Using these three input files, we create the three-level SSM file within HLM. As in the two-level example, a number of output files are generated. One of these files, HLM2SSM.STS, captures preliminary descriptive statistics for variables at each level. The contents of this file are displayed in Table 8.1.

We provide the test of this model in Table 8.2. There is one within-organization predictor of leadership at level-2 (*role*), and one between-organization predictor at level-3 (*organizational effectiveness*) to explain variance in the level-2 intercepts. There is consistency in findings from our structural model in chapter 7. More specifically, the unstandardized LISREL coefficient for organizational role on leadership was .43, and for organizational effectiveness on leadership it was .36. Similarly, the HLM coefficients are .43 and .35, respectively.

TABLE 8.1
Descriptive Statistics for the Three-Level Leadership Model

LEVEL-1 DESCRIPTIVE STATISTICS

VARIABLE NAME	N	MEAN	SD	MINIMUM	MAXIMUM
LEAD	1152	3.84	0.74	1.17	5.00

LEVEL-2 DESCRIPTIVE STATISTICS

VARIABLE NAME	N	MEAN	SD	MINIMUM	MAXIMUM
ROLE	384	0.13	0.34	0.00	1.00

LEVEL-3 DESCRIPTIVE STATISTICS

VARIABLE NAME	N	MEAN	SD	MINIMUM	MAXIMUM
EFFECT_1	56	0.52	0.50	0.00	1.00

TABLE 8.2
Final Statistics for the Three-Level Model

Fixed Effect	Coefficient	Standard Error	t-Ratio	p-Value
For INTRCPT1, P0				
For INTRCPT2, B00				
INTRCPT3, G000	3.870977	0.041493	93.292	.000
EFFECT_1, G001	0.348944	0.077810	4.485	.000
For ROLE, B01				
INTRCPT3, G010	0.434501	0.096250	4.514	.000

Random Effect	Standard Deviation	Variance Component	df	Chi-Square	p-Value
Final estimation of level-1 and level-2 variance components:					
INTRCPT1, R0	0.49431	0.24434	272	1167.474	.000
level-1, E	0.40388	0.16312			
Final estimation of level-3 variance components:					
INTRCPT1/INTRCPT2, U0	0.22449	0.05040	48	90.595	.000

Essentially, the three-level multivariate regression model and the two-level SEM both correct the structural relationships for measurement error. As we observed in the last chapter, the error structure can be quite different at each level. For example, at the individual level, reliability depends on the number of items in a construct and the relative interitem agreement (Bryk & Raudenbush, 1992). At the organization level, reliability depends more on the number of individuals sampled per unit and the level of agreement within groups. The three-level model can also provide empirical Bayes (shrinkage) estimates of random coefficients at levels 2 and 3 (Bryk & Raudenbush, 1992).

We can also estimate the true variance that is between groups [.05/(.16 + .05)], after correcting for measurement (about 24%). This is only slightly different from the 22% between-group factor variance reported in the last chapter, owing to a couple of organizational units being dropped from the HLM analysis due to insufficient within-group variation. The structural model presented in chapter 7 and the three-level multivariate regression model can therefore be seen to give very similar estimates. We note in passing that the three-level multivariate formulation would also allow the analyst to examine between-group variation in role-leadership slopes.

Synthesizing the Methods

We hope that the reader can see that there is considerable similarity in the methods we demonstrated to investigate multilevel data structures. The multilevel regression and SEM approaches and models presented in this book provide an introduction to some of the uses of multilevel models within educational and organizational research settings. How are these approaches different? One view (Raudenbush, 1998) suggests that the multilevel regression approach (e.g., HLM) allows considerable flexibility in examining data structures for a limited class of models (e.g., random coefficients), while the SEM approach (i.e., latent variables, simultaneous equations both within and between groups) offers a wide variety of models for a more limited set of data structures. In the past, this distinction was partly a function of the commercial software available. Currently, attention is being given to expanding the types of multilevel models that can be estimated (e.g., nonlinear structural models, nonnormal probabilistic models, simultaneous equations models between groups, models with missing data). These models can use data distributions other than normal (e.g., binary data, ordinal data). With software for estimating multilevel models developing rapidly, as Raudenbush argues, a more complete view for understanding the advantages of each approach centers on determining the research design (e.g., research questions, data structure, scale of outcome variables), before considering the estimation theory (e.g., ordinary least squares, maximum likelihood, empirical Bayes, quasilikelihood) and algorithms appropriate for various designs and data, and finally considering the software that would be most useful in conducting the analysis.

In chapter 1, we presented one general framework for considering quantitative analysis alternatives. The framework was based on the type of theoretical model to be investigated (e.g., number of outcome variables), data structures present in organizational and educational research settings, and the overall goal of the analysis (i.e., explanation or prediction). We believe that the framework should be considered independently from the computer software available to estimate the models. In fact, most researchers currently use several software programs, depending upon their research problem—the theoretical model they are investigating, the design of the study (single level, multilevel, longitudinal), the number and scale of the outcome variables, the presence of missing data, and the goals of their analyses. Where researchers examine relationships between constructs such as leadership, organizational culture, and outcomes across organizational units, SEM or the multivariate (three-level) regression model (i.e., incorporating a level-1 measurement model) are likely methodological choices because of the researcher's ability to incorporate measurement error into the multivariate model. This leads to a more exact assessment of the structural relationships among constructs because they have been corrected for measurement errors. As we have argued, ignoring measurement error can substantially bias other parameter estimates in the model (Rigdon, 1998).

Until recently, however, factor analyses of educational and organizational data routinely ignored the nested nature of the data. The techniques we demonstrated in chapters 7 and 8 allow us to incorporate both factor models and regression models into the multivariate multilevel framework of clustered data. In the multilevel context, these techniques can be used to test hypotheses about the means of latent variables and observed variables across groups. In fact, the researcher can develop separate structural models at each level that account for variation in latent variables of interest. Moreover, the SEM approach also has the capability of incorporating intervening variables into the multilevel model, so that direct, indirect (effects through other paths), and total effects (i.e., the sum of direct and indirect effects) can be determined. The range of output from testing the models is extensive (e.g., estimates of parameters, estimates of standard errors, significance tests of individual parameters, measurement errors, variance accounted for in dependent variables, various types of goodness-of-fit indices, model diagnostics) and can add much to our understanding of social phenomena.

A second situation where the multilevel multivariate approach might be useful is to incorporate variables that are highly correlated into a model. As the reader may realize, often in regression analyses variables that are multicollinear (e.g., several measures of socioeconomic status) can create biased parameter estimates and inflated standard errors (Rigdon, 1998). The solution is generally to eliminate one of the variables, which can lead to a loss of theoretically important information from the model. In the SEM framework, the highly correlated variables can be modeled as indicators of a latent factor, and therefore, all the information can be contained within one socioeconomic status construct in the model. The ability to retain multiple indicators that are highly correlated allows one to model their simultaneous effects and should result in the creation of more reliable and valid constructs.

Another advantage of multilevel modeling in general is that it allows researchers to define a research problem in such a way that they can ask substantively important questions about how group variables affect individuals. Most of the social sciences are concerned with these types of relationships on some level; hence, multilevel techniques are an important means of linking our theories about how social processes work to observations collected at several levels. Humans are by nature social and, as such, are members of many social groupings (e.g., families, churches, workplaces, cultural groups, nations). Multilevel modeling allows us a means to extend our theories to incorporate ways in which these higher order social and environmental processes are posited to affect individuals.

If social contexts are hypothesized to affect individuals, these effects are likely mediated by intervening processes that relate to characteristics of the macrolevel processes. Such cross-level interactions require the specification of processes within individuals that allow these individuals to be differentially affected by their contexts (Hox, 1995). These types of theoretical processes require the careful attention to individual and group processes. There is much to learn through explicit attention to the exploration of individual processes within wider social groupings and cultural contexts. The accumulation of knowledge in any field requires the application of more powerful theoretical models. One example of this is Creemers' (1994) model of educational effectiveness. Building on several decades of studies that examined student learning from various levels (individual students, classes, schools, district or state), Creemers outlined a multilevel theory about how these contextual processes may affect individual student learning through cross-level interactions.

Empirically testing a complex theory of cross-level interactions will prove challenging to researchers, however, because of the need to adequately model all of these interactions. The explication of the theory requires researchers to think carefully about how to model these processes correctly with the data they collect. In this type of a multilevel model, there is a clear advantage currently to the multilevel regression approach because of the possibility of examining both regression slopes and intercepts across several organizational or educational levels. Of course, any complete test of the theory will also require a large amounts of data at each level to ensure representativeness. Often, in more complex models, data analysis should begin with the careful examination of variables that may be used in the model using univariate (descriptive) and bivariate relationships. Prior to fitting multilevel models, such analyses would be done at each level. Exploratory analyses can also be conducted within each organization to identify possible outlier organizations—that is, organizations that may have implausible regression slopes or intercepts (Bryk & Raudenbush, 1992).

It is also likely that individuals affect the groups of which they are members. One interesting use of multilevel SEM techniques, which allow very flexible modeling of direct and indirect effects as well as reciprocal effects, may be to conceptualize and test a model that estimates some of these reciprocal effects between context and individual.

Limitations

We have raised a number of issues that remain important to consider in using these multilevel approaches. One issue is sampling strategies with respect to the level-2 units. As we suggested, the number of level-2 units in a study affects the appropriate methods of estimation used to test the model, the stability of estimates, and the power to detect effects if they are indeed present. These are issues that are by no means settled. There are, however, a number of sources that we have mentioned where the interested reader can obtain more information about sample size in level-2 units. Especially with SEM designs, large numbers of level-2 units may be required to provide stable estimates, or even to get the model to converge. If models with relatively few level-2 units do converge, however, it is quite likely that they will appear to fit better than they actually would in the population.

For multilevel SEM analyses, model identification issues are also important to consider. Multilevel SEM models contain many parameters and, because of this, can easily become underidentified. This means that it is not possible to find a unique solution to the set of equations (see chap. 5). Because of the large number of parameters, it is important to give great care to their specification, so that the a correct number of paths can be restricted, thereby ensuring positive degrees of freedom in the model test. Correct specification is important because it is easy for some software programs (e.g., LISREL) to produce incorrect degrees of freedom in situations where means are estimated or when there are several group-level observed variables that must be defined in the within-group covariance matrix.

We also raised several issues related to how to conceptualize and estimate these models. SEM techniques are dependent on analyzing covariance in a set of observed predictors. The idea of comparing covariance matrices across a number of groups was attractive in earlier work, but in practice is difficult to accomplish past a few groups. It is also difficult to determine what between-group variables might account for invariance or variance across the matrices. Muthén (1989) and others successfully adapted the multiple group SEM method to look at the matrices in a two-group (within and between) configuration. These efforts look promising, but specification and estimation of these models remain difficult (e.g., trying to model random slopes across units, getting the models to converge). Problems of nonconvergence due to poor choices for initial estimates and small sample sizes appear to be very common in conducting these analyses.

A related issue in multilevel SEM analysis is the software needed to develop the between- and within-group matrices for unbalanced data. Without special software, one is generally limited to investigating balanced data. Muthén and Muthén (1998) recently developed a new software program (*Mplus*) that has in our opinion made conducting multilevel SEM analyses easier. The models are relatively easy to specify, but there is not a full range of fit indices available yet. Muthén's quasi-likelihood estimator will likely undergo further tests in a variety of conditions regarding missing data, severe departures from common group sizes, and violations of multivariate normality. The fit indices in most programs should be considered as approximate only. We also point out that the two-group means of testing SEM models can result in an asymmetric amount of information about the within- and between-group models, because there are usually many more cases at the individual level than at the group level. This can cause difficulties in interpreting the goodness-of-fit indices (Gustafsson & Stahl, 1996). EQS (Bentler, 1989) is also set to release version 6, which will include multilevel SEM capabilities (Bentler, personal communication, April 25, 1999). Moreover, there are still relatively few examples of multilevel factor and SEM models in the literature—a problem related to researchers' limited access to appropriate software.

SUMMARY

Of course, the bottom line is whether or not we gain new insights by employing these analytic tools. Organizational and educational scholarship has benefitted over the past several decades from improvements in the application of both theory and methodology. Multilevel methods are important analytic tools in the investigation of a variety of substantive and methodological research problems (educational improvement, organizational leadership, measurement, and construct validation). It is obvious that we can get refined estimates by acknowledging the clustered nature of educational and organizational data. Over the past several years, for example, multilevel regression models have certainly heightened our understanding of how school processes impact student learning.

It is important to keep in mind the role of theory in defining and testing multilevel models. For example, multilevel SEM is a powerful statistical tool, but it can be easily misused. One common misuse is the sole reliance on model modification indices to improve the fit of a structural model. We must always be mindful that the ultimate test of a theory is its usefulness—does it help us to understand the phenomenon we are studying?

We have discussed a number of issues regarding judgments that are made about a model's adequacy in representing the data. Harvey (1989) outlined some useful principles that we can adapt for use in evaluating the suitability of a multilevel model (as summarized in Hershberger, Molenaar, & Corneal, 1996). Harvey suggested a model should be *parsimonious;* that is, it should describe the data in relatively few parameters. The model should be *consistent with prior knowledge*—or should tend to confirm accepted theory and prior knowledge. The model should have *data admissibility;* that is, it should not have impossible values for the data. It should also have *structural stability*, or fit across the contexts (or times) tested. Finally, the model should be *encompassing*—it should encompass competing models by explaining aspects in the data accounted for by competing models and should provide additional explanation.

We caution that multilevel SEM is still in its early stages. We have discussed a number of ways that clustered sampling (e.g., small numbers of groups, large intraclass correlations) can affect the multilevel structural equation model estimated with maximum likelihood including biasing the calculation of fit indices, parameter estimates, and standard errors. Consequently, it is probably best to treat solutions as tentative until more empirical work has been completed.

Multilevel modeling techniques provide us with a powerful means for investigating the types of processes referred to by our theories in more refined ways. From this standpoint, they allow us to create and test more complex models. Although the models presented in this book were necessarily simple, complexity can be added by increasing the number of observed variables, the numbers of latent variables, the complexity of interrelations across levels, and so forth. Moreover, the techniques are being rapidly extended to analyses of growth models and time-series data. Although remembering that any statistical model is not a substitute for reality, and in many cases can actually be a severe reduction of reality, we are optimistic that progress will continue to be made where it is simultaneously defined on both conceptual and methodological fronts.

References

Aitken, M., & Longford, N. (1986). Statistical modeling issues in school effectiveness studies. *Journal of Royal Staistical Society, Series A, 149,* 1–43.

Arbuckle, J. (1996). Full information estimation in the presence of incomplete data. In G. A. Marcoulides & R. Schumacker (Eds.), *Advanced structural equation modeling: Issues and techniques* (pp. 243–278). Mahwah, NJ: Lawrence Erlbaum Associates.

Arbuckle, J. (1997). *Amos users' guide.* Chicago: SmallWaters Corporation.

Barcikowski, R. (1981). Statistical power with group mean as the unit of analysis. *Journal of Educational Statistics, 6*(3), 267–285.

Barnett, R., Marshall, N., Raudenbush, S., & Brennan, R. (1993). Gender and the relationship between job experiences and psychological distress: A study of dual-earner couples. *Journal of Personality and Social Psychology, 64,* 794–806.

Bashaw, W., & Findley, W. (1968). *Symposium on general linear model approach to the analysis of experimental data in educational research* (Project No. 7-8096). Washington, DC: U.S. Department of Health, Education, and Welfare.

Bassiri, D. (1988). *Large and small sample properties of maximum likelihood estimates for the hierarchical model.* Unpublished doctoral dissertation, Michigan State University, East Lansing.

Bentler, P. (1989). *EQS structural equations program manual.* Los Angeles: BMDP Statistical Software.

Bentler, P., & Chou, C. (1987). Practical issues in structural modeling. *Sociological Methods and Research, 16,* 78–117.

Bock, R. D. (1989). *Multilevel analysis of educational data.* San Diego: Academic Press.

Bollen, K. (1989). *Structural equations with latent variables.* New York: Wiley.

Bollen, K., & Long, J. (1993). *Testing structural equation models.* Newbury Park, CA: Sage.

Boomsma, A. (1987). The robustness of maximum likelihood estimation in structural equation models. In P. Cuttance & R. Ecobe (Eds.), *Structural modeling by example* (pp. 160–188). Cambridge: Cambridge University Press.

Bryk, A. S., & Raudenbush, S. W. (1992). *Hierarchical linear models: Applications and data analysis methods.* Newbury Park, CA: Sage.

Bryk, A. S., Raudenbush, S. W., & Condon, R. (1996). *HLM: Hierarchical linear and nonlinear modeling with the HLM/2L and HLM/3L programs.* Chicago: Scientific Software.

Burstein, L. (1980). The analysis of multilevel data in educational research in evaluation. *Review of Research in Education, 8,* 158–233.

Busing, F. M. (1993). *Distribution characteristics of variance estimates in two-level models* (Preprint PRM 93-04). Department of Psychometrics and Research Methodology, University of Leiden, The Netherlands.

Byrne, B. (1995). One application of structural equation modeling from two perspectives: Exploring with EQS and LISREL. In R. Hoyle (Ed.), *Structural equation modeling: Concepts, issues and applications* (pp. 138–157). Newbury Park, CA: Sage.

Chou, C. P., & Bentler, P. (1990). Model modification in covariance structure modeling: A comparison among likelihood ratio, Lagrange multiplier, and Wald tests. *Multivariate Behavioral Research, 25,* 115–136.

Chou, C. P., & Bentler, P. (1995). Estimates and tests in structural equation modeling. In R. Hoyle (Ed.), *Structural equation modeling: Concepts, issues, and applications* (pp. 37–55). Newbury Park, CA: Sage.

Chou, C. P., Bentler, P., & Pentz, M. (1998). A two-stage approach to multilevel structural equation models: Application to longitudinal data. Unpublished paper, Department of Preventive Medicine, University of Southern California, Los Angeles.

Cohen, J. (1988). *Statistical power analysis for the behavioral sciences* (2nd ed.). Hillsdale, NJ: Lawrence Erlbaum Associates.

Creemers, B. (1994). *The effective classroom.* London: Cassell.

Cronbach, L. J. (1976). *Research in classrooms and schools: Formulation of questions, designs and analysis.* Stanford, CA: Occasional Paper, Stanford Evaluation Consortium.

Cronbach, L. J., & Meehl, P. (1955). Construct validity in psychological tests. *Psychological Bulletin, 52,* 281–302.

Cronbach, L. J., & Webb, N. (1975). Between and within class effects in a reported aptitude-by-treatment interaction: Reanalysis of a study by G. L. Anderson. *Journal of Educational Psychology, 6,* 717–724.

de Finetti, B. (1964). Foresight: Its logical laws, its subjective sources. In H. E. Kyberg & H. E. Smokler (Eds.), *Studies in subjective probability* (pp. 93–158). New York: Wiley.

de Leeuw, J. (1992). Series Editor's introduction to hierarchical linear models. In A. Bryk & S. Raudenbush, *Hierarchial linear models: Applications and data analysis methods* (pp. xiii–xvi). Newbury Park, CA: Sage.

de Leeuw, J., & Kreft, I. (1986). Random coefficient models for multilevel analysis. *Journal of Educational Statistics, 11*(1), 57–85.

de Leeuw, J., & Kreft, I. G. (1995). Questioning multilevel models. *Journal of Educational Statistics, 20*(2), 171–189.

Dempster, A., Laird, N., & Rubin, D. (1977). Maximum likelihood from incomplete data via the EM algorithm. *Journal of the Royal Statistical Society, Series B, 30,* 1–38.

Dempster, A., Rubin, D., & Tsutakawa, R. (1981). Estimation in covariance components models. *Journal of the American Statistical Association, 76,* 341–353.

Draper, D. (1995). Inference and hierarchical modeling in the social sciences. *Journal of Educational Statistics, 20*(2), 115–148.

Duncan, S. C., & Duncan, T. E. (1996). A multivariate growth curve analysis of adolescent substance abuse. *Structural Equation Modeling, 3,* 323–347.

Ecob, R., & Cuttance, P. (1987). An overview of structural equation modeling. In P. Cuttance & R. Ecob (Eds.), *Structural modeling by example* (pp. 9–23). Cambridge: Cambridge University Press.

Efron, B., & Morris, C. (1975). Data analysis using Stein's estimator and its generalizations. *Journal of the American Statistical Association, 74,* 311–319.

Fisher, R. A. (1918). The correlation between relatives on the supposition of Mendelian inheritance. *Transactions of the Royal Society of Edinburgh, 52,* 399–433.

Fisher, R. A. (1925). *Statistical methods for research workers.* London: Oliver & Boyd.

Fotiu, R. (1989). *A comparison of the EM and data augmentation algorithms on simulated small sample hierarchical data from research on education.* Unpublished doctoral dissertation, Michigan State University, East Lansing.

Goldstein, H. (1986). Multilevel mixed linear model analysis using iterative generalized least squares. *Biometrika, 73*(1), 43–56.

Goldstein, H. (1987). *Multilevel models in educational and social research.* London: Oxford University Press.

Goldstein, H. (1995a). *Multilevel statistical models.* New York: Halsted.

Goldstein, H. (1995b). Hierarchical data modeling in the social sciences. *Journal of Educational Statistics, 20*(2), 201–204.

Goldstein, H., & McDonald, R. (1988). A general model for the analysis of multilevel data. *Pyschometrika, 53,* 455–467.

Goldstein, H., & Woodhouse, G. (1996, July). Multilevel models with missing data. Paper presented at the Eleventh International Workshop on Statistical Modeling, Orvieto, Italy.

Gustafsson, J. E., & Stahl, P. A. (1996). *STREAMS User's Guide.* Version 1.6 for Windows. Mölndal, Sweden: Multivariate Ware.

Hartley, H. O., & Rao, J. N. (1967). Maximum likelihood estimation for the mixed analysis of variance model. *Biometrika, 54,* 93–108.

Harvey, A. (1989). *Forecasting, structural time series models and the Kalman filter.* Cambridge, MA: Cambridge University Press.

Harville, D. A. (1977). Maximum likelihood approaches to variance component estimation and to related problems. *Journal of the American Statistical Association, 72,* 320–340.

Heck, R. H. (1998). Factor analysis: Exploratory and confirmatory approaches. In G. A. Marcoulides (Ed.), *Modern methods for business research* (pp. 177–216). Mahwah, NJ: Lawrence Erlbaum Associates.

Heck, R. H., & Marcoulides, G. A. (1996). School culture and performance: Testing the invariance of an organizational model. *School Effectiveness and School Improvement, 7*(1), 76–95.

Hershberger, S. L., Molenaar, P. C., & Corneal, S. E. (1996). A hierarchy of univariate and multivariate time series models. In G. Marcoulides & R. Schumacker (Eds.), *Advanced structural equation modeling: Issues and techniques* (pp. 159–194). Mahwah, NJ: Lawrence Erlbaum Associates.

Hofstede, G., Neuijen, B., Ohayv, D., & Sanders, E. (1990). Measuring organizational cultures: A qualitative and quantitative study across twenty cases. *Administrative Science Quarterly, 35,* 286–316.

Hox, J. (1993). Factor analysis of multilevel data: Gauging the Muthén model. In J. Oud & R. van Blokland-Vogelesang (Eds.), *Advances in longitudinal and multivariate analysis in the behavioural sciences.* Nijmegen, Netherlands: ITS.

Hox, J. J. (1995). *Applied multilevel analysis.* Amsterdam: T. T. Publikaties.

Hoyle, R., & Panter, A. (1995). Writing about structural equation models. In R. Hoyle (Ed.), *Structural equation modeling: Concepts, issues, and applications* (pp. 158–176). Newbury Park, CA: Sage.

Hu, L., & Bentler, P. (1995). Evaluating model fit. In R. Hoyle (Ed.), *Structural equation modeling: Concepts, issues, and applications* (pp. 76–99). Newbury, CA: Sage.

Jöreskog, K. G. (1977). Structural equation modeling in the social sciences: Specification, estimation, and testing. In P. R. Krishnaih (Ed.), *Applications of statistics* (pp. 265–287). Amsterdam: North-Holland.

Jöreskog, K. G., & Sörbom, D. (1989). *LISREL 7: User's reference guide.* Chicago: Scientific Software.

Jöreskog, K. G., & Sörbom, D. (1993a). *LISREL 8: User's reference guide.* Chicago: Scientific Software.

Jöreskog, K. G., & Sörbom, D. (1993b). *PRELIS 2: User's reference guide.* Chicago: Scientific Software.

Jöreskog, K. G., & Sörbom, D. (1999). *LISREL 8.30.* Chicago: Scientific Software.

Kaplan, D. (1995). Statistical power in SEM. In R. Hoyle (Ed.), *Structural equation modeling: Concepts, issues, and applications* (pp. 100–117). Newbury Park, CA: Sage.

Kaplan, D. (1998). Methods for multilevel data analysis. In G. A. Marcoulides (Ed.), *Modern methods for business research* (pp. 337–358). Mahwah, NJ: Lawrence Erlbaum Associates.

Kaplan, D., & Elliott, P. R. (1997). A didactic example of multilevel structural equation modeling applicable to the study of organizations. *Structural Equation Modeling, 4*(1), 1–23.

Kiecolt-Glaser, J. K. (1997). Studying multivariate change using multilevel models and latent curve models. *Multivariate Behavioral Research, 32,* 215–254.

Kirk, R. E. (1982). *Experimental design. Procedures of the social sciences.* Belmont, CA: Wadsworth.

Kish, L. (1957). Confidence limits for cluster samples. *American Sociological Review, 22,* 154–165.

Kish, L. (1965). *Survey sampling.* New York: Wiley.

Kreft, I., & De Leeuw, J. (1998). *Introducing multilevel modeling.* Newbury Park, CA: Sage.

Kreft, I., de Leeuw, J., & Aiken, L. (1995). The effects of different forms of centering in hierarchical linear models. *Multivariate Behavioral Research, 30,* 1–22.

Kreft, I. G., de Leeuw, J., & Kim, K. (1990). *Comparing four different statistical packages for hierarchical linear regression: Genmod, HLM, ML2, and VARCL* (Statistical Series No. 50) Los Angeles: University of California at Los Angeles.

Laird, N. M., & Ware, J. H. (1982). Random-effects models for longitudinal data. *Biometrics, 38,* 963–974.

Lawley, D., & Maxwell, A. (1963). *Factor analysis as a statistical method.* London: Butterworth.

Lee, V., & Bryk, A. (1989). A multilevel model of the social distribution of high school achievement. *Sociology of Education, 62,* 172–192.

Lindley, D., & Smith, A. (1972). Bayes estimates for the linear model. *Journal of the Royal Statistical Society, B34,* 1–41.

Little, R., & Rubin, D. (1987). *Statistical analysis with missing data.* New York: Wiley.

Long, S. (1983). *Confirmatory factor analysis* (Sage Series on Quantitative Applications in the Social Sciences, No. 13). Newbury Park, CA: Sage.

Longford, N. (1993). *Random coefficient models.* Oxford: Clarendon Press.

MacCallum, R. C., Roznowski, M., & Necowitz, L. B. (1992). Model modifications in covariance structure analysis. The problem of capitalization on chance. *Psychological Bulletin, 111,* 490–504.

Marcoulides, G. A. (1987). *An alternative method for variance component estimation: Applications to generalizability theory.* Unpublished doctoral dissertation, University of California, Los Angeles.

Marcoulides, G. A. (1993). Maximizing power in generalizability studies under budget constraints. *Journal of Educational Statistics, 18*(2), 197–206.

Marcoulides, G. A. (1994). Selecting weighting schemes in multivariate generalizability studies. *Educational and Psychological Measurement, 54*(1), 3–7.

Marcoulides, G. A. (1998). Applied generalizability theory models. In G. A. Marcoulides (Ed.), *Modern methods for business research* (pp. 1–22). Mahwah, NJ: Lawrence Erlbaum Associates.

Marcoulides, G. A., & Heck, R. H. (1993). Organizational culture and performance: Proposing and testing a model. *Organization Science, 4*(2), 209–225.

Marcoulides, G. A., & Hershberger, S. (1997). *Multivariate statistical methods: A first course.* Mahwah, NJ: Lawrence Erlbaum Associates.

Marcoulides, G. A., & Schumacker, R. E. (1996). *Advanced structural equation modeling: Issues and techniques.* Mahwah, NJ: Lawrence Erlbaum Associates.

Mason, W. (1995). Comment. *Journal of Educational and Behavioral Statistics, 20,* 2, 221–227.

McArdle, J. (1998). Modeling longitudinal data by latent growth curve methods. In G. Marcoulides (Ed.), *Modern methods for business research* (pp. 359–406). Mahwah, NJ: Lawrence Erlbaum Associates.

McArdle, J., & Hamagami, F. (1996). Multilevel models from a multiple group structural equation perspective. In G. Marcoulides & R. Schumacker (Eds.), *Advanced Structural equation modeling: Issues and techniques* (pp. 89–124). Mahwah, NJ: Lawrence Erlbaum Associates.

McDonald, R. P. (1994). The bilevel reticular action model for path analysis with latent variables. *Sociological Methods and Research, 22*, 399–413.

McDonald, R. P., & Goldstein, H. (1989). Balanced versus unbalanced designs for linear structural relations in two-level data. *British Journal of Mathematical and Statistical Psychology, 42*, 215–232.

Mok, M. (1995). *Sample size requirements for 2-level designs in educational research.* Sydney, Australia: Macquarie University.

Morris, C. (1995). Hierarchical models for educational data: An overview. *Journal of Educational Statistics, 20*(2), 190–200.

Muthén, B. O. (1989). Latent variable modeling in heterogenous populations. *Psychometrika, 54*, 557–585.

Muthén, B. O. (1990, June). *Mean and covariance structure analysis of hierarchical data.* Paper presented at the Psychometric Society Meeting, Princeton, NJ.

Muthén, B. O. (1991). Multilevel factor analysis of class and student achievement components. *Journal of Educational Measurement, 28*, 338–354.

Muthén, B. O. (1992, September). *Latent variable modeling of growth with missing data and multilevel.* Paper presented at the Seventh International Conference on Multivariate Analysis, Barcelona, Spain.

Muthén, B. O. (1994). Multilevel covariance structure analysis. *Sociological Methods & Research, 22*(3), 376–398.

Muthén, B. O. (1997). Latent variable modeling with longitudinal and multilevel data. In Raftery (Ed.), *Sociological methodology* (pp. 453–480). Boston: Blackwell.

Muthén, B. O., & Muthén, L. (1998). *Mplus* [Computer software]. Los Angeles: Authors.

Muthén, B. O., & Satorra, A. (1989). Multilevel aspects of varying parameters in structural models. In R. D. Bock (Ed.), *Multilevel analysis of educational data* (pp. 87–99). San Diego: Academic Press.

Muthén, B. O., & Satorra, A. (1995). Complex sample data in structural equation modeling. In P. Marsden (Ed.), *Sociological methodology* (pp. 267–316). Washington, DC: American Sociological Association.

National Council on Measurement. (1984). *Standards for educational and psychological testing.* Washington, DC: American Psychological Association.

Pedhazur, E., & Schmelkin, L. (1991). *Measurement, design, and analysis: An integrated approach.* Hillsdale, NJ: Lawrence Erlbaum Associates.

Raudenbush, S. W. (1988). Educational applications of hierarchical linear model: A Review. *Journal of Educational Statistics, 13*(2), 85–116.

Raudenbush, S. W. (1995). Reexamining, reaffirming, and improving application of hierarchical models. *Journal of Educational Statistics, 20*(2), 210–220.

Raudenbush, S. W., & Bryk, A. S. (1986). A hierarchical model for studying school effects. *Sociology of Education, 59*, 1–17.

Raudenbush, S. (1998, October). Toward a coherent framework for comparing trajectories of individual change. Paper presented for the conference, New Methods for the Analysis of Change, held at Pennsylvania State University.

Raudenbush, S. W., Rowan, B., & Kang, S. J. (1991). A multilevel multivariate model for school climate and estimation via the EM algorithm and application to U.S. high school data. *Journal of Education Statistics, 1*, 295–330.

Rigdon, E. (1998). Structural equation models. In G. Marcoulides (Ed.), *Modern methods for business research* (pp. 251–294). Mahwah, NJ: Lawrence Erlbaum Associates.

Robinson, W. S. (1950). Ecological correlations and the behavior of individuals. *Sociological Review, 15*, 351–357.

Rogosa, D., & Saner, H. (1995). Longitudinal data analysis examples with random coefficient models. *Journal of Educational and Behavioral Statistics, 20*(2), 149–170.

Rubin, H. (1950). Note on random coefficients. In T. C. Koopmans (Ed.), *Statistical inference in dynamic economic models* (pp. 419–421). New York: Wiley.

Saris, W. E., den Ronden, J., & Satorra, A. (1987). Testing structural equation models. In P. Cuttance & R. Ecob (Eds.), *Structural modeling by example: Applications in educational, sociological, and behavioral research* (pp. 202–220). Cambridge: Cambridge University Press.

Saris, W. E., & Satorra, A. (1993). Power evaluations in structural equation models. In K. Bollen & J. S. Long (Eds.), *Testing structural equation models* (pp. 181–204). Newbury Park, CA: Sage.

Satorra, A. (1989). Alternative test criteria in covariance structure analysis. A unified approach. *Psychometrika, 54*, 131–151.

Satorra, A., & Saris, W. E. (1985). Power of the likelihood ratio test in covariance structure analysis. *Psychometrika, 50*, 83–90.

Schein, E. (1990). Organizational culture. *American Psychologist, 45*(2), 109–119.

Schmidt, W., & Wisenbaker, J. (1986). Hierarchical data analysis: An approach based on structural equations (Tech. Rep. No. 4). East Lansing, MI: Department of Counseling Psychology and Special Education.

Schumacker, R., & Lomax, R. (1996). *Structural equation modeling for beginners.* Mahwah, NJ: Lawrence Erlbaum Associates.

Schmidt, W. H. (1969). *Covariance structure analysis of the multivariate random effects model.* Unpublished doctoral dissertation, University of Chicago.

Shavelson, R. J., & Webb, N. M. (1991). *Generalizability theory: A primer.* Newbury Park, CA: Sage.

Shigemasu, K. (1976). Development and validation of a simplified m-group regression model. *Journal of Educational Statistics, 1*(2), 157–180.

Silva, E., & McCallum, R. (1988). Some factors affecting the success of specification searches in covariance structure modeling. *Multivariate Behavioral Research, 23*, 297–326.

Smart, J., & St. John, E. (1996). Organizational culture and effectiveness in higher education: A test of the "culture type" and "strong culture" hypotheses. *Educational Evaluation and Policy Analysis, 18*(3), 219–241.

Smith, A. F. (1973). A general Bayesian linear model. *Journal of the Royal Statistical Society, Series B, 35*, 61–75.

Stoolmiller, M., Duncan, T., & Patterson, G. (1995). Predictors of change in antisocial behavior during elementary school for boys. In R. Hoyle (Ed.), *Structural equation modeling: Concepts, issues, and applications* (pp. 236–253). Newbury Park, CA: Sage.

Strenio, J. L. (1981). *Empirical Bayes estimation for a hierarchical linear model.* Unpublished doctoral dissertation, Department of Statistics, Harvard University.

Supovitz, J. A., & Brennan, R. T. (1997). Mirror, mirror on the wall, which is the fairest test of all? An examination of the equitability of portfolio assessment relative to standardized tests. *Harvard Educational Review, 67*(3), 472–505.

Wald, A. (1947). A note on regression analysis. *Annals of Mathematical Statistics, 18*, 586–589.

Walsh, J. E. (1947). Concerning the effect of the intraclass correlation on certain significance tests. *Annals of Mathematical Statistics, 18*, 88–96.

Ware, J. (1985). Linear models for the analysis of longitudinal studies. *American Statistician, 39*(2), 95–101.

Willett, J., & Sayer, A. (1996). Cross-domain analysis of change overtime: combining growth modeling and covariance structure analysis. In G. Marcoulides & R. Schumacker (Eds.), *Advanced structural equation modeling: Issues and techniques* (pp. 125–158). Mahwah, NJ: Lawrence Erlbaum Associates.

Woodhouse, G., Yang, M., Goldstein, H., & Rasbash, J. (1996). Adjusting for measurement error in multilevel analysis. *Journal of the Royal Statistical Society, A, 159*, 201–212.

Wong, G. T., & Mason, W. M. (1985). The hierarchical logistic regression model for multilevel analysis. *Journal of the American Statistical Association, 80*(391), 513–524.

Author Index

201

Subject Index